THE DISPOSABLE WORKER

HOW AMERICAN COMPANIES ARE DESTROYING THE PRODUCTIVE AMERICAN WORKFORCE

HERBERT P. RICARDO

THE DISPOSABLE WORKER

"The modern corporation has not lost its humanity by accident, it has engineered its removal. The disposable worker is not a byproduct of progress, but the outcome of a system that values efficiency over dignity, profit over people, and short-term gain over long-term societal stability."

~Herbert P. Ricardo

Acknowledgments

Writing a book is never a solitary journey, and I am deeply grateful to those who have supported me along the way.

I am grateful to my colleagues and friends, including Tom Kindred, Phil Galdys, Richard Grego and Dan Wigley, for their valuable feedback and insights during the early stages of writing. Your honesty and thoughtful suggestions helped shape this book into what it is today.

To my editor and the publishing team at Kime Consulting for their guidance and attention to detail, ensuring this book reached its full potential. And to the many leaders and professionals I have had the privilege to work with, you have taught me that true greatness lies not only in results but in the way we treat people along the way.

Thank you all for being part of this journey.

~Herbert Ricardo

THE DISPOSABLE WORKER:
How American Companies are Destroying the Productive American Workforce

By Herbert P. Ricardo

Published by: KIME Consulting, a division of
Enzo and Philips Managing Partners LLC
This Book can be purchased for educational, trade and business use through Kime Consulting

First Edition: May, 2026
Printed in the United States of America

ISBN: 979-8-9889172-8-1

Published by Herbert P. Ricardo

1.Leadership 2.Management 3.Organizational Change 4.Business Ethics

Preface

Decades of focusing on short-term gains and maximizing profits have fractured the corporate landscape. The modern workplace is often unrecognizable from the era when loyalty was rewarded and jobs could support a family. Today, the corporate world is obsessed with maximizing output while minimizing cost, creating a system where "efficiency trumps humanity" and workers are treated as "disposable cogs".

This devastating shift was cemented by the rise of shareholder primacy, which prioritized maximizing profits for stockholders over investing in employees and customers.

The alarming results are visible across the economy:

Employees are treated as temporary expenses rather than long-term assets, facing grueling demands, stagnant wages, and eroded benefits.

Consumers have been devalued, encountering hidden fees, poor service, and deceptive corporate practices in everything from airlines to banking.

Business Owners and Managers struggle daily to maintain ethical leadership in a world dominated by the demand for shareholder returns.

The Disposable Worker challenges readers not just to understand the current system, but to change it. It argues that restoring the balance between profit and people is not just a moral goal, it is a strategic imperative for long-term success.

This book is your essential guide to understanding the root causes of corporate detachment and implementing lasting change.

Table of Contents

Introduction

Imagine racing against the clock to meet impossible delivery quotas, knowing that stopping, even for a bathroom break, could mean falling behind. For some Amazon drivers, that pressure is so intense that they've resorted to urinating in bottles just to stay on schedule[1].

This isn't a dystopian novel, it's the reality of modern corporate efficiency. The same company that delivers packages at lightning speed has also been fined millions for imposing grueling productivity quotas on its workers.[2] In an age where businesses celebrate automation, artificial intelligence, and record-breaking profits, the people behind those numbers, the employees who keep companies running, are often pushed to their physical and mental limits.

At its core, the corporate world has become obsessed with one thing: maximizing output while minimizing cost. That obsession has created a system where efficiency trumps humanity, where workers are treated less as valuable assets and more as disposable cogs in an ever-churning machine. From warehouses to call centers, from gig workers to retail employees, the evidence is everywhere: productivity targets have grown higher, benefits have shrunk, and job security has eroded, all in the name of profit.

---

1. Paul, Kari. "Leaked memo shows Amazon knows delivery drivers resort to urinating in bottles." *The Guardian*, 25 March 2021

2. SupplyChainBrain. "Amazon Fined Nearly $6M over Warehouse Quotas in California." SupplyChainBrain, 21 June 2024.

This book explores how corporations arrived at this breaking point, how the shift from people-first to profit-first thinking reshaped the modern workplace and what must change to restore balance. Because the question we should all be asking isn't just how much companies can grow, but who pays the price for that growth?

Why This Book?

Not long ago, the corporate world operated on a simple premise: take care of your employees and they will take care of your customers. Companies like IBM, General Motors, and Sears built their reputations by offering stable jobs, competitive wages, and benefits that rewarded long-term loyalty.[3] Employers understood that investing in workers wasn't just ethical, it was good business. Customers, too, were valued partners in this equation, with businesses prioritizing quality service, fair pricing, and strong brand relationships.

But something changed.

The rise of shareholder primacy in the 1970s, fueled by economist Milton Friedman's assertion that a company's sole responsibility is to maximize profits for its shareholders, reshaped corporate priorities.[4] Instead of long-term investment in employees and customers, businesses pivoted toward quarterly earnings reports, stock buybacks, and aggressive cost-cutting. The result? A corporate culture where people became secondary to profit.

Today, that shift is felt in every sector of the economy. Stable, full-time jobs have been replaced by gig work and short-term contracts. Companies now treat employees as temporary expenses rather than long-term assets, keeping wages low, reducing benefits, and automating roles whenever possible.[5] Warehouse workers, once protected by labor

---

3. Chandler, A. D. (1977). *The Visible Hand: The Managerial Revolution in American Business.* Harvard University Press.

4. Friedman, M. (1970). *The Social Responsibility of Business is to Increase its Profits.* The New York Times Magazine.

5. Kalleberg, A. L. (2009). *Precarious Work, Insecure Workers: Employment Relations in Transition. American Sociological Review, 74(1),* 1-22.

unions, now race against algorithm-driven quotas.[6] Retail and customer service employees face unrealistic demands while enduring verbal abuse from frustrated customers. Even white-collar professionals are not immune, record layoffs and mass outsourcing have destabilized entire industries.

And what about the customers? They, too, have been devalued. Loyalty no longer matters in an era of hidden fees, deceptive marketing, and outsourced customer service. Banks impose unexpected charges, airlines slash service while raising prices, and even hospitals prioritize billing over patient care.[7]

So, what happens when corporations treat people as disposable? This book explores the forces that led to this shift, the consequences of prioritizing profit over people, and the urgent need to restore balance. Because in a world where businesses thrive while workers and customers suffer, the real question isn't just how much profit is enough, it's how much damage are we willing to accept?

Who This Book Is For, Understanding the System and Changing It

This book isn't just for boardroom executives or Wall Street analysts. It's for the people who keep the corporate world running, workers, business owners, and consumers, who all feel the effects of an increasingly profit-driven system.

- **For Employees:** If you've ever felt like your job treats you as replaceable, that your wages haven't kept up with inflation, or that your employer demands more while offering less, this book is for you. Whether you're a warehouse worker under constant surveillance, a gig worker struggling with unstable income, or an office employee watching jobs disappear to automation, you're not imagining things. The system has shifted, at your expense.

---

6. Kantor, J., & Streitfeld, D. (2015). *Inside Amazon: Wrestling Big Ideas in a Bruising Workplace.* The New York Times.

7. Zuboff, S. (2019). *The Age of Surveillance Capitalism: The Fight for a Human Future at the New Frontier of Power.* PublicAffairs.

- **For Business Owners and Managers:** Many leaders want to do right by their employees and customers, but in a world where shareholder returns dictate decision-making, ethical leadership feels like an uphill battle. This book explores how companies can remain competitive without exploiting their workforce or deceiving their customers, and why doing so is a long-term advantage, not a disadvantage.
- **For Consumers:** Ever been frustrated by hidden fees, poor service, or deceptive corporate practices? You're not alone. Customers have become an afterthought in the relentless pursuit of cost-cutting. From airlines to telecom providers, businesses increasingly prioritize squeezing out profits over maintaining relationships. If you're tired of being treated as just another transaction, this book explains how we got here, and what you can do about it.
- **For Anyone Who Wants to Understand the Bigger Picture:** The forces reshaping work and business affect all of us. Automation, globalization, the gig economy, and the decline of corporate accountability are not isolated trends, they're interconnected. Whether you're an investor, a student, or someone just trying to navigate an economy that feels increasingly hostile to the average person, this book provides a roadmap to understanding how corporate priorities shifted, and how they might be realigned.

What This Book Will Not Do

This is not a book of complaints without solutions. It won't just rehash corporate greed or paint an unchangeable dystopia.

Instead, it will:

☑ **Break down the system**, explaining in clear, accessible terms how we got here.

☑ **Examine case studies**, both of companies that exploit workers and those proving ethical business can thrive.

✅ **Explore real solutions**, for employees, business owners, and consumers alike.

Because understanding the system is the first step to changing it.

How This Book Is Structured, A Roadmap for Change

The corporate world didn't always operate this way. There was a time when companies understood that taking care of employees and customers wasn't just the right thing to do, it was smart business, but that mindset shifted. This book will take you through that transformation, why it happened, what it means for all of us, and how we can fix it.

Part 1: The Rise and Fall of People-First Business Models

To understand how we got here, we first need to look at where we started. This section explores:

- How companies like IBM and General Motors once valued their employees and customers, investing in stable careers, pensions, and long-term relationships.[8]
- The turning point, how shareholder primacy and short-term profit incentives took hold, shifting corporate priorities away from people and toward quarterly earnings.[9]
- How globalization and deregulation accelerated the move toward outsourcing, cost-cutting, and automation, at the expense of workers and consumers.[10]

---

8. Chandler, A. D. (1977). *The Visible Hand: The Managerial Revolution in American Business.* Harvard University Press.

9. Friedman, M. (1970). *The Social Responsibility of Business is to Increase its Profits.* The New York Times Magazine.

10. Lazonick, W. (2009). *Sustainable Prosperity in the New Economy? Business Organization and High-Tech Employment in the United States.* Upjohn Institute.

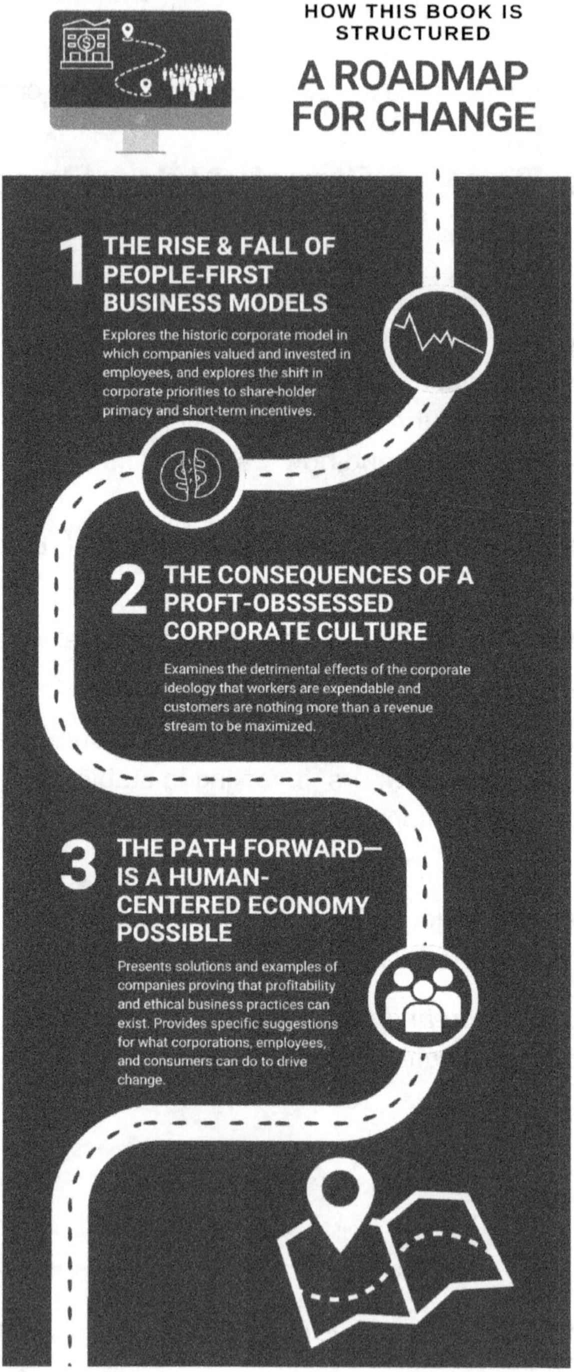

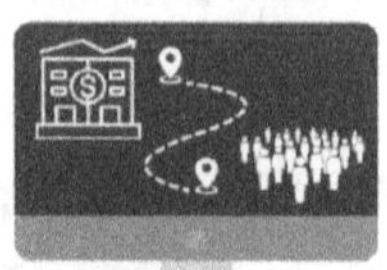

HOW THIS BOOK IS STRUCTURED

A ROADMAP FOR CHANGE

1 THE RISE & FALL OF PEOPLE-FIRST BUSINESS MODELS

Explores the historic corporate model in which companies valued and invested in employees, and explores the shift in corporate priorities to share-holder primacy and short-term incentives.

2 THE CONSEQUENCES OF A PROFT-OBSSESSED CORPORATE CULTURE

Examines the detrimental effects of the corporate ideology that workers are expendable and customers are nothing more than a revenue stream to be maximized.

3 THE PATH FORWARD—IS A HUMAN-CENTERED ECONOMY POSSIBLE

Presents solutions and examples of companies proving that profitability and ethical business practices can exist. Provides specific suggestions for what corporations, employees, and consumers can do to drive change.

Figure 1

Part 2: The Consequences of a Profit-Obsessed Corporate Culture

Today, businesses often see workers as expendable and customers as revenue streams to be maximized. This section uncovers the real cost of this shift:

- The rise of gig work and precarious employment, where companies like Uber and Amazon sidestep labor protections by misclassifying workers as independent contractors.[11]
- The erosion of customer trust through deceptive marketing, hidden fees, and poor service, as companies chase short-term gains instead of long-term loyalty.[12]
- The wider implications: rising income inequality, economic instability, and growing public distrust in corporations that prioritize profit above all else.

Part 3: The Path Forward, Is a Human-Centered Economy Possible?

This book isn't just about diagnosing the problem, it's about finding solutions. In the final section, we explore:

- Companies proving that profitability and ethical business practices can coexist. Brands like Costco, Patagonia, and Trader Joe's show that investing in employees and customers leads to long-term success.[13]
- What corporations, employees, and consumers can do to drive change. Whether it's through ethical leadership, responsible consumer choices, or policy advocacy, we are not powerless.
- Rebuilding trust in business, how companies can move beyond short-term thinking and regain the loyalty of workers and customers.

---

11. Rosenblat, A., & Stark, L. (2016). *Algorithmic Labor and Information Asymmetries: A Case Study of Uber's Drivers.* International Journal of Communication, 10, 3758-3784.

12. Zuboff, S. (2019). *The Age of Surveillance Capitalism: The Fight for a Human Future at the New Frontier of Power.* PublicAffairs.

13. B Corps Annual Report. (2023). *The Business Case for Ethical Corporate Practices.*

A Spark of Hope

This book is designed to be both eye-opening and practical. By the time you turn the last page, you'll have a clearer understanding of how we reached this moment, and, more importantly, what can be done to reshape the future of work and business.

Because while corporations may have created this system, we have the power to demand something better.

Chapter 1

From Principles to Profit, Balancing Empathy and Enterprise

A warehouse worker scans items under the glow of fluorescent lights, his every movement tracked by an algorithm dictating his pace. A gig worker swipes at their phone, anxiously waiting for the next ride request, knowing that a slow day could mean skipping rent. A call center employee follows a rigid script, aware that too much deviation could cost them their job.

Work didn't always look like this.

There was a time when employment meant stability, when companies invested in their workers and customers, not just their bottom line. But today, corporations operate differently.

This chapter explores the shift from people-first business models to profit-first corporate strategies, why it happened, who benefited, and what it has cost employees, customers, and society as a whole.

Because when companies stop seeing people as their greatest asset, the consequences aren't just economic, they're deeply human.

The evolution of business practices over the past few decades has seen a significant shift from models that prioritize employees and customers to those primarily driven by profit. This transformation, driven by globalization, technological advances, and changing corporate governance structures, has had profound implications for the workplace, the economy, and society at large.

Employee-Centric and Customer-Centric Models

In the mid-20th century, many companies operated with a strong focus on employee welfare and customer satisfaction. Known as the "Golden Age of Capitalism," this era saw companies realize how crucial it was to retain a motivated and devoted workforce in addition to cultivating enduring relationships with clients.

Companies like IBM and General Motors, for example, were known for their generous employee benefits, including pensions, health care, and job security, which in turn ensured high levels of productivity and innovation.[14] Similarly, businesses understood the importance of customer loyalty and satisfaction.[15]

THE SHAREHOLDER REVOLUTION

BEFORE 1970	AFTER 1970
• Companies reinvested profits into workers, customers, and innovation. • Employees had stable jobs, pensions, and benefits. • Customer service focused on long-term loyalty rather than short-term gains.	• Stockholders became the primary focus. • Employee benefits and customer service were cut to reduce costs. • Short-term stock price became the only measure of success.

Figure 2

---

14. Chandler, A. D. (1977). *The Visible Hand: The Managerial Revolution in American Business.* Harvard University Press.

15. Lazonick, W. (2009). *Sustainable Prosperity in the New Economy? Business Organization and High-Tech Employment in the United States.* Upjohn Institute.

Brands like Sears and Coca-Cola invested heavily in customer service and product quality, aiming to build lasting relationships with consumers.[16] The idea was that by taking care of employees and customers, profitability would follow naturally as a result of increased productivity, innovation, and brand loyalty.

Rise of Profit-Driven Approaches

The shift towards profit-driven models began in the late 20th century, largely driven by changes in corporate governance and the rise of shareholder primacy. This new approach, which prioritized the interests of shareholders above all else, was popularized by economist Milton Friedman in his seminal 1970 article, "The Social Responsibility of Business is to Increase its Profits."

Friedman argued that the primary responsibility of a business was to maximize returns for its shareholders, within the bounds of the law.[17] This shift was further reinforced by the rise of institutional investors and the growing influence of financial markets. Companies began to focus on short-term profits and share price maximization, often at the expense of employees and customers.[18] The era of mergers and acquisitions in the 1980s and 1990s saw many companies cutting costs aggressively, including downsizing their workforces, to boost their bottom lines.[19]

Wider Social Effects

The shift towards profit-driven models has also had broader implications for society. The focus on shareholder value has contributed to growing income inequality, as executives and shareholders reap the benefits of cost-cutting measures while employees face stagnating wages and

---

16. Colby, C. L., & Parasuraman, A. (2003). *Technology Still Matters: Eighty-one Percent of Consumers Believe They Can Get Better Deals from Brands with Good Customer Service.. Journal of Service Research*, 6(1), 55-70.

17. Friedman, M. (1970). The Social Responsibility of Business is to Increase its Profits. *The New York Times Magazine*.

18. Useem, M. (1993). *Executive Defense: Shareholder Power and Corporate Reorganization*. Harvard University Press.

19. Kalleberg, A. L. (2009). Precarious Work, Insecure Workers: Employment Relations in Transition. *American Sociological Review*, 74(1), 1-22.

diminished job security.[20] This trend is evident in the increasing disparity between CEO compensation and average worker wages, which has widened significantly over the past two decades.

Customers are also becoming increasingly disillusioned as a result of the decline in corporate trust. As companies prioritize profits over people, customers are becoming increasingly skeptical of corporate motives and are more likely to seek out brands that demonstrate genuine commitment to ethical practices and social responsibility.

How the Modern Business Environment Undervalues Employees and Customers

In recent decades, the corporate landscape has shifted significantly, influenced by technological advancements, globalization, and evolving corporate governance practices. These changes have brought efficiency and profitability but have also contributed to a culture where employees and customers are increasingly devalued.[21] Manifestations of this devaluation include precarious employment, job insecurity, diminished customer service quality, and a focus on short-term profits over long-term relationships.[22]

Devaluation of Employees

A major shift in the corporate environment has been the rise of precarious employment, work that is unpredictable and lacks the security of traditional full-time jobs. The gig economy, exemplified by companies like Uber and Lyft, relies heavily on classifying workers as independent contractors rather than employees.[23] This designation allows companies to sidestep obligations such as health insurance, paid leave, and retirement plans, effectively devaluing the worker's role.

---

20. Piketty, T. (2014). *Capital in the Twenty-First Century*. Harvard University Press.

21. Lazonick, W. (2009). *Sustainable Prosperity in the New Economy? Business Organization and High-Tech Employment in the United States*. Upjohn Institute.

22. Brynjolfsson, E., & McAfee, A. (2014). *The Second Machine Age: Work, Progress, and Prosperity in a Time of Brilliant Technologies*. W.W. Norton & Company.

23. Rosenblat, A., & Stark, L. (2016). Algorithmic Labor and Information Asymmetries: A Case Study of Uber's Drivers. *International Journal of Communication*, 10, 3758-3784.

The trend of outsourcing and offshoring further contributes to job insecurity as companies move jobs to countries with cheaper labor, causing job losses in developed economies. For instance, offshoring has contributed to substantial declines in U.S. manufacturing employment, leaving many workers with limited job prospects and decreasing the value placed on their labor.[24]

Stagnant Wages and Diminished Benefits

Despite increasing corporate profits and productivity, wages for many workers have stagnated or declined in real terms. The rise of shareholder primacy, where the primary goal is maximizing returns for shareholders, has often come at the cost of fair wages and benefits for employees. CEOs and top executives have seen significant increases in their compensation, while average worker wages barely keep up with inflation, widening income inequality.[25]

Figure 3

Employee devaluation has also been exacerbated by benefit reductions. Many companies have cut back on health benefits, retirement plans, and other perks that were once standard. A decline in union membership has

24. Kalleberg, A. L. (2009). Precarious Work, Insecure Workers: Employment Relations in Transition. *American Sociological Review*, 74(1), 1-22.

25. Piketty, T. (2014). *Capital in the Twenty-First Century*. Harvard University Press.

also weakened workers' bargaining power, making it harder for them to secure better pay and benefits.[26]

Rise of Automation and the Dehumanization of Work

Automation and technological advancements have transformed the workplace, often to the detriment of workers. While automation boosts efficiency and reduces costs, it poses a threat to jobs, particularly those involving routine or manual tasks.

For instance, self-checkout machines in retail stores have reduced the need for cashiers, leading to job losses and reduced hours for remaining employees.[27] A constant emphasis on efficiency and cost-cutting has also dehumanized labor, treating workers like cogs with little care for their welfare. Amazon's warehouse workers, for example, report grueling conditions with high productivity demands and limited consideration for their physical and mental health.[28]

Devaluation of Customers

As businesses increasingly focus on cost-cutting and efficiency, the quality of customer service has often suffered as a result. Many companies have reduced their customer service teams or outsourced these operations to countries with lower labor costs, leading to longer wait times, reduced service quality, and heightened customer frustration. Customers are left waiting in long queues or dealing with unresponsive or unqualified representatives, which leads to an overall negative experience.

In particular, the telecommunications industry, including well-known companies like Comcast and AT&T, has faced criticism for poor customer service. Customers often report frustrating experiences such as long

---

26. Kalleberg, A. L. (2009). Precarious Work, Insecure Workers: Employment Relations in Transition. *American Sociological Review*, 74(1), 1-22.

27. Brynjolfsson, E., & McAfee, A. (2014). *The Second Machine Age: Work, Progress, and Prosperity in a Time of Brilliant Technologies*. W.W. Norton & Company.

28. Kantor, J., & Streitfeld, D. (2015). Inside Amazon: Wrestling Big Ideas in a Bruising Workplace. *The New York Times*.

wait times, unhelpful representatives, and recurring billing issues, all of which contribute to dissatisfaction.[29]

The quality of customer interactions has also declined as a result of the growing use of automated phone systems and chatbots for customer service. While these systems can be helpful for addressing simple inquiries or performing basic tasks, they frequently fail to resolve more complex or nuanced issues. This leaves customers feeling undervalued and ignored, as they are unable to engage with a real person who can fully address their concerns.[30]

Deceptive Practices and Hidden Fees

Deceptive practices and hidden fees are other ways that modern corporations devalue customers. Companies frequently use misleading marketing to attract customers, only to impose hidden fees or restrictive terms after they sign up. The banking and financial services sectors, in particular, have faced criticism for such tactics. The Wells Fargo scandal, where employees opened millions of unauthorized accounts to meet aggressive sales targets, is a prominent example of exploiting customers for profit.[31]

Deterioration of Trust

The cumulative effect of declining service quality, deceptive practices, and a profit-centric focus has led to an erosion of customer trust. Customers increasingly view corporate motives with skepticism, leading them to switch brands or seek alternatives they perceive as more transparent and customer-focused.

---

29. Brodkin, J. (2014). Comcast and AT&T Are America's Most Hated ISPs, Study Finds. *Ars Technica*.

30. Colby, C. L., & Parasuraman, A. (2003). *Technology Still Matters: Eighty-one Percent of Consumers Believe They Can Get Better Deals from Brands with Good Customer Service.*. *Journal of Service Research*, 6(1), 55-70.

31. Egan, M. (2016). Wells Fargo's 5,300 Fired Employees: Where Are They Now? *CNN Money*.

Patients frequently feel that the financial interests of insurance companies and healthcare providers come before their own needs in sectors like healthcare, where this breakdown of trust is particularly evident.[32] Data security worries have also been exacerbated by the increase in privacy violations and data breaches. For example, Facebook faced backlash for its handling of user data, raising widespread privacy concerns.[33]

Need for a Balanced Approach

The shift from employee-centric and customer-centric models to profit-driven approaches has undoubtedly transformed the corporate landscape, often to the detriment of both employees and customers. However, this trend is not sustainable in the long term. Companies that continue to prioritize short-term profits at the expense of their workforce and customer base risk alienating the very people who drive their success.

There is a growing recognition that businesses must return to a more balanced approach, where the well-being of employees and customers is considered alongside profitability. By investing in their people and fostering genuine relationships with customers, these companies have demonstrated that long-term success and profitability are best achieved through a holistic approach that values all stakeholders.

These shifts in corporate priorities reveal a troubling imbalance, where the pursuit of efficiency and profitability has compromised the essential human values of trust, loyalty, and respect. As companies increasingly prioritize short-term gains and shareholder returns, both employees and customers find themselves undervalued and disempowered, leading to dissatisfaction, disengagement, and a widening trust gap.

In response, a growing movement advocates for a reimagining of corporate responsibility. By prioritizing ethical practices, fair treatment, and transparent customer relations, companies have an opportunity to rebuild trust and foster a more sustainable, human-centered approach.

---

32. Sandel, M. J. (2012). *What Money Can't Buy: The Moral Limits of Markets*. Farrar, Straus and Giroux.

33. Zuboff, S. (2019). *The Age of Surveillance Capitalism: The Fight for a Human Future at the New Frontier of Power*. PublicAffairs.

Realigning corporate goals with the well-being of workers, customers, and the communities they serve could set a new standard, one that balances profit with purpose and restores the integrity of the business-consumer relationship.

KEY TAKEAWAYS

- **The Golden Age of Employee and Customer-Centric Business**
During the mid-20th century, businesses valued employee welfare and customer loyalty, seeing long-term investment in people as key to productivity, innovation, and trust.

- **The Rise of Shareholder Primacy Reshaped Corporate Values**
Milton Friedman's 1970s shareholder primacy theory shifted corporate focus to maximizing stockholder returns, driving cost-cutting, outsourcing, and short-term gains over sustainability.

- **Employees Became Disposable, and Job Security Declined**
With companies seeking greater efficiency and lower costs, workforce stability eroded. The rise of gig work, automation, and offshoring resulted in precarious employment, stagnant wages, and fewer benefits.

- **Customers Are Increasingly Treated as Revenue Streams, Not Relationships**
As businesses optimized for profit, customer service declined. Companies outsourced support, implemented automated systems, and introduced deceptive pricing models such as hidden fees. As a result, consumer trust has eroded, with customers often feeling undervalued and exploited.

- **The Shift to Profit-First Models Is Not Sustainable**
The relentless pursuit of short-term shareholder gains has led to wider income inequality, economic instability, and public distrust in corporations. However, a growing movement advocates for a return to balanced business models that invest in employees, rebuild customer relationships, and prioritize ethical, long-term success.

Chapter 2

Foundations of Modern Management, The Legacy of Scientific Efficiency

The dawn of the 20th century marked a significant transformation in the field of management, with the advent of scientific management playing a pivotal role in reshaping organizational practices. Spearheaded by Frederick Winslow Taylor, scientific management introduced a systematic approach to improving efficiency and productivity in industrial settings.

Although its main goal was to optimize management structures and work processes, it also unintentionally brought attention to the significance of employee welfare and motivation, which in turn increased engagement and productivity.

Origins of Scientific Management

Scientific management, or Taylorism, emerged in the late 19th and early 20th centuries as a response to inefficiency and disorganization in industrial workplaces. Frederick Winslow Taylor, widely regarded as its founder, was deeply concerned with the wastefulness and lack of structured methods in manufacturing.[34] His observations and experiments, particularly at Midvale Steel Company, led him to develop principles focused on enhancing productivity by applying scientific methods to work processes.

34. Taylor, F. W. (1911). *The Principles of Scientific Management*. Harper & Brothers.

Key Principles of Scientific Management

Taylor's scientific management was built on several core principles, which can be summarized as follows:

- **Scientific Study of Work:** Taylor advocated for the systematic study of work processes to identify the most efficient ways of performing tasks. This involved breaking down tasks into their simplest components and analyzing the time and motions required to complete them.
- **Standardization of Work Practices:** Once the most efficient methods were identified, they were standardized and implemented across the workforce. This standardization ensured consistency in output and reduced variability in performance.
- **Selection and Training of Workers:** Taylor emphasized the importance of selecting the right workers for specific tasks and providing them with proper training to perform those tasks efficiently. This principle recognized the role of skill and aptitude in achieving optimal performance.
- **Division of Labor:** Scientific management introduced a clear separation between planning and execution. Managers were responsible for planning and organizing work, while workers were tasked with executing the tasks according to the prescribed methods.
- **Incentive Systems:** Taylor believed in the use of monetary incentives to motivate workers. He proposed that workers should be paid based on their productivity, with higher wages offered to those who met or exceeded performance standards.

These principles were encapsulated in Frederick Winslow Taylor's seminal work, *The Principles of Scientific Management*, which became the cornerstone for the widespread adoption of scientific management practices across industries. Taylor's ideas sparked a shift in management philosophy, and his approach, though criticized at times for its rigidity and dehumanizing effects on workers, laid the groundwork for many of the management practices that remain in use today. His influence reached beyond the manufacturing sector, touching nearly every industry and creating a lasting legacy in both the world of business and labor.[35]

Impacts of Scientific Management on Management Structure

The implementation of scientific management had a profound impact on the structure of organizations. It introduced a hierarchical management structure with clearly defined roles and responsibilities, which became a hallmark of modern industrial organizations.

Managerial Role in Scientific Management

Under scientific management, managers assumed a central role in the planning and organization of work. Their responsibilities included the following:

- **Planning:** Managers were tasked with developing detailed plans for each work process, based on the scientific study of tasks. This planning process involved determining the most efficient methods, tools, and sequences of operations.
- **Coordination:** Managers coordinated the work of different departments and workers to ensure that production flowed smoothly and efficiently. This coordination minimized delays and bottlenecks in the production process.
- **Supervision:** Scientific management emphasized close supervision of workers to ensure that they adhered to the standardized work practices. Managers were responsible for monitoring performance and providing feedback to workers.
- **Control:** Managers exercised control over the work environment, ensuring that all necessary resources were available and that work was carried out according to the prescribed methods. This control extended to enforcing discipline and maintaining order in the workplace.

35. Taylor, F. W. (1911). *The Principles of Scientific Management*. Harper & Brothers.

The hierarchical structure introduced by scientific management placed managers at the top of the organizational pyramid, with workers occupying the lower levels. This clear delineation of roles and responsibilities facilitated efficient decision-making and accountability within the organization.

TAYLORISM IN ACTION: THEN vs. NOW

EARLY 20TH CENTURY	TODAY
• Factories used stopwatches and clipboards to measure worker efficiency. • Managers standardized every task, down to the smallest movement. • Incentive pay encouraged faster, more efficient work.	• Algorithms track productivity in warehouses and call centers. • AI-driven workforce management assigns tasks in real-time. • Performance-based pay still dominates gig work and retail.

RESULT: The efficiency revolution continues—but so do concerns about worker burnout and dehumanization.

Figure 4

Evolution of Management Theories

While scientific management laid the groundwork for modern management practices, it also spurred the development of alternative management theories that sought to address some of its limitations. One such theory was the Human Relations Movement, which emerged in the 1930s and emphasized the importance of social and psychological factors in the workplace.

Elton Mayo's Hawthorne Studies, conducted at the Western Electric Hawthorne Works during the 1920s and 1930s, demonstrated that workers' productivity was shaped not only by physical work conditions but also by social interactions, group dynamics, and the attention they received from management.[36] These findings challenged the mechanistic view of workers as mere cogs in a machine, as proposed by Taylorism, and

36. Mayo, E. (1933). *The Human Problems of an Industrial Civilization*. Macmillan.

emphasized the importance of addressing employees' emotional and social needs within management practices.

The Human Relations Movement laid the groundwork for more employee-focused management theories, such as Douglas McGregor's Theory X and Theory Y.[37] Theory Y, in particular, highlighted the potential for intrinsic motivation among workers and promoted a participative, empowering approach to management. These theories built upon the principles of scientific management by incorporating employee motivation and welfare into organizational structures.

Employee Welfare and Motivation's Impact on Productivity

While scientific management was primarily concerned with optimizing work processes and efficiency, it also indirectly highlighted the importance of employee motivation and welfare in driving productivity. Taylor's emphasis on incentive systems, for example, recognized the role of motivation in influencing worker performance.

Psychological Impacts of Work on Employees

The adoption of scientific management practices, with its emphasis on standardization and close supervision, had both positive and negative impacts on employees. The standardization of work processes helped reduce ambiguity, providing workers with clear guidelines, which in turn could boost their sense of competence and mastery.[38] However, the repetitive and mechanistic nature of tasks under scientific management often resulted in job dissatisfaction and alienation, as employees were confined to monotonous tasks with limited autonomy or creative input.[39]

To address these challenges, subsequent management theories and practices began to focus more on the psychological and emotional needs of workers. The Human Relations Movement, for example, emphasized

37. McGregor, D. (1960). *The Human Side of Enterprise*. McGraw-Hill.

38. Locke, E. A., & Latham, G. P. (1990). *A Theory of Goal Setting & Task Performance*. Prentice-Hall.

39. Braverman, H. (1974). *Labor and Monopoly Capital: The Degradation of Work in the Twentieth Century*. Monthly Review Press.

the importance of social interactions and recognition in motivating workers. This shift in focus laid the groundwork for the development of modern theories of motivation, such as Abraham Maslow's Hierarchy of Needs and Frederick Herzberg's Two-Factor Theory.

Maslow's Hierarchy of Needs posits that individuals are motivated by a series of needs, starting with basic physiological requirements and advancing to higher-order needs, such as self-actualization. According to Maslow, once fundamental needs are satisfied, individuals turn their attention to fulfilling needs related to social belonging, esteem, and ultimately, self-actualization.[40] In the workplace, this translates to a desire for meaningful work, opportunities for personal and professional growth, and a sense of purpose.

Herzberg's Two-Factor Theory built on motivation research by identifying two key categories that influence job satisfaction: hygiene factors and motivators. Hygiene factors, such as pay, working conditions, and job security, are essential to prevent dissatisfaction but do not inherently drive motivation.[41] In contrast, motivators are intrinsic elements of the work itself, such as accountability, achievement, and recognition, which have the potential to boost engagement and motivation.

Employee Welfare Programs' Effects

The contemporary business environment acknowledged the value of employee welfare initiatives in boosting productivity in addition to addressing motivation. Welfare programs, such as health benefits, retirement plans, and wellness initiatives, contribute to the overall well-being of employees, which in turn has a positive impact on their performance and engagement.

For instance, companies such as Google and Microsoft have introduced robust employee welfare programs that encompass health and wellness initiatives, flexible work policies, and opportunities for personal and professional growth.[42] These initiatives enhance employee satisfaction

---

40. Maslow, A. H. (1943). A theory of human motivation. *Psychological Review*, 50(4), 370-396.
41. Herzberg, F. (1959). *The Motivation to Work*. John Wiley & Sons.
42. Laszlo, B. (2014). *Work Rules!: Insights from Inside Google That Will Transform How You Live and Lead*. Twelve.

while cultivating a positive organizational culture that drives productivity and innovation.

According to research, companies that invest in the welfare of their employees experience increased engagement, reduced turnover, and improved overall performance.[43] This demonstrates the strong connection between employee welfare and organizational success.

Employee Engagement and Productivity: A Correlation

Employee engagement is a critical factor in driving productivity and organizational success. Engaged employees are those who are emotionally invested in their work and are committed to the organization's goals and values. They are more likely to go above and beyond in their roles, contributing to higher levels of productivity, innovation, and customer satisfaction. This was the work environment back in the 1970s and 80s, which also spurred the quality movement.

Management's Function in Promoting Employee Engagement

Management plays a crucial role in fostering employee engagement. The principles of scientific management, with their emphasis on clear communication, goal-setting, and feedback, laid the groundwork for modern management practices that prioritize employee engagement.

For example, goal-setting theory, developed by Edwin Locke and Gary Latham, highlights the significance of establishing specific, challenging, and attainable goals to drive employee motivation and engagement.[44] When employees are provided with clear objectives and understand how their efforts align with organizational success, they tend to be more committed and enthusiastic about their work.

---

43. Harter, J. K., Schmidt, F. L., & Hayes, T. L. (2002). Business-unit-level relationship between employee satisfaction, employee engagement, and business outcomes: A meta-analysis. *Journal of Applied Psychology*, 87(2), 268-279.

44. Locke, E. A., & Latham, G. P. (1990). *A Theory of Goal Setting & Task Performance*. Prentice-Hall.

Effective management involves not only setting clear goals but also providing employees with regular feedback and recognition. Acknowledging a job well done serves as a powerful motivator, significantly boosting engagement and satisfaction. The rise of continuous feedback practices in recent years has encouraged managers to deliver real-time feedback and recognition, cultivating a culture of constant improvement and heightened involvement.[45] This approach mirrors the dynamic between coaches and athletes, where tailored feedback and motivation help individuals and teams perform at their best.

Granting workers autonomy and opportunities for growth is a crucial strategy for fostering empowerment and engagement. Studies reveal that employees who feel a sense of control over their tasks and have access to skill development and career advancement are significantly more motivated and invested in their work.[46]

How Employee Engagement Affects Organizational Effectiveness

The relationship between employee engagement and organizational performance is well-documented in the literature. Engaged employees are more productive, deliver higher quality work, and are less likely to leave the organization, leading to lower turnover rates and reduced recruitment and training costs.[47]

Employee engagement also increases the likelihood that they will support a positive company culture, which can foster innovation, teamwork, and collaboration. A study by Gallup found that organizations with high levels of employee engagement outperformed their competitors in terms of profitability, customer satisfaction, and productivity.[48]

---

45. Braverman, H. (1974). *Labor and Monopoly Capital: The Degradation of Work in the Twentieth Century*. Monthly Review Press.

46. Maslow, A. H. (1943). A theory of human motivation. *Psychological Review*, 50(4), 370-396.

47. Harter, J. K., Schmidt, F. L., & Hayes, T. L. (2002). Business-unit-level relationship between employee satisfaction, employee engagement, and business outcomes: A meta-analysis. *Journal of Applied Psychology*, 87(2), 268-279.

48. Gallup. (2013). *State of the American Workplace: Employee Engagement Insights for U.S. Business Leaders*. Gallup.

Management Practices' Development: From Scientific Management to Contemporary Methods

While scientific management laid the foundation for modern management practices, it is important to recognize that management theories and practices have continued to evolve. The limitations of scientific management, particularly its focus on efficiency at the expense of employee autonomy and creativity, have led to the development of more holistic and employee-centric approaches.

Movement for Human Relations

As mentioned earlier, the Human Relations Movement emerged as a response to the mechanistic and dehumanizing aspects of scientific management. The movement highlighted the significance of social and psychological factors in the workplace, including employee morale, group dynamics, and leadership styles.[49] This shift in focus contributed to the development of management practices that prioritized employee well-being and motivation, ultimately laying the foundation for modern human resource management.

Theories of Motivation and Leadership

The evolution of management practices led to the development of various theories of motivation and leadership, which built upon the principles of scientific management while addressing its limitations. Theories such as Maslow's Hierarchy of Needs, Herzberg's Two-Factor Theory, and McGregor's Theory Y emphasized the importance of understanding and addressing the intrinsic needs of employees to drive motivation and engagement.[50, 51, 52]

In the realm of leadership, transformational leadership emerged as a popular approach, emphasizing the role of leaders in inspiring and

49. Mayo, E. (1933). *The Human Problems of an Industrial Civilization*. Macmillan.
50. Maslow, A. H. (1943). A theory of human motivation. *Psychological Review*, 50(4), 370-396.
51. McGregor, D. (1960). *The Human Side of Enterprise*. McGraw-Hill.
52. Herzberg, F. (1959). *The Motivation to Work*. John Wiley & Sons.

motivating employees to reach their full potential. Transformational leaders focus on creating a vision, fostering a positive organizational culture, and empowering employees to take ownership of their work.[53] This approach stands in contrast to the more directive and authoritarian leadership styles associated with scientific management.

The Emergence of Agile and Employee-Centric Management Methods

In recent years, some companies have adopted employee-centric and agile management approaches, which prioritize flexibility, collaboration, and employee empowerment. Agile management, originally developed in the software industry, promotes iterative and adaptive processes, cross-functional teams, and a focus on customer value. This approach has since been embraced by various industries and has proven effective in fostering innovation and responsiveness in dynamic environments.[54]

Employee-centric approaches, adopted by companies like Google and Zappos, prioritize the well-being and development of employees as essential to organizational success. These strategies focus on creating a positive work environment, offering opportunities for learning and growth and nurturing a culture of trust and collaboration.[55, 56]

A paradigm shift in management practices occurred with the introduction of scientific management, which introduced a methodical approach to productivity and process optimization. While scientific management initially focused on efficiency and standardization, it also laid the foundation for the development of more employee-centric approaches that recognize the importance of motivation, welfare, and engagement in driving organizational success.

---

53. Bass, B. M. (1985). *Leadership and Performance Beyond Expectations*. Free Press.

54. Rigby, D. K., Sutherland, J., & Takeuchi, H. (2016). Embracing Agile. *Harvard Business Review*, 94(5), 40-50.

55. Laszlo, B. (2014). *Work Rules!: Insights from Inside Google That Will Transform How You Live and Lead*. Twelve.

56. Hsieh, T. (2010). *Delivering Happiness: A Path to Profits, Passion, and Purpose*. Business Plus.

Modern management techniques, as opposed to Taylorism, demonstrate the increasing understanding of the intricate and varied nature of work and the vital role that employees play in accomplishing company objectives. By integrating the principles of scientific management with a focus on employee motivation and welfare, organizations can create environments that foster productivity, innovation, and long-term success.

Employee motivation, engagement, and productivity are known to be correlated, and companies that put these elements first are more likely to succeed in the cutthroat and quickly evolving business environment of today. As management practices continue to evolve, the lessons learned from the inception of scientific management will remain relevant, serving as a reminder of the importance of balancing efficiency with the human elements of work.

KEY TAKEAWAYS

- **Taylor's Scientific Management standardized work**, Breaking tasks into measurable steps increased efficiency but reduced worker autonomy.
- **Management became hierarchical and rigid**, Planning and execution were separated, with managers controlling workflows while workers followed strict guidelines.
- **Modern workplaces still use Taylorism**, Gig work, AI-driven tracking, and performance-based pay reflect its lasting impact on labor today.

Chapter 3

The Golden Era of Employee Commitment and Loyalty

The latter half of the 20th century, particularly the 1970s, 1980s, and 1990s, witnessed a significant transformation in the corporate world with a growing emphasis on employee motivation, quality improvement, and customer service. This period was marked by the emergence of influential thought leaders such as Zig Ziglar, Tom Peters, Wayne Dyer, Stephen Covey, Denis Waitley, Ken Blanchard, John Maxwell, and Jim Collins.

Their contributions played a pivotal role in shaping management practices and organizational culture, leading to a more motivated workforce, higher-quality products, and enhanced customer experiences. Here we explore the evolution of these concepts during this era, highlighting the impact of these thought leaders on creating a better work environment and driving organizational success.

The Context of the 1970s, 1980s, and 1990s

Before delving into the specific contributions of these thought leaders, it is essential to understand the broader context of the 1970s, 1980s, and 1990s. These decades were marked by profound social, technological, and economic shifts that affected management techniques and business strategies.

The 1970s were marked by economic challenges, including the oil crisis, stagflation, and increased global competition. Companies faced pressure to improve efficiency and reduce costs while maintaining product quality. The 1980s saw the rise of globalization, deregulation, and the proliferation of information technology, which further intensified competition.

By the 1990s, the advent of the internet and the digital revolution transformed the business landscape, creating new opportunities and challenges for organizations.[57] In response to these changes, companies began to recognize the importance of employee motivation and engagement in driving productivity and innovation. Also, as companies looked to stand out in a more competitive market, the emphasis on quality and customer service became critical.

Shifting Towards Employee Motivation and Quality

The economic pressures of the 1970s and 1980s led to a shift in management thinking, with a growing recognition that employee motivation and quality were critical to organizational success. This period saw the emergence of Total Quality Management (TQM) as a key management philosophy, emphasizing the importance of continuous improvement, employee involvement, and customer satisfaction.[58]

Simultaneously, the concept of employee motivation gained prominence, with thought leaders and motivational speakers advocating for a more human-centric approach to management. The work of these leaders emphasized the role of leadership, personal development, and intrinsic motivation in creating a more engaged and productive workforce.

How Thought Leaders Influence Employee Quality and Motivation

The thought leaders played a critical role in shaping management practices related to employee motivation, quality improvement, and customer service. These individuals, through their books, speeches, and training programs, provided valuable insights and practical tools that helped

57. Drucker, P. F. (1993). *Post-Capitalist Society*. HarperBusiness.

58. Deming, W. E. (1986). *Out of the Crisis*. MIT Press.

organizations create a better work environment and deliver superior products and services.

Figure 5

Zig Ziglar: The Power of Positive Thinking and Motivation

Zig Ziglar, one of the most well-known motivational speakers and authors of the late 20th century, was a pioneer in the field of personal development and motivation. Ziglar's philosophy was encapsulated in his famous quote, "You can have everything in life you want if you will just help enough other people get what they want."[59] His work focused on the power of positive thinking, goal setting, and the importance of a positive attitude in achieving success.

Ziglar's teachings emphasized the importance of self-belief, perseverance, and a strong work ethic. He believed that motivated and optimistic employees were more likely to be productive, innovative, and committed to delivering high-quality work. His training programs, seminars, and books, such as *See You at the Top* (1974) and *Top Performance* (1986), were widely adopted by organizations seeking to improve employee motivation and performance.[60, 61]

Beyond motivating individuals, Ziglar's impact was felt at the corporate level, where his ideas were used to improve organizational culture. Companies that embraced Ziglar's teachings reported increased employee satisfaction, higher productivity, and improved customer service, demonstrating the link between motivation, quality, and customer experience.

Tom Peters: Excellence in Management and Customer Service

Tom Peters, a management consultant, gained widespread recognition in the 1980s with the publication of his seminal book *In Search of Excellence* (1982), co-authored with Robert H. Waterman Jr. The book highlighted the practices of successful companies and introduced the concept of "management by walking around" (MBWA), which emphasized the importance of hands-on leadership and close engagement, distinct from

---

59. Ziglar, Z. (1982). Top Performance: How to Develop Excellence in Yourself and Others. Baker Books.

60. Ibid.

61. Ziglar, Z. (1974). See You at the Top. Pelican Publishing.

the micromanagement practices prevalent today, with employees and customers.[62]

Peters' work was instrumental in promoting the idea that excellence in management and customer service was the key to long-term success. He maintained that rather than concentrating on immediate financial gains, businesses should prioritize innovation, customer satisfaction, and ongoing improvement. Businesses in the 1980s and 1990s responded favorably to Peters' emphasis on customer service as a differentiator in the marketplace, which increased attention to quality and customer-centric tactics.

Later writings by Peters, including *Thriving on Chaos* (1987) and T*he Pursuit of WOW!* (1994), persisted in promoting a culture of excellence, innovation, and customer-focused responsiveness. His ideas influenced a generation of managers and executives, inspiring them to prioritize employee engagement, quality improvement, and customer service in their organizations.

Wayne Dyer: Personal Development and Self-Actualization

Wayne Dyer, a psychologist, emerged as a leading figure in the personal development movement of the 1970s and 1980s. His best-selling book *Your Erroneous Zones* (1976) introduced millions of readers to the concept of self-actualization, emphasizing the importance of taking control of one's thoughts and emotions to achieve personal and professional fulfillment.[63]

Dyer's teachings on self-empowerment and personal responsibility resonated with individuals and organizations alike. He believed that employees who were self-motivated and focused on personal growth were more likely to be engaged, productive, and committed to delivering high-quality work. Dyer's emphasis on the power of the mind and the importance of a positive mindset influenced the way organizations approached employee motivation and development.

---

62. Peters, T., & Waterman, R. H. (1982). *In Search of Excellence: Lessons from America's Best-Run Companies*. Harper & Row.

63. Dyer, W. W. (1976). *Your Erroneous Zones*. Funk & Wagnalls.

His later works, such as *The Power of Intention* (2004) and *Inspiration: Your Ultimate Calling* (2006), continued to explore the connection between personal development and professional success. His teachings inspired companies to invest in employee development programs that focused on enhancing self-awareness, emotional intelligence, and resilience, leading to a more motivated and engaged workforce.

Stephen Covey: Leadership and Principle-Centered Management

Stephen Covey made a significant impact on the corporate world with the publication of his best-selling book *The 7 Habits of Highly Effective People* (1989). Covey's work introduced the concept of principle-centered leadership, which emphasized the importance of aligning personal and organizational values with ethical principles to achieve long-term success.[64] His book provided a practical framework for personal and professional development, focusing on habits such as proactive behavior, goal setting, prioritization, and continuous improvement.

In his emphasis on character, integrity, and service-oriented leadership, organizations seeking to create a positive and values-driven culture found resonance. The ideas highlighted by Covey's principles extended to the realm of quality management and customer service, where his concepts of leadership and personal responsibility were applied to drive continuous improvement and customer satisfaction.[65] Organizations that adopted Covey's teachings reported increased employee engagement, improved teamwork, and a stronger focus on delivering high-quality products and services.

Denis Waitley: The Psychology of Winning and Peak Performance

Denis Waitley, a motivational speaker and author, is best known for his work on the psychology of winning and peak performance. His book *The*

---

64. Covey, S. R. (1989). *The 7 Habits of Highly Effective People: Powerful Lessons in Personal Change*. Simon & Schuster.

65. Covey, S. R. (1989). *The 7 Habits of Highly Effective People: Powerful Lessons in Personal Change*. Simon & Schuster.

Psychology of Winning (1979) explored the mindset and behaviors of successful individuals, emphasizing the importance of self-discipline, goal-setting, and a positive mental attitude.[66] Waitley's teachings focused on the mental and emotional aspects of performance, encouraging individuals to develop a winning mindset and overcome self-limiting beliefs.

Because his ideas were used to improve performance, motivation, and resilience, his work had a particularly significant impact on the domains of sales, leadership, and personal development. His influence extended to the corporate world, where his principles were used to create a culture of excellence and high performance. Businesses that adopted Waitley's lessons saw improvements in customer satisfaction, sales, and employee motivation, proving the connection between quality, mindset, and customer experience.

Ken Blanchard: Situational Leadership and Empowerment

Ken Blanchard is best known for his work on situational leadership and empowerment. His book *The One Minute Manager* (1982), co-authored with Spencer Johnson, introduced the concept of situational leadership, which emphasizes the importance of adapting leadership styles to the needs and development levels of employees.[67] Blanchard's situational leadership model provided a practical framework for managers to assess the competence and commitment of their employees and to provide the appropriate level of direction and support.

His writings highlighted the value of encouraging teamwork, empowering workers, and establishing a positive work atmosphere. Blanchard's later works, such as *Leadership and the One Minute Manager* (1985) and *The Empowerment Explosion* (1996), continued to advocate for a more flexible and empowering approach to leadership. Because of his lessons, organizations implemented management strategies that placed a higher priority on employee autonomy, engagement, and development, which improved customer satisfaction, quality, and motivation.

---

66. Waitley, D. (1979). *The Psychology of Winning: Ten Qualities of a Total Winner*. Berkley Publishing.

67. Blanchard, K., & Johnson, S. (1982). *The One Minute Manager*. HarperCollins.

John Maxwell: Leadership Development and Influence

John Maxwell has made significant contributions to the field of leadership development. His books, such as *The 21 Irrefutable Laws of Leadership* (1998) and *Developing the Leader Within You* (1993), provide practical guidance on how to develop leadership skills, build influence, and create a positive impact within organizations.[68, 69] Maxwell's teachings emphasize the importance of character, vision, and communication in effective leadership.

He advocates for a servant leadership approach, where leaders prioritize the needs and development of their employees, creating a culture of trust, collaboration, and continuous improvement. The widespread adoption of Maxwell's leadership principles by businesses looking to boost team performance, increase employee engagement, and provide high-quality goods and services is evidence of his influence in the business sector. His work has inspired a generation of leaders to focus on personal growth, ethical leadership, and the empowerment of their teams.

Jim Collins: Building Enduring Organizations and the Flywheel Effect

Jim Collins is known for his work on building enduring organizations and the concept of the "flywheel effect." His book *Good to Great* (2001) explored how companies transition from being good to becoming great, emphasizing the importance of disciplined people, disciplined thought, and disciplined action.[70] Collins introduced the concept of the "flywheel effect," which describes the process of building momentum through consistent and incremental improvements.

According to Collins, great businesses focus on the right people, develop a disciplined culture, and never compromise on quality and customer service if they want to succeed in the long run.

---

68. Maxwell, J. C. (1993). *Developing the Leader Within You.* Thomas Nelson.

69. Maxwell, J. C. (1998). *The 21 Irrefutable Laws of Leadership: Follow Them and People Will Follow You.* Thomas Nelson.

70. Collins, J. (2001). *Good to Great: Why Some Companies Make the Leap... and Others Don't.* HarperBusiness.

Collins' work has had a profound impact on organizations seeking to achieve sustainable growth and excellence. His principles of leadership, strategic focus, and continuous improvement have been widely adopted by companies across various industries, leading to higher levels of employee engagement, product quality, and customer satisfaction.

The Impact of Thought Leadership on Organizational Practices

The teachings and principles of these thought leaders had a transformative impact on organizational practices during the 1970s, 1980s, and 1990s. Their emphasis on employee motivation, quality, and customer service influenced management strategies, leadership styles, and corporate cultures, leading to a more engaged workforce, higher-quality products, and enhanced customer experiences.

Corporate Culture and Employee Motivation Integration

The work of motivational speakers and authors such as Zig Ziglar, Wayne Dyer, and Denis Waitley played a significant role in integrating employee motivation into corporate culture. Their teachings encouraged organizations to recognize the importance of intrinsic motivation, personal development, and a positive mindset in driving employee performance and satisfaction. As a result, many companies began to invest in employee development programs, training initiatives, and wellness programs that focused on enhancing motivation, resilience, and overall well-being. These programs not only improved employee morale but also contributed to a more positive and productive work environment.

Emphasis on Quality and Continuous Improvement

The adoption of Total Quality Management (TQM) principles and the implementation of continuous improvement processes became widespread during this period. Companies such as Toyota, General Electric, and

Motorola became pioneers in quality management, demonstrating how a relentless focus on quality could lead to competitive advantage and customer loyalty.

Customer service emerged as a critical competitive differentiator during the 30 years mentioned. Their work emphasized the importance of understanding customer needs, delivering exceptional service, and building long-term relationships with customers.

Organizations that embraced these principles, such as Nordstrom, Ritz-Carlton, and Southwest Airlines, became known for their outstanding customer service and customer-centric cultures. These companies demonstrated that by prioritizing customer satisfaction, organizations could achieve higher levels of customer loyalty, repeat business, and positive word-of-mouth.

TOTAL QUALITY MANAGEMENT (TQM)

A Game-Changer in the 1980s and 1990s

- **Customer Focus:** Delivering what customers truly want
- **Continuous Improvement:** Small, steady improvements lead to excellence
- **Employee Involvement:** Workers at every level contribute ideas
- **Data-Driven Decisions:** Quality measured and tracked

REAL-WORLD EXAMPLE

- Toyota became a global leader by using TQM to eliminate waste, boost efficiency, and ensure product quality.

Figure 6

Toyota: The Power of Continuous Improvement and Quality

Toyota's success in the 1980s and 1990s can be attributed to its relentless focus on quality and continuous improvement. The company adopted the principles of Total Quality Management (TQM) and Lean Manufacturing, which emphasized the importance of eliminating waste, improving processes, and delivering high-quality products.[71]

Toyota's commitment to quality and continuous improvement was influenced by the teachings of thought leaders such as W. Edwards Deming, who advocated for a systems approach to quality management. The company's "Toyota Production System" became a model for other organizations, demonstrating how a focus on quality could lead to increased efficiency, customer satisfaction, and market success.

Ritz-Carlton: Creating a Culture of Excellence in Customer Service

Ritz-Carlton's reputation for excellence in customer service is a testament to the impact of thought leadership on organizational practices. The company adopted a customer-centric approach, inspired by the teachings of Tom Peters and Ken Blanchard, which emphasized the importance of delivering personalized and exceptional service to every guest.[72]

Ritz-Carlton's "Gold Standards" and "Employee Promise" created a culture of excellence and empowerment, where employees were encouraged to take ownership of the guest experience and go above and beyond to meet customer needs. The company's commitment to customer service earned it numerous accolades and a loyal customer base, demonstrating the power of a customer-focused culture.

The Continued Relevance of Employee Motivation

Employee motivation remains a critical focus for modern organizations, as companies recognize the importance of engaged and motivated employees in driving innovation, productivity, and customer satisfaction. Companies like Google, Salesforce, and Zappos have embraced these principles, creating work environments that prioritize employee well-being,

---

71. Liker, J. K. (2004). *The Toyota Way: 14 Management Principles from the World's Greatest Manufacturer*. McGraw-Hill.

72. Michelli, J. A. (2008). *The New Gold Standard: 5 Leadership Principles for Creating a Legendary Customer Experience Courtesy of the Ritz-Carlton Hotel Company*. McGraw-Hill.

empowerment, and growth. These organizations have demonstrated that a motivated and engaged workforce is a key driver of competitive advantage and long-term success.

The 1970s, 1980s, and 1990s were transformative decades for the corporate world, marked by a growing emphasis on employee motivation, quality improvement, and customer service. The contributions of these thought leaders played a pivotal role in shaping management practices and organizational culture during this period. Their teachings provided valuable insights and practical tools that helped organizations create better work environments, deliver higher-quality products, and enhance customer experiences.

The principles of employee motivation, quality, and customer service that emerged during this era continue to influence modern organizations, shaping the way companies operate and compete in the global marketplace.

As organizations continue to navigate the challenges of the 21st century, the lessons learned from these thought leaders need to remain relevant, guiding the pursuit of excellence, innovation, and customer satisfaction. By embracing these principles, organizations can create a culture of continuous improvement, employee engagement, and customer-centricity, driving long-term success and sustainability.

KEY TAKEAWAYS

- The 1970s,1990s saw a shift toward employee motivation and quality. Companies recognized that engaged employees and continuous improvement were essential for long-term success.
- Total Quality Management (TQM) became a dominant philosophy. Businesses like Toyota and Motorola adopted systematic approaches to improving efficiency, reducing waste, and enhancing customer satisfaction.
- Thought leaders reshaped workplace culture. Influential figures like Zig Ziglar, Stephen Covey, and Tom Peters emphasized motivation, leadership, and customer-centric strategies.
- Customer service became a key differentiator. Companies like Ritz-Carlton and Nordstrom built reputations around exceptional service, proving that investing in customers drives profitability.
- The principles from this era still influence modern business. Many organizations continue to focus on leadership development, employee engagement, and quality management as critical success factors.

Chapter 4

When Success Breeds Distance, The Growth of Corporate Detachment

Many people attribute a rise in corporate indifference to the contemporary corporate environment, marked by a greater emphasis on profitability at the expense of workers and customers. The devaluation of labor, poor customer service, and the preference for short-term shareholder value over sustainability and social responsibility are just a few of the problems that are encompassed by this term.

Historical Context: From Welfare Capitalism to Shareholder Primacy

To understand the rise of corporate indifference, it is essential to explore the historical evolution of corporate practices and ideologies. In the early to mid-20th century, many companies operated under a model of welfare capitalism, where businesses took an active role in the well-being of their employees and communities. This approach was influenced by the paternalistic attitudes of the time, as well as the belief that a content and loyal workforce would contribute to long-term business success.

Era of Welfare Capitalism

Welfare capitalism emerged in the United States during the late 19th and early 20th centuries as a response to growing labor unrest and the threat of socialism. Companies like Ford Motor Company, under the leadership of Henry Ford, introduced programs such as the $5 workday, profit-sharing, and various employee benefits, including healthcare and housing.[73] These initiatives were designed to improve worker satisfaction, reduce turnover, and increase productivity.

During this period, businesses were often seen as stewards of the community, with a responsibility to contribute to the public good. This sense of corporate social responsibility was reflected in the long-term investments companies made in their employees, communities, and the environment. While these practices were not without their flaws, they represented a more balanced approach to corporate governance where the interests of multiple stakeholders were considered.

The Shift to Shareholder Primacy

The mid-20th century saw the gradual erosion of welfare capitalism and the rise of a new corporate ideology: shareholder primacy. This shift was influenced by several factors, including changes in corporate governance, economic theory, and the broader political and social context. Even though it started in the mid- to late 20th century, it has clearly been magnified during the 21st century.

One of the key turning points was the publication of economist Milton Friedman's 1970 article, "The Social Responsibility of Business is to Increase its Profits." In this article, Friedman argued that the primary responsibility of a business is to maximize returns for its shareholders, within the bounds of the law.[74] He dismissed the idea that corporations should engage in activities aimed at social or environmental good unless these actions directly contributed to profitability.

---

73. Jacoby, S. M. (1997). *Modern Manors: Welfare Capitalism Since the New Deal.* Princeton University Press.

74. Friedman, M. (1970). The Social Responsibility of Business is to Increase its Profits. *The New York Times Magazine.* Retrieved from https://www.nytimes.com/1970/09/13/archives/article-15-no-title.html

Friedman's ideas gained widespread acceptance in the corporate world, particularly during the 1980s, as businesses faced increasing pressure to deliver short-term financial results. This era was marked by the rise of institutional investors, the proliferation of stock options as executive compensation, and the dominance of financial markets in shaping corporate strategies.[75] The focus shifted from long-term growth and sustainability to maximizing shareholder value, often at the expense of other stakeholders.

Globalization's Effects

Globalization, defined as the increasing interconnectedness of economies and cultures through trade, investment, and communication, has had a profound impact on corporate behavior and governance. While globalization has brought about significant economic growth and development, it has also contributed to the rise of corporate indifference by amplifying the focus on cost-cutting, efficiency, and short-term profits.

Drive for Efficiency and Cost-Cutting

One of the primary drivers of globalization has been the pursuit of efficiency and lower production costs. As companies expanded their operations across borders, they sought to take advantage of cheaper labor, materials, and regulatory environments in developing countries. This led to the widespread offshoring and outsourcing of manufacturing and services, resulting in significant job losses and wage stagnation in developed economies.[76] The relentless focus on cost-cutting has often come at the expense of workers' rights and well-being.

In many cases, multinational corporations have been accused of exploiting workers in developing countries, where labor laws and protections are weaker. The garment industry, for example, has faced criticism for its reliance on sweatshops in countries like Bangladesh, where workers endure poor working conditions and low wages to produce cheap clothing

---

75. Lazonick, W. (2014). Profits Without Prosperity. *Harvard Business Review*, 92(9), 46-55.

76. Levy, D. L. (2005). Offshoring in the New Global Political Economy. *Journal of Management Studies*, 42(3), 685-693.

for Western markets.[77] This emphasis on efficiency has also contributed to the dehumanization of labor in developed economies.

The rise of the gig economy, characterized by temporary, freelance, and contract work, has led to the erosion of traditional employment benefits and job security. Companies like Uber and Amazon have been criticized for treating their workers as disposable resources, prioritizing efficiency and profitability over employee welfare.[78]

The Race to the Bottom

Globalization has also led to what is often referred to as a "race to the bottom," where countries and companies compete to offer the lowest costs and the most favorable conditions for business, often at the expense of labor standards, environmental protections, and social welfare. This dynamic has incentivized corporations to prioritize short-term financial gains over long-term sustainability and social responsibility.

For example, the electronics industry has been plagued by reports of poor working conditions and environmental degradation in countries like China, where many of the world's electronic goods are produced.[79] Companies like Apple have faced scrutiny for their reliance on suppliers like Foxconn, where workers have reported long hours, low wages, and unsafe working conditions.

The race to the bottom has also had a significant impact on environmental sustainability. In their pursuit of lower costs, many corporations have moved their operations to countries with lax environmental regulations, leading to increased pollution and environmental degradation. The oil and gas industry, for instance, has been criticized for its role in deforestation, water contamination, and carbon emissions, particularly in developing countries where regulatory oversight is limited.

---

77. Kabeer, N., & Mahmud, S. (2004). Globalization, Gender and Poverty: Bangladeshi Women Workers in Export and Local Markets. *Journal of International Development*, 16(1), 93-109.

78. Rosenblat, A., & Stark, L. (2016). Algorithmic Labor and Information Asymmetries: A Case Study of Uber's Drivers. *International Journal of Communication*, 10, 3758-3784.

79. Chan, J., Pun, N., & Selden, M. (2013). The Politics of Global Production: Apple, Foxconn and China's New Working Class. *New Technology, Work and Employment*, 28(2), 100-115.

Modern Technological Advancements

Technological advancements, particularly in information technology and automation, have played a dual role in shaping the modern corporate environment. While technology has driven innovation, efficiency, and economic growth, it has also contributed to the rise of corporate indifference by exacerbating income inequality, job displacement, and the erosion of privacy and data security.

Automation and Job Displacement

The automation of work processes has been one of the most significant technological trends of the past few decades. Advances in robotics, artificial intelligence, and machine learning have enabled companies to automate tasks that were once performed by human workers, leading to increased efficiency and cost savings.[80] However, these technological advancements have also resulted in significant job displacement, particularly in industries like manufacturing, retail, and transportation.

The rise of automation has led to concerns about the future of work and the potential for widespread unemployment. As machines and algorithms become increasingly capable of performing complex tasks, many workers face the prospect of losing their jobs to automation.[81] This has contributed to a sense of insecurity and anxiety among workers, particularly those in low-skilled and routine jobs.

More often than not, the emphasis on automation has come at the expense of worker upskilling and retraining. While some companies have invested in programs to help workers transition to new roles, many have not, leaving displaced workers with limited options for reemployment.[82] Because those who possess the skills necessary to prosper in the new economy are rewarded while others are left behind, this has made social polarization and income inequality worse.

---

80. Brynjolfsson, E., & McAfee, A. (2014). *The Second Machine Age: Work, Progress, and Prosperity in a Time of Brilliant Technologies.* W.W. Norton & Company.

81. Ford, M. (2015). *Rise of the Robots: Technology and the Threat of a Jobless Future*. Basic Books.

82. Acemoglu, D., & Restrepo, P. (2018). Artificial Intelligence, Automation, and Work. *National Bureau of Economic Research*. https://doi.org/10.3386/w24196

Erosion of Privacy and Data Security

The rise of the digital economy has brought with it new challenges related to privacy and data security. As companies increasingly rely on data to drive their business strategies, concerns have emerged about the ways in which personal information is collected, stored, and used.[83] High-profile data breaches and scandals, such as those involving Facebook and Equifax, have highlighted the risks associated with the widespread collection and commercialization of personal data.

Corporate indifference to data security and privacy has eroded trust between companies and their customers. The Cambridge Analytica scandal, in which the data of millions of Facebook users was harvested without their consent for political purposes, is a prime example of how the misuse of data can have far-reaching consequences.[84] Many other organizations have been accused of prioritizing profit over the protection of personal information, leading to a growing backlash from consumers and regulators alike.

The lack of transparency and accountability in the digital economy has raised concerns about the ethical implications of data-driven business models. As companies continue to monetize personal information, questions arise about the balance between innovation and the protection of individual rights. This tension has become a defining feature of the modern corporate landscape, contributing to the perception of corporate indifference to the welfare of customers and society as a whole.

---

83. Zuboff, S. (2019). *The Age of Surveillance Capitalism: The Fight for a Human Future at the New Frontier of Power*. PublicAffairs.

84. Cadwalladr, C., & Graham-Harrison, E. (2018). Revealed: 50 million Facebook profiles harvested for Cambridge Analytica in major data breach. *The Guardian*. Retrieved from https://www.theguardian.com/news/2018/mar/17/cambridge-analytica-facebook-influence-us-election

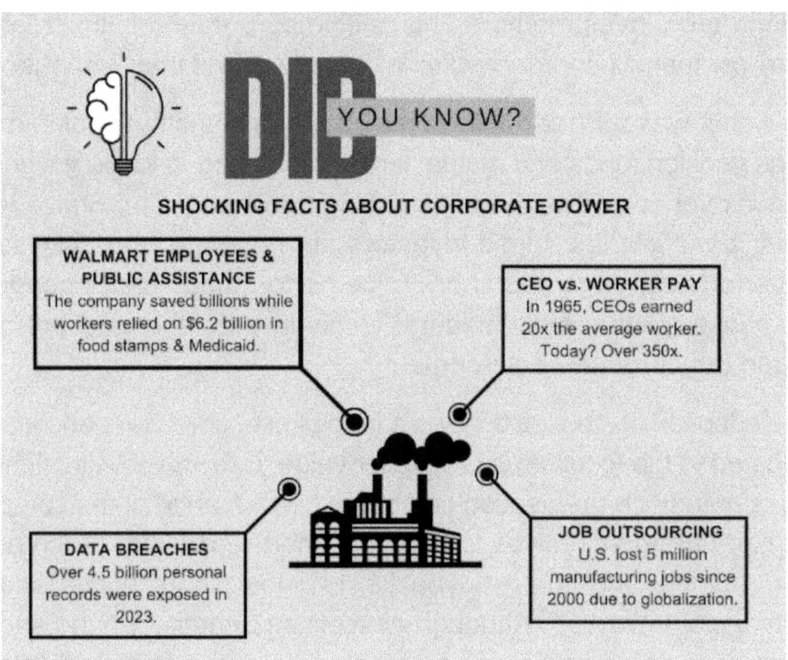

Figure 7

Focus on Shareholder Value

The emphasis on maximizing shareholder value has been one of the most significant factors contributing to the rise of corporate indifference. This focus has reshaped corporate priorities, leading to a relentless pursuit of short-term profits at the expense of long-term sustainability, employee welfare, and social responsibility.

Origins of Shareholder Primacy

Milton Friedman's economic theories and the emergence of financial markets as powerful players in corporate governance served as the impetus for the idea of shareholder primacy. Shareholder primacy asserts that the primary responsibility of a corporation is to generate returns for its shareholders, often leading to decisions that prioritize short-term gains over long-term investments.[85] This shift in corporate thinking reshaped the way companies approached their operations and their responsibilities.

This shift was further reinforced by the rise of institutional investors, such as pension funds and mutual funds, which began to exert significant influence over corporate decision-making.[86] In order to maximize returns for their beneficiaries, these investors put pressure on businesses to put quarterly earnings and share price performance first, frequently at the expense of other stakeholders. These investors' impact profoundly changed the corporate environment.

The adoption of stock options as a form of executive compensation also contributed to the focus on shareholder value. Executives with significant portions of their compensation tied to the performance of the company's stock had strong incentives to prioritize short-term gains, such as cost cutting, layoffs, and share buybacks, to boost share prices and their own financial rewards.[87] Although executives benefited in the short run from this practice, businesses and their employees frequently suffered long-term negative effects.

Consequences of Shareholder Primacy

Corporate governance and behavior have been significantly impacted by the focus on shareholder value. One of the most significant impacts has been the short-termism that now characterizes many corporate strategies. Companies are often more focused on meeting quarterly earnings targets and maintaining high stock prices than on investing in long-term growth, innovation, and sustainability.[88] This shift in priorities has shaped much of corporate decision-making in recent decades.

This short-term focus has led to a range of negative outcomes, including underinvestment in research and development, reduced capital expenditures,

85. Jensen, M. C., & Meckling, W. H. (1976). Theory of the Firm: Managerial Behavior, Agency Costs and Ownership Structure. *Journal of Financial Economics*, 3(4), 305-360.

86. Useem, M. (1996). *Investor Capitalism: How Money Managers are Changing the Face of Corporate America*. Basic Books.

87. Bebchuk, L. A., & Fried, J. M. (2004). *Pay Without Performance: The Unfulfilled Promise of Executive Compensation*. Harvard University Press.

88. Lazonick, W. (2014). Profits Without Prosperity. *Harvard Business Review*, 92(9), 46-55.

and the neglect of employee training and development. Companies that prioritize shareholder value above all else are more likely to engage in cost-cutting measures such as layoffs and outsourcing, which can have detrimental effects on employee morale, productivity, and long-term competitiveness.[89] Employees and the company's long-term prospects are frequently affected by these practices.

Growing income inequality has also been exacerbated by the emphasis on shareholder value, as executives and shareholders profit from rising stock prices while workers experience stagnant wages and job insecurity. The increasing disparity between CEO compensation and average worker wages has become a symbol of the broader inequalities that characterize the modern economy.[90] This growing divide highlights the disconnect between the corporate elite and the broader workforce.

It is important to note that social and environmental responsibility has frequently suffered as a result of the focus on shareholder value. Companies that prioritize short-term profits may be less likely to invest in sustainable practices, community development, or corporate social responsibility initiatives.

This has led to a growing disconnect between corporations and the broader society, contributing to the perception of corporate indifference to the needs and welfare of communities and the environment.[91] In the long term, this approach may hinder a company's ability to maintain positive relationships with stakeholders and the broader public.

Current State of Affairs and the Future of Corporate Governance

The rise of corporate indifference has led to widespread criticism of the current state of corporate governance and a growing call for change. As companies continue to prioritize shareholder value at the expense

89. Stout, L. A. (2012). *The Shareholder Value Myth: How Putting Shareholders First Harms Investors, Corporations, and the Public*. Berrett-Koehler Publishers.

90. Piketty, T. (2014). *Capital in the Twenty-First Century*. Harvard University Press.

91. Freeman, R. E. (2010). *Strategic Management: A Stakeholder Approach*. Cambridge University Press.

of other stakeholders, there is increasing pressure from regulators and the public to rethink corporate priorities and adopt more sustainable and inclusive business practices.

Rise of Stakeholder Capitalism

In response to the criticisms of shareholder primacy, there has been a growing movement towards stakeholder capitalism, which advocates for a more balanced approach to corporate governance. Stakeholder capitalism asserts that companies should consider the interests of all stakeholders, including employees, customers, suppliers, communities, and the environment, in their decision-making processes. This shift represents an evolving understanding of corporate responsibility, where businesses are expected to balance financial success with social and environmental considerations.

Environmental, social, and governance (ESG) considerations are becoming increasingly important in business strategy and investment choices, which reflects this change. Companies are increasingly being held accountable for their impact on society and the environment, with investors and consumers demanding greater transparency and responsibility from businesses.

The rise of *socially responsible investing* (SRI) and impact investing are examples of how financial markets are beginning to align with the principles of stakeholder capitalism.[92] However, despite these advancements, the influence of the investor class remains strong, often pushing companies to prioritize short-term returns over long-term sustainability and broader stakeholder interests.

Public Policy and Regulation's Role

Regulation and public policy also play a critical role in shaping corporate behavior and addressing the rise of corporate indifference. Governments and regulatory bodies are increasingly focused on holding companies accountable for their actions and ensuring that they contribute to the broader public good. This includes initiatives to strengthen labor rights,

---

92. Eccles, R. G., & Klimenko, S. (2019). The Investor Revolution. *Harvard Business Review*, 97(3), 106-116.

enhance environmental protections, and promote corporate transparency and accountability.[93]

In recent years, there has been a growing trend towards mandating corporate social responsibility (CSR) and sustainability reporting, requiring companies to disclose their impact on society and the environment. These regulations are designed to encourage companies to adopt more sustainable and socially responsible practices, as well as to provide stakeholders with the information they need to hold companies accountable.[94] These thoughts and actions continue to move slowly. As corporations are encouraged and less to a point required to change their practices.

The Role of Corporate Leadership

Corporate leadership plays a crucial role in driving change and addressing the rise of corporate indifference. Leaders who prioritize ethical decision-making, long-term sustainability, and stakeholder engagement can help reshape corporate culture and governance.[95] The rise of purpose-driven leadership, which emphasizes the alignment of corporate goals with broader societal values, is an example of how corporate leaders can lead the way in creating more responsible and inclusive businesses.

Leaders who embrace the principles of stakeholder capitalism and sustainable business practices can help build trust with employees, customers, and communities and contribute to the long-term success and resilience of their organizations. As the corporate landscape continues to evolve, the role of leadership in shaping the future of corporate governance will be critical.

The rise of corporate indifference, characterized by a focus on shareholder value at the expense of employees, customers, and society, has its roots in the historical evolution of corporate governance and the

---

93. Vogel, D. (2005). *The Market for Virtue: The Potential and Limits of Corporate Social Responsibility*. Brookings Institution Press.

94. Ioannou, I., & Serafeim, G. (2017). The Consequences of Mandatory Corporate Sustainability Reporting. *Harvard Business School Research Working Paper*, No. 11-100.

95. Mayer, C. (2018). *Prosperity: Better Business Makes the Greater Good*. Oxford University Press.

broader economic, technological, and social changes of the past few decades.

Globalization, technological advancements, and the relentless pursuit of short-term profits have reshaped corporate priorities, leading to a range of negative outcomes, including job displacement, income inequality, and environmental degradation. As companies and society grapple with the challenges of the 21st century, the future of corporate governance will likely depend on the ability to balance the interests of all stakeholders and to create value in a way that is sustainable, equitable, and responsible.

KEY TAKEAWAYS

- The shift from welfare capitalism to shareholder primacy has fueled corporate indifference.
- Globalization and automation have increased short-term profit focus, often at the expense of employees.
- The "disposable employee" model has led to job insecurity, wage stagnation, and eroded worker benefits.
- Data privacy concerns and the monetization of personal information have weakened consumer trust.
- Stakeholder capitalism is emerging as a response, urging businesses to consider social and environmental impacts.

Chapter 5

Valuing People Over Positions, Moving Beyond a Disposable Workforce

The concept of the "disposable employee" has become increasingly relevant in discussions about the modern workplace. This term refers to workers who are treated as easily replaceable by their employers, with little regard for their job security, career development, or overall well-being. Disposable employment practices have proliferated due to the rise of globalization, technological advancements, and a shift towards profit-driven business models. These practices put short-term gains ahead of long-term employee relationships.

Defining the Disposable Employee

The term "disposable employee" refers to workers viewed as expendable by their employers, often placed in precarious working conditions with minimal job security and limited opportunities for career advancement. These individuals are frequently hired under short-term contracts, as temporary workers, or as part of the ever-expanding gig economy. While this employment model traditionally emphasized flexibility and cost-cutting over stability, the trend has evolved to include even long-term workers in roles previously thought to offer greater security.

Characteristics of Disposable Employment

Disposable employment signifies a fundamental shift in the relationship between employer and employee, prioritizing profit margins over workforce welfare. This model undermines the traditional expectation of stable, long-term employment relationships, forcing workers to navigate an unpredictable and often exploitative job market. The defining features of disposable employment paint a sobering picture of modern labor practices.

A stark example of these trends can be seen in Amazon's warehouse operations, where efficiency and cost-cutting have led to widespread concerns about worker treatment.

Job Insecurity

At its core, disposable employment thrives on instability. Workers in these roles often find themselves employed on a part-time, temporary, or contract basis, with no guarantee of continued employment.[96] This lack of stability fosters a persistent sense of vulnerability and anxiety among employees, who live with the constant fear that their jobs could disappear at any moment.

Low Wages and Limited Benefits

Disposable employees typically earn significantly lower wages than their permanent counterparts. Their compensation often excludes crucial benefits such as health insurance, retirement plans, and paid leave.[97] This disparity not only highlights the diminished value placed on their labor but also deepens income inequality within the workforce.

Restricted Career Advancement

Opportunities for growth and career advancement are often scarce for disposable employees. Employers rarely view these workers as long-term investments, leaving them trapped in roles

96. Kalleberg, A. L. (2009). Precarious Work, Insecure Workers: Employment Relations in Transition. *American Sociological Review*, 74(1), 1-22.

97. Standing, G. (2011). *The Precariat: The New Dangerous Class*. Bloomsbury Academic.

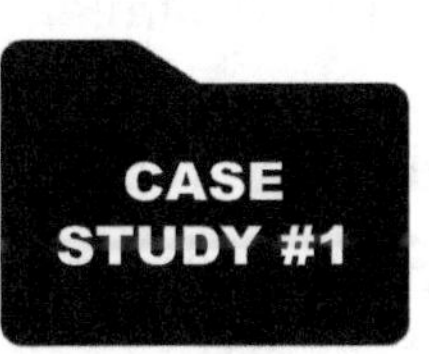

Amazon Warehouse Working Conditions

Amazon, one of the world's largest and most influential corporations, has revolutionized e-commerce with its relentless drive for efficiency and innovation. However, this success has not come without controversy. Critics often highlight the company's treatment of its warehouse employees, who are frequently described as "disposable", a term used to denote workers seen as easily replaceable, with minimal consideration for their job security, career development, or overall well-being.

In Amazon's fulfillment centers, where the speed and precision of operations drive the company's dominance, reports of harsh working conditions, high turnover rates, and employee mistreatment have cast a shadow over its achievements. In-depth analysis of Amazon's labor practices in its warehouses is provided in this case study, which also explores the wider ramifications for the contemporary workforce and the disposable employee model.

The Physical Demands of Warehouse Work

The working conditions in Amazon's warehouses have drawn widespread criticism for being physically demanding and, at times, dangerous. Employees are often required to walk several miles daily, lifting and moving heavy packages while working under strict time constraints. These demands, combined with the pressure to meet performance targets tracked by sophisticated monitoring systems, frequently lead to exhaustion and physical strain.[98]

98. Bensinger, G. (2013, September 17). Amazon's Warehouse Staffing Model Under Fire. *The Wall Street Journal.* Retrieved from https://www.wsj.com/articles/amazon-faces-criticism-for-using-temporary-workers-1379379876

A 2019 investigation by The Guardian uncovered that Amazon warehouse workers were suffering from various injuries, including back pain, joint problems, and repetitive strain injuries, largely attributed to the physically taxing nature of their tasks.[99] The report revealed that injury rates in some Amazon warehouses significantly exceeded the industry average, raising serious concerns about worker safety and the company's commitment to employee well-being.

Impacts of Productivity Targets

One of the most controversial aspects of working in an Amazon warehouse is the company's relentless focus on productivity. Employees are required to meet strict performance targets, commonly referred to as "rate," which dictate the number of tasks they must complete within a given timeframe. These targets are monitored in real-time by automated systems that track workers' movements and productivity levels.[100] Failure to meet these targets often results in disciplinary action, including termination, fostering a high-pressure environment where workers feel constantly monitored and fear losing their jobs.

Former Amazon employees have reported that this intense pressure creates a stressful and anxiety-inducing workplace, where taking breaks or even using the restroom can feel risky due to the potential of falling behind.[101] This unyielding focus on productivity at all costs has raised concerns about the dehumanization of workers. Employees are often treated as interchangeable cogs in a machine rather than as individuals with needs and limitations, exemplifying the characteristics of a disposable employee model.[102]

---

99. Sainato, M., & Davies, R. (2019, November 25). Amazon Warehouse Workers Suffer Serious Injuries at Higher Rates Than Other Firms. *The Guardian.* Retrieved from https://www.theguardian.com/technology/2019/nov/25/amazon-warehouse-workers-serious-injuries

100. Rosenblat, A., & Stark, L. (2016). Algorithmic Labor and Information Asymmetries: A Case Study of Uber's Drivers. *International Journal of Communication, 10*, 3758-3784.

101. Scholz, T. (2016). *Uberworked and Underpaid: How Workers Are Disrupting the Digital Economy.* Polity Press.

102. Bensinger, G. (2013, September 17). Amazon's Warehouse Staffing Model Under Fire. *The Wall Street Journal.* Retrieved from https://www.wsj.com/articles/amazon-faces-criticism-for-using-temporary-workers-1379379876

Reports of Unsafe Working Conditions

Numerous reports of hazardous working conditions have been made in conjunction with the physical demands and high-pressure atmosphere of Amazon warehouses. Workers have described being exposed to extreme temperatures, with some facilities lacking adequate heating or cooling systems. In one widely reported incident, an Amazon warehouse in Pennsylvania hired ambulances to wait outside the facility during a heatwave, prepared to treat workers who collapsed from heat exhaustion.[103] Critics argue that these incidents highlight a systemic disregard for employee well-being.

While Amazon has frequently downplayed the severity of these issues, emphasizing its commitment to worker safety, its responses have often been seen as insufficient.[104] Observers point to the company's focus on efficiency and cost-cutting measures as contributing factors, further reinforcing the perception of its employees as disposable assets rather than valued individuals.

High Turnover Rates and Reports of Employee Mistreatment

High turnover rates and allegations of employee mistreatment serve as critical markers of a disposable workforce, issues that have been consistently documented in Amazon's warehouse operations. These concerns reveal the challenges faced by the company's labor force and reflect a broader critique of its approach to workforce management.

---

103. Graham, K. (2011, September 18). Inside Amazon's Warehouse. *The Morning Call.* Retrieved from https://www.mcall.com/news/local/mc-allentown-amazon-complaints-20110917-story.html

104. Rosenblat, A., & Stark, L. (2016). Algorithmic Labor and Information Asymmetries: A Case Study of Uber's Drivers. *International Journal of Communication, 10*, 3758-3784.

Comprehending the High Turnover Rates at Amazon

A striking feature of Amazon's warehouse workforce is its extraordinarily high turnover rate. In 2020, The New York Times reported that Amazon's warehouse turnover was approximately 150% annually, indicating that the company effectively replaces its entire workforce more than once a year.[105] This alarming figure underscores the strain placed on workers and raises questions about the sustainability of Amazon's labor model.

The demanding nature of the job is one significant factor driving this turnover. Warehouse workers are often pushed to their physical limits, tasked with meeting productivity targets that can lead to burnout and exhaustion.[106] The intense pace, coupled with the high-pressure environment, frequently results in employees leaving after only a few months. Temporary and seasonal workers, who make up a significant portion of Amazon's workforce, face additional challenges. These positions often lack permanence, creating job insecurity and contributing to the perception of employees as easily replaceable.[107]

Further contributing to discontent is the fact that many employees report few prospects for promotion. With few pathways to career growth, employees often feel stuck in their roles, leading them to seek more promising opportunities elsewhere.[108] This revolving door of workers not only destabilizes the workforce but also carries

---

105. Soper, S. (2020, June 16). Amazon's Turnover Problem: Delivery Drivers Quit at Higher Rates Than Other Workers. *The New York Times.* Retrieved from https://www.nytimes.com/2020/06/16/business/amazon-warehouse-turnover.html

106. Scholz, T. (2016). *Uberworked and Underpaid: How Workers Are Disrupting the Digital Economy.* Polity Press.

107. Rosenblat, A., & Stark, L. (2016). Algorithmic Labor and Information Asymmetries: A Case Study of Uber's Drivers. *International Journal of Communication, 10*, 3758-3784.

108. Bensinger, G. (2013, September 17). Amazon's Warehouse Staffing Model Under Fire. *The Wall Street Journal.* Retrieved from https://www.wsj.com/articles/amazon-faces-criticism-for-using-temporary-workers-1379379876

significant costs for Amazon, including increased expenses for recruitment and training and the loss of experienced personnel.[109]

Reports of Employee Mistreatment

Beyond turnover rates, Amazon has faced widespread accusations of mistreating its warehouse employees. From claims of unfair labor practices to reports of inadequate breaks, these allegations paint a troubling picture of the conditions many workers endure.

Unfair labor practices are among the most contentious issues. Amazon's use of "flex" scheduling, for example, allows the company to alter workers' shifts with minimal notice, leaving employees struggling to plan their personal lives.[110] This unpredictability fosters a sense of instability, further compounding the stress associated with the job.

Another frequent complaint has been about insufficient breaks. Particularly during peak demand periods, workers often report skipping meals or breaks altogether in an effort to meet their productivity targets.[111] This practice not only compromises physical well-being but also heightens mental exhaustion, creating a work environment that feels punishing rather than supportive.

Perhaps most troubling is the perceived lack of respect and dignity afforded to workers. Many employees describe feeling dehumanized under Amazon's constant surveillance and relentless focus on efficiency. The pressure to meet rigorous performance metrics, paired with a lack of consideration for workers' basic needs, fosters an environment where employees feel undervalued and replaceable.[112]

---

109. Katz, L. F., & Krueger, A. B. (2016). The Rise and Nature of Alternative Work Arrangements in the United States, 1995-2015. *National Bureau of Economic Research.* https://doi.org/10.3386/w22667

110. Scholz, T. (2016). *Uberworked and Underpaid: How Workers Are Disrupting the Digital Economy.* Polity Press.

111. Bensinger, G. (2013, September 17). Amazon's Warehouse Staffing Model Under Fire. *The Wall Street Journal.* Retrieved from https://www.wsj.com/articles/amazon-faces-criticism-for-using-temporary-workers-1379379876

112. Rosenblat, A., & Stark, L. (2016). Algorithmic Labor and Information Asymmetries: A Case Study of Uber's Drivers. *International Journal of Communication, 10*, 3758-3784.

These issues have sparked widespread criticism of Amazon's labor practices, with many calling for increased regulation and oversight of the company's operations. Critics argue that Amazon's relentless focus on cost-cutting and efficiency has come at a profound cost to its workforce, perpetuating a system where employees are treated as disposable assets rather than as individuals with inherent worth.[113]

The Broader Implications of Amazon's Employment Practices

The challenges faced by Amazon's warehouse workers are not isolated to the company but reflect broader trends shaping the modern labor market. The rise of a disposable workforce, defined by high turnover, job insecurity, and the devaluation of labor, carries profound implications for workers, organizations, and society at large.

Impact on Workers

Amazon's employment practices have a significant effect on the well-being of its warehouse workers. The combination of physically demanding tasks, mental stress, and a lack of job security often leads to adverse outcomes such as anxiety, burnout, and chronic stress. The absence of opportunities for career advancement exacerbates these issues, leaving employees feeling trapped in roles that offer little long-term stability.[114] High turnover rates and consistent reports of mistreatment only amplify this instability, making it difficult for workers to establish fulfilling and sustainable careers.

Beyond the immediate challenges, the perception of being disposable has far-reaching consequences for employees' mental health and self-worth. When workers sense that they are

113. Scholz, T. (2016). *Uberworked and Underpaid: How Workers Are Disrupting the Digital Economy.* Polity Press.

114. Benach, J., Vives, A., Amable, M., Vanroelen, C., Tarafa, G., & Muntaner, C. (2014). Precarious Employment: Understanding an Emerging Social Determinant of Health. *Annual Review of Public Health, 35*, 229-253.

easily replaceable and undervalued, it fosters a deep sense of disillusionment and disengagement.[115] Over time, this can diminish their quality of life, with long-term effects on their mental health and their ability to pursue meaningful opportunities outside the workplace.

Effects on Organizations

For Amazon and other companies relying on a disposable workforce, the short-term benefits of temporary labor, such as cost savings and operational flexibility, are often outweighed by long-term drawbacks. Frequent turnover leads to increased recruitment and training expenses, while the loss of experienced workers undermines institutional knowledge and operational continuity.[116]

The public perception of a business is also significantly impacted by reports of employee abuse. Negative publicity surrounding unfair labor practices can erode trust and brand loyalty, especially in today's market, where consumers are increasingly mindful of ethical standards.[117] Companies that fail to prioritize employee welfare risk public backlash, which can translate into diminished customer loyalty and declining sales.

Its Effect on Society

Equally worrisome are the social repercussions of a disposable workforce. Precarious employment and the devaluation of labor exacerbate social and economic inequality, leaving low-wage workers struggling to achieve financial security and upward mobility. This disparity contributes to broader social challenges, including rising poverty rates, heightened social unrest, and a decline in overall quality of life.[118]

---

115. Cappelli, P. (1999). *The New Deal at Work: Managing the Market-Driven Workforce.* Harvard Business School Press.

116. Katz, L. F., & Krueger, A. B. (2016). The Rise and Nature of Alternative Work Arrangements in the United States, 1995-2015. *National Bureau of Economic Research.* https://doi.org/10.3386/w22667

117. Freeman, R. E. (2010). *Strategic Management: A Stakeholder Approach.* Cambridge University Press.

118. Standing, G. (2011). *The Precariat: The New Dangerous Class.* Bloomsbury Academic.

The social fabric is also weakened by the dependence on precarious labor. Workers who feel undervalued and disposable are less likely to invest in their communities or participate in civic activities, eroding social cohesion and trust.[119] This disconnect can have a ripple effect, deepening the societal divides that already challenge modern economies and governance.

Addressing the Challenges of a Disposable Workforce

Given the significant implications of a disposable workforce, it is essential to explore potential solutions to address these challenges. These solutions may include policy interventions, changes in corporate governance, and efforts to strengthen worker protections and support systems.

Policy Interventions and Labor Market Reforms

Policy changes and labor market reforms can play a crucial role in tackling the systemic problems that lead to exploitative work conditions. Governments have the power to implement policies that improve job security, fair wages, and access to essential benefits for all workers, no matter their employment status. For example, increasing the minimum wage, making healthcare and retirement plans more accessible, and strengthening labor rights are key steps toward supporting vulnerable workers.[120]

Reforming the labor market to prioritize stable, long-term employment can also curb the rise of disposable labor. This could include tightening regulations around temporary and contract jobs to prevent employers from bypassing critical worker protections.[121] Programs for workforce development can also help employees

---

119. Putnam, R. D. (2000). *Bowling Alone: The Collapse and Revival of American Community.* Simon & Schuster.

120. Baccaro, L., & Howell, C. (2011). A Common Neoliberal Trajectory: The Transformation of Industrial Relations in Advanced Capitalism. *Politics & Society, 39*(4), 521-563.

121. Kalleberg, A. L. (2011). *Good Jobs, Bad Jobs: The Rise of Polarized and Precarious Employment Systems in the United States, 1970s-2000s.* Russell Sage Foundation.

acquire the knowledge and training they need to move into higher-paying, more secure positions.

Changes in Corporate Governance and Business Practices

Changes in corporate governance are crucial to tackling the issues of a disposable workforce. Companies like Amazon can focus on long-term employee well-being by investing in development, career advancement, and creating supportive, inclusive environments.[122] Adopting stakeholder-oriented governance, which considers the interests of employees, customers, and communities, rather than just shareholders, can lead to more equitable and sustainable practices.[123]

Strengthening Worker Protections and Support Systems

Strengthening worker protections is key to addressing the negative effects of a disposable workforce. Ensuring fair wages, benefits, and job security for all workers, regardless of employment status, can be achieved through stronger labor laws that protect against exploitation.[124] Rebuilding labor unions and collective bargaining rights empowers workers to negotiate for better conditions, particularly those in precarious, low-wage jobs.[125]

Amazon's reliance on temporary labor and its focus on cost-cutting have led to high turnover and reports of mistreatment, highlighting the challenges of a disposable workforce. To address these issues, a multifaceted approach is needed, combining policy reforms, corporate governance changes, and strengthened worker

---

122. Freeman, R. E. (2010). *Strategic Management: A Stakeholder Approach.* Cambridge University Press.

123. Lazonick, W. (2014). Profits Without Prosperity. *Harvard Business Review, 92*(9), 46-55.

124. Baccaro, L., & Howell, C. (2011). A Common Neoliberal Trajectory: The Transformation of Industrial Relations in Advanced Capitalism. *Politics & Society, 39*(4), 521-563.

125. Kalleberg, A. L. (2011). *Good Jobs, Bad Jobs: The Rise of Polarized and Precarious Employment Systems in the United States, 1970s-2000s.* Russell Sage Foundation.

protections. This would create a more equitable and sustainable economy for all.

that offer little chance for upward mobility[126]. This stagnation breeds frustration, as employees feel their efforts are neither recognized nor rewarded.

High Turnover Rates

A hallmark of disposable employment is its high turnover. Workers cycle in and out of roles, often leaving or being dismissed once their contracts expire[127]. This constant churn disrupts continuity, erodes institutional knowledge, and diminishes overall productivity and morale within organizations.

The Growing Prevalence of Disposable Employment

In recent decades, disposable employment has surged across industries as companies increasingly adopt flexible labor practices to cut costs and boost efficiency. The rise of the gig economy has been instrumental in spreading this model[128]. Companies like Uber, Lyft, and TaskRabbit rely on independent contractors rather than traditional employees, sidestepping the financial responsibilities associated with benefits, job security, and long-term employment.

Beyond the gig economy, sectors such as retail, hospitality, and manufacturing have embraced similar practices. Temporary workers, part-time employees, and outsourced labor have become the norm in these industries, where the emphasis remains on minimizing costs

126. Cappelli, P. (1999). The New Deal at Work: Managing the Market-Driven Workforce. Harvard Business School Press.

127. Katz, L. F., & Krueger, A. B. (2016). The Rise and Nature of Alternative Work Arrangements in the United States, 1995-2015. National Bureau of Economic Research. https://doi.org/10.3386/w22667

128. Rosenblat, A., & Stark, L. (2016). Algorithmic Labor and Information Asymmetries: A Case Study of Uber's Drivers. International Journal of Communication, 10, 3758-3784.

and maximizing operational flexibility[129]. These trends demand critical examination and call for a reevaluation of labor practices to ensure fairness and sustainability in the modern workplace.

Nowhere is the disposable employment model more evident than in the gig economy, where companies like Uber redefine labor structures while sidestepping worker protections.

129. Kalleberg, A. L. (2011). Good Jobs, Bad Jobs: The Rise of Polarized and Precarious Employment Systems in the United States, 1970s-2000s. Russell Sage Foundation.

Examining Uber's Disposable Workforce

Uber, the ride-hailing giant, is one of the most prominent examples of the gig economy, a labor market characterized by short-term contracts or freelance work as opposed to permanent jobs. While Uber has revolutionized transportation and created new opportunities for earning income, it has also been at the center of intense debates and legal battles over the classification and rights of its drivers.

The term *"disposable employee"* aptly describes the treatment of these workers, who are often considered independent contractors rather than employees, leading to significant implications for their rights, benefits, and job security. With an emphasis on the gig economy's effects on driver rights and the continuous legal battles over employee classification, this case study examines the idea of the disposable employee in the context of Uber.

The Gig Economy and Its Impact on Driver Rights

The gig economy, which includes companies like Uber, Lyft, TaskRabbit, and others, has transformed the labor market by providing flexible work opportunities for millions of people worldwide. However, this flexibility often comes at the cost of worker rights, benefits, and job security.

Uber drivers are classified as independent contractors rather than employees, which means they do not receive many of the protections and benefits that traditional employees enjoy. This classification allows Uber to avoid the costs associated with full-time employment, such as health insurance, paid leave, unemployment benefits, and retirement plans.[130] Instead, drivers are paid per ride, with Uber taking a commission on each fare.

While the independent contractor model provides drivers with the flexibility to choose their working hours, it also places them in a precarious position. Drivers bear the full responsibility for expenses such as fuel, vehicle maintenance, insurance, and taxes. They also lack the job security and stability that come with traditional employment, making them vulnerable to fluctuations in demand, changes in Uber's policies, and other external factors.[131]

Economic Insecurity and Exploitation

The gig economy model has faced criticism for fostering economic insecurity among workers. Uber drivers, like many gig workers, experience unpredictable income due to fluctuating demand and the company's pricing strategies. Surge pricing can boost earnings during peak periods, but drivers have little control over when these times occur or how long they last.[132]

Uber's dynamic pricing model and frequent changes to pay structures have frustrated many drivers. Allegations suggest Uber has reduced per-mile or per-minute rates while increasing its share of the fare, ultimately lowering driver earnings.[133] This has led to claims that Uber treats its drivers as disposable resources rather than valued workers.

The lack of benefits and protections for Uber drivers only worsens their financial instability. Without access to health insurance, paid leave, or unemployment benefits, drivers are left to manage health

130. De Stefano, V. (2016). The Rise of the "Just-in-Time Workforce": On-Demand Work, Crowdwork, and Labor Protection in the "Gig-Economy". *Comparative Labor Law & Policy Journal, 37*(3), 471-504.

131. Rosenblat, A., & Stark, L. (2016). Algorithmic Labor and Information Asymmetries: A Case Study of Uber's Drivers. *International Journal of Communication, 10*, 3758-3784.

132. Rosenblat, A. (2018). *Uberland: How Algorithms are Rewriting the Rules of Work.* University of California Press.

133. Berg, J., & Johnston, H. (2019). Too Good to Be True? A Call for Reform in the Gig Economy. *International Labour Organization.*

and financial crises on their own.[134] This creates significant hardships for those who rely on Uber as their primary source of income.

Psychological and Social Impacts on Drivers

Significant psychological and social repercussions may result from the gig economy's economic instability and lack of job security. Uber drivers often experience stress, anxiety, and frustration due to unpredictable income and long hours needed to make ends meet.[135] The isolation of gig work also impacts mental health, as drivers work alone with limited social interaction or support, unlike traditional employees who regularly interact with colleagues and managers. This lack of connection can lead to feelings of alienation and disconnection from the broader workforce.

The absence of legal protections and the perception of being easily replaceable can further create a sense of powerlessness among drivers. Many fear retaliation or deactivation if they speak out about unfair treatment.[136] This power imbalance reinforces their status as disposable workers, valued only for their ability to generate profits.

Legal Battles Over Employee Classification and Benefits

Uber drivers, labor activists, and regulators have all contested the company's practices, leading to multiple legal disputes over the classification of Uber drivers as independent contractors. These legal disputes center on the question of whether Uber drivers should be classified as employees, entitled to benefits and protections under labor laws, or as independent contractors, with fewer rights and responsibilities.

---

134. Sundararajan, A. (2016). *The Sharing Economy: The End of Employment and the Rise of Crowd-Based Capitalism.* MIT Press.

135. Freeman, R. E. (2010). *Strategic Management: A Stakeholder Approach.* Cambridge University Press.

136. Rosenblat, A. (2018). *Uberland: How Algorithms are Rewriting the Rules of Work.* University of California Press.

The distinction between employees and independent contractors is a crucial one, as it determines the rights and protections afforded to workers under labor laws. Employees are entitled to a range of benefits, including minimum wage, overtime pay, unemployment insurance, and workers' compensation, among others.[137] Independent contractors, on the other hand, are generally excluded from these protections and are responsible for managing their own taxes, insurance, and benefits.

The Legal Framework: Employee vs. Independent Contractor

Uber has consistently argued that its drivers are independent contractors because they have the freedom to set their own schedules, choose when and where to work, and use their own vehicles. The company contends that it operates as a technology platform that connects riders with drivers rather than as an employer that exerts control over its workforce.[138]

However, many drivers and labor advocates have challenged this classification, arguing that Uber exerts significant control over drivers' work through its app, pricing algorithms, and performance monitoring systems.[139] These critics argue that Uber drivers should be classified as employees because they are subject to company-imposed rules, such as dress codes, customer service standards, and penalties for declining too many rides.

Major Legal Cases and Decisions

The classification of Uber drivers has been central to several high-profile legal cases, raising important questions about workers' rights in the gig economy. These cases have varied in outcome, with some courts ruling in favor of drivers, granting them employee

---

137. Cherry, M. A., & Aloisi, A. (2017). Dependent Contractors in the Gig Economy: A Comparative Approach. *American University Law Review, 66*(3), 635-689.

138. Sundararajan, A. (2016). *The Sharing Economy: The End of Employment and the Rise of Crowd-Based Capitalism.* MIT Press.

139. Rosenblat, A. (2018). *Uberland: How Algorithms are Rewriting the Rules of Work.* University of California Press.

status and benefits, while others have upheld Uber's independent contractor model. The legal decisions not only impact Uber's operations but also influence the broader gig economy, shaping the rights and protections of workers in similar industries.

California's Assembly Bill 5 (AB5)

A key moment in the debate over Uber driver classification came with the passage of Assembly Bill 5 (AB5) in California in 2019. This law introduced the "ABC test," a three-part framework to decide if a worker should be classified as an employee or an independent contractor.[140] According to the test, a worker qualifies as an employee unless they are free from the company's control, perform work outside the company's usual business, and operate an independently established business.

Uber and other gig economy companies strongly opposed AB5, arguing that it threatened the flexibility drivers rely on and would lead to significant financial burdens for the companies. In response, Uber, Lyft, and other gig companies supported Proposition 22, a ballot initiative designed to exempt them from AB5.[141] This initiative allowed them to continue classifying drivers as independent contractors. Despite strong opposition from labor advocates, Proposition 22 passed in November 2020, effectively overriding AB5 for Uber and similar companies.

O'Connor v. Uber Technologies, Inc.

In one of the earliest and most significant class-action lawsuits against Uber, drivers in California filed a case in 2013, seeking employee status and the benefits that come with it. The plaintiffs argued that Uber's control over key aspects of their work, such as setting fares, managing customer interactions, and enforcing rules, made them employees rather than independent contractors.[142]

140. Dubal, V. B. (2020). Winning the Battle, Losing the War: Assessing the Impact of Proposition 22 on Gig Workers. *California Law Review Online,* 11-14.

141. *Ibid.*

142. Cherry, M. A., & Aloisi, A. (2017). Dependent Contractors in the Gig Economy: A Comparative Approach. *American University Law Review, 66*(3), 635-689.

Although the case initially seemed headed for a settlement, the Ninth Circuit Court of Appeals ultimately decided that the drivers must resolve their claims through arbitration, which limited the broader implications of the lawsuit.

United Kingdom Supreme Court Ruling

In February 2021, the UK Supreme Court ruled that Uber drivers should be classified as "workers" instead of independent contractors, recognizing Uber's control over fares, terms, and penalties. As a result, UK drivers are now entitled to benefits like minimum wage, paid vacation, and pension contributions.[143] These legal battles reveal the challenges of regulating gig economy work, with some regions recognizing gig workers as employees while others maintain the independent contractor model, leaving many without traditional employment benefits.

The Broader Implications of Legal Battles

The legal battles over Uber driver classification have broader implications for the gig economy and the future of work. The outcomes of these cases and legislative efforts could set important precedents for how gig workers are treated and protected under labor laws.

Impact on Other Gig Economy Companies

Companies like Lyft, DoorDash, and Instacart have faced similar legal challenges and have closely followed the developments in Uber's cases.[144] A shift towards recognizing gig workers as employees could lead to significant changes in the business models of these companies, including higher labor costs and increased regulatory scrutiny.

---

143. Prassl, J. (2021). The UK Uber Decision: What Next for the Gig Economy? *Oxford Business Law Blog.* Retrieved from https://www.law.ox.ac.uk/business-law-blog/blog/2021/03/uk-uber-decision-what-next-gig-economy

144. Cherry, M. A., & Aloisi, A. (2017). Dependent Contractors in the Gig Economy: A Comparative Approach. *American University Law Review, 66*(3), 635-689.

The Future of Worker Protections

The debate over Uber driver classification has also raised important questions about the adequacy of existing labor laws in addressing the needs of gig workers. As the gig economy continues to grow, there is increasing recognition that traditional employment classifications may not fully capture the realities of gig work.[145] This has led to calls for new legal frameworks that provide gig workers with basic protections and benefits, regardless of their classification as employees or independent contractors.

Implications for Economic Inequality

Economic inequality is significantly impacted when gig workers are categorized as independent contractors. Without access to benefits such as health insurance, retirement plans, and unemployment insurance, gig workers are often left in precarious financial situations.[146] This can exacerbate existing inequalities, particularly for workers from marginalized communities who are disproportionately represented in gig work.

The Disposable Employee: The Case of Uber Drivers

Since Uber drivers are frequently seen as easily replaceable and receive few benefits or protections, their treatment is a prime example of the disposable employee concept. This model has significant implications for both the drivers and the broader workforce. Uber's reliance on a disposable workforce has significant economic and social consequences for its drivers.[147] The lack of job security, benefits, and legal protections places drivers in a vulnerable position, where they are constantly at risk of financial instability and exploitation.

---

145. Dubal, V. B. (2020). Winning the Battle, Losing the War: Assessing the Impact of Proposition 22 on Gig Workers. *California Law Review Online,* 11-14.

146. Ravenelle, A. J. (2019). *Hustle and Gig: Struggling and Surviving in the Sharing Economy.* University of California Press.

147. Rosenblat, A., & Stark, L. (2016). Algorithmic Labor and Information Asymmetries: A Case Study of Uber's Drivers. *International Journal of Communication, 10*, 3758-3784.

The Economic and Social Impact on Drivers

The economic insecurity faced by Uber drivers can lead to a range of negative outcomes, including stress, anxiety, and burnout. Many drivers report working long hours, often in unsafe or unhealthy conditions, in order to make ends meet.[148] This can have serious consequences for their physical and mental health, as well as their overall quality of life.

Drivers may feel disenfranchised and alienated due to gig work's disposable nature. The lack of social support, opportunities for advancement, and recognition for their work can create feelings of powerlessness and frustration.[149] This can contribute to a broader sense of disconnection from the workforce and society, further exacerbating the challenges faced by gig workers.

The Broader Implications for the Workforce

The gig economy, exemplified by Uber, presents broader challenges for the future of work. The classification of workers as independent contractors could undermine labor rights, as more companies adopt this model to cut costs and increase flexibility.[150] This shift may worsen economic inequality, widening the gap between stable, well-paying jobs and precarious gig work, leading to greater social disparities and instability.[151]

While platforms like Uber offer new opportunities, they also raise concerns about worker rights and the dehumanization of labor.[152]

---

148. Ravenelle, A. J. (2019). *Hustle and Gig: Struggling and Surviving in the Sharing Economy.* University of California Press.

149. Sundararajan, A. (2016). *The Sharing Economy: The End of Employment and the Rise of Crowd-Based Capitalism.* MIT Press.

150. De Stefano, V. (2016). The Rise of the "Just-in-Time Workforce": On-Demand Work, Crowdwork, and Labor Protection in the "Gig-Economy". *Comparative Labor Law & Policy Journal, 37*(3), 471-504.

151. Ravenelle, A. J. (2019). *Hustle and Gig: Struggling and Surviving in the Sharing Economy.* University of California Press.

152. Sundararajan, A. (2016). *The Sharing Economy: The End of Employment and the Rise of Crowd-Based Capitalism.* MIT Press.

Uber's classification of drivers as independent contractors, without benefits or job security, has sparked legal battles that highlight the need for stronger protections for gig workers. As the gig economy grows, developing new legal frameworks to protect workers is essential for creating a more equitable and sustainable economy.

Factors Contributing to the Rise of Disposable Employment

As disposable employment becomes more entrenched, its effects ripple across both the workforce and society. The model not only erodes traditional notions of job security but also fosters inequality, stagnates career growth, and compromises organizational stability. Several factors have contributed to the rise of disposable employment, including globalization, technological advancements, and changes in corporate governance and labor market policies.

Globalization and Offshoring

Globalization has played a significant role in the rise of disposable employment by encouraging companies to seek out lower-cost labor markets and outsource jobs to countries with weaker labor protections. The offshoring of manufacturing jobs to countries like China, Mexico, and Vietnam has led to the displacement of workers in developed economies where job security and wages have declined.[153]

The pressure to remain competitive in a globalized economy has also driven companies to adopt more flexible employment practices, such as the use of temporary and contract workers.[154] By reducing labor costs and avoiding long-term commitments, companies can respond more quickly to changes in demand and market conditions, but this often comes at the expense of worker security and well-being.

---

153. Levy, D. L. (2005). Offshoring in the New Global Political Economy. *Journal of Management Studies*, 42(3), 685-693.

154. Kalleberg, A. L. (2011). *Good Jobs, Bad Jobs: The Rise of Polarized and Precarious Employment Systems in the United States, 1970s-2000s.* Russell Sage Foundation.

Technological Advancements and Automation

Technological advancements, particularly in automation and digital platforms, have also contributed to the rise of disposable employment. Automation has enabled companies to replace human workers with machines and algorithms, reducing the need for full-time employees and increasing reliance on temporary and contract workers.[155]

The rise of digital platforms, such as those used by gig economy companies, has further facilitated the shift towards disposable employment by allowing companies to manage large, flexible workforces with minimal overhead.[156] These platforms enable companies to scale up or down their labor force quickly and efficiently, but they also create a sense of impermanence and disposability among workers, who are often treated as interchangeable units of labor.

Corporate Governance and Shareholder Value

Disposable employment has increased as a result of corporate governance's shift toward shareholder value as its main goal. Companies are increasingly pressured to deliver short-term financial results to satisfy shareholders, leading to cost-cutting measures such as layoffs, outsourcing, and the use of temporary labor.[157]

This emphasis on short-term profitability has often come at the expense of long-term employee relationships and investments in workforce development. As a result, employees are viewed as costs to be minimized rather than assets to be developed, leading to a devaluation of labor and the proliferation of disposable employment practices.[158]

---

155. Brynjolfsson, E., & McAfee, A. (2014). *The Second Machine Age: Work, Progress, and Prosperity in a Time of Brilliant Technologies*. W.W. Norton & Company.

156. De Stefano, V. (2016). The Rise of the "Just-in-Time Workforce": On-Demand Work, Crowdwork, and Labor Protection in the "Gig-Economy". *Comparative Labor Law & Policy Journal*, 37(3), 471-504.

157. Lazonick, W. (2014). Profits Without Prosperity. *Harvard Business Review*, 92(9), 46-55.

158. Cappelli, P. (1999). *The New Deal at Work: Managing the Market-Driven Workforce*. Harvard Business School Press.

Labor Market Policies and Deregulation

Changes in labor market policies and deregulation have also played a role in the rise of disposable employment. The weakening of labor unions and the erosion of collective bargaining rights have reduced workers' ability to negotiate for better wages, benefits, and job security. This has made it easier for employers to adopt flexible employment practices and treat workers as disposable.[159] Deregulation of the labor market has also increased the number of non-traditional employment arrangements, including gig, temporary, and part-time work.

The Implications of Disposable Employment

The rise of disposable employment has significant implications for workers, organizations, and society as a whole. These implications include the impact on worker well-being, organizational performance, and social and economic inequality.

Impact on Worker Well-Being

Disposable employment erodes worker well-being, as the pervasive insecurity and lack of benefits leave employees feeling vulnerable and undervalued.[160] This precarious environment fosters chronic stress and anxiety, compounding mental and physical health challenges.

The limited opportunities for career growth, coupled with the constant threat of job loss, lead many employees to experience frustration, disengagement, and eventual burnout, which directly undermine job performance and workplace morale.[161] A lot of people also struggle to save for the future, invest in self-improvement, or meet basic needs due

---

159. Baccaro, L., & Howell, C. (2011). A Common Neoliberal Trajectory: The Transformation of Industrial Relations in Advanced Capitalism. *Politics & Society*, 39(4), 521-563.

160. Benach, J., Vives, A., Amable, M., Vanroelen, C., Tarafa, G., & Muntaner, C. (2014). Precarious Employment: Understanding an Emerging Social Determinant of Health. *Annual Review of Public Health*, 35, 229-253.

161. Cappelli, P. (1999). *The New Deal at Work: Managing the Market-Driven Workforce*. Harvard Business School Press.

to financial instability brought on by low wages and limited benefits, which feeds cycles of insecurity and hardship.[162]

Impact on Organizational Performance

The widespread use of disposable employment practices can have negative consequences for organizational performance. High turnover rates, which are common in organizations that rely heavily on temporary and contract workers, can lead to a loss of institutional knowledge and a decline in overall productivity and efficiency.[163]

A disengaged and demotivated workforce can have a detrimental effect on work quality and customer satisfaction if there is a lack of investment in career advancement and employee development. Organizations that treat their employees as disposable may also struggle to attract and retain top talent, as workers are likely to seek more stable and supportive employment opportunities elsewhere.[164]

Impact on Social and Economic Inequality

The rise of disposable employment has intensified social and economic inequality by disproportionately affecting low-wage workers and marginalized groups. These individuals often face precarious jobs with low pay, inadequate benefits, and minimal job security, exacerbating disparities in income and access to opportunities while perpetuating cycles of poverty and exclusion. Women, people of color, and immigrants are particularly vulnerable, as they are more likely to occupy non-standard and low-paying roles, which entrenches systemic inequities and limits their prospects for economic stability and upward mobility.[165]

---

162. Kalleberg, A. L. (2011). *Good Jobs, Bad Jobs: The Rise of Polarized and Precarious Employment Systems in the United States, 1970s-2000s*. Russell Sage Foundation.

163. Katz, L. F., & Krueger, A. B. (2016). The Rise and Nature of Alternative Work Arrangements in the United States, 1995-2015. *National Bureau of Economic Research*. https://doi.org/10.3386/w22667

164. Cappelli, P. (1999). *The New Deal at Work: Managing the Market-Driven Workforce*. Harvard Business School Press.

165. Kalleberg, A. L. (2009). Precarious Work, Insecure Workers: Employment Relations in Transition. *American Sociological Review*, 74(1), 1-22.

The societal consequences of disposable employment extend beyond individual workers to broader societal impacts. The erosion of stable jobs and benefits places additional strain on social safety nets, increases poverty rates, and undermines social cohesion. This weakening of community bonds can contribute to unrest, fostering instability, and reducing the overall quality of life.[166] Addressing the systemic factors that allow disposable employment to persist is crucial to building a more equitable and sustainable future.

166. Standing, G. (2011). *The Precariat: The New Dangerous Class*. Bloomsbury Academic.

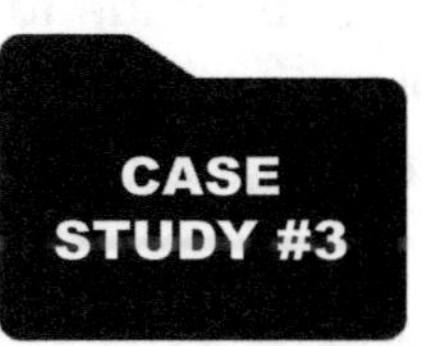

Walmart and the Cost of Keeping Things Low

Walmart, the world's largest retailer, is known for its massive scale, low prices, and efficient supply chain. Yet, it faces criticism for its labor practices, including low wages, part-time work, and strong opposition to unionization. These practices have fueled the image of Walmart employees as disposable workers, easily replaceable with little job security or career growth. This case study dives into Walmart's labor practices, examining the impact of low pay, part-time hours, and anti-union policies on both workers and local economies.

Low Wages and Part-Time Work at Walmart

Walmart's business model revolves around providing customers with low prices, a goal it achieves in part by minimizing labor costs. This approach has drawn significant criticism, particularly for its reliance on low wages and part-time positions. While the company's cost-saving tactics have allowed it to dominate the retail market, they have also raised concerns about the impact on employees, including job insecurity, limited benefits, and a lack of career advancement opportunities.

Low Wages

Walmart has long been criticized for paying its employees low wages, particularly those in entry-level positions. According to a 2020 report by the Economic Policy Institute (EPI), Walmart's average hourly wage for full-time employees was around $14.26, which is below the national average for retail workers.[167] Many Walmart employees earn close to the federal minimum wage, which has not kept pace with the cost of living in many parts of the United States.

The low wages paid by Walmart have significant implications for its employees, many of whom struggle to make ends meet. A 2013 study by the University of California, Berkeley, found that many Walmart employees rely on public assistance programs, such as food stamps and Medicaid, to supplement their incomes.[168] The study estimated that Walmart employees cost U.S. taxpayers an estimated $6.2 billion annually in public assistance due to their low wages.

Walmart's low wages also contribute to economic inequality, as the company's executives and shareholders reap substantial profits while many of its workers live in poverty. The wage gap between Walmart's CEO and its average worker is one of the largest in the retail industry, further highlighting the disparity between the company's upper management and its frontline employees.[169]

Part-Time Work

Walmart relies heavily on part-time workers, who form a substantial portion of its workforce. This approach provides the company with flexibility, as part-time employees can be scheduled to meet fluctuating demand while avoiding the costs of overtime pay or full-time benefits.[170]

However, part-time positions often come with few or no benefits, leaving workers without access to health insurance, retirement

---

167. McNicholas, C., Shierholz, H., & Poydock, M. (2020). Wages Have Risen in the Pandemic, But Not for Everyone. *Economic Policy Institute.*

168. Jacobs, K., Graham-Squire, D., & Luce, S. (2013). Living Wage Policies and Big-Box Retail: How a Higher Wage Standard Would Impact Walmart Workers and Shoppers. *UC Berkeley Labor Center.*

169. McNicholas, C., Shierholz, H., & Poydock, M. (2020). Wages Have Risen in the Pandemic, But Not for Everyone. *Economic Policy Institute.*

170. De Stefano, V. (2016). The Rise of the "Just-in-Time Workforce": On-Demand Work, Crowdwork, and Labor Protection in the "Gig-Economy". *Comparative Labor Law & Policy Journal, 37*(3), 471-504.

plans, or paid leave, further exacerbating financial insecurity.[171] These employees must navigate low wages and unpredictable schedules without the safety net of comprehensive benefits.

Walmart's high turnover rates are also a result of its reliance on part-time workers, many of whom depart in quest of more secure and stable jobs. This turnover results in increased recruitment and training costs, as well as a loss of institutional knowledge and experience.[172]

The Impact on Employee Well-Being

The combination of low wages and part-time work has significant implications for the well-being of Walmart employees. Many workers struggle to afford basic necessities, such as housing, food, and healthcare, and are forced to rely on public assistance programs to make ends meet.[173] This financial insecurity can lead to a range of negative outcomes, including stress, anxiety, and poor physical and mental health.

The lack of job security and benefits associated with part-time work can also contribute to a sense of powerlessness and alienation among Walmart employees.[174] Many workers feel that they are easily replaceable and have little control over their schedules or working conditions, leading to feelings of frustration and disengagement from their work.

Walmart's Resistance to Unionization

Walmart has a long history of resisting unionization efforts, both in the United States and abroad. The company's aggressive stance against unions is driven by a desire to maintain control

---

171. Rosenblat, A. (2018). *Uberland: How Algorithms are Rewriting the Rules of Work.* University of California Press.

172. Cappelli, P. (1999). *The New Deal at Work: Managing the Market-Driven Workforce.* Harvard Business School Press.

173. Benach, J., Vives, A., Amable, M., Vanroelen, C., Tarafa, G., & Muntaner, C. (2014). Precarious Employment: Understanding an Emerging Social Determinant of Health. *Annual Review of Public Health, 35*, 229-253.

174. Lichtenstein, N. (2013). *The Retail Revolution: How Wal-Mart Created a Brave New World of Business.* Picador.

over labor costs and avoid the potential for collective bargaining, which could lead to higher wages and better working conditions for employees.

Anti-Union Tactics

Walmart has long been recognized for its steadfast opposition to unionization, a stance that has sparked controversy and drawn significant criticism from labor advocates. The company views unions as a potential threat to its business model, which is built on low costs, operational flexibility, and centralized control. To maintain this model, Walmart has implemented a range of strategies designed to discourage union activity and prevent collective bargaining among its employees.

- **Surveillance and Monitoring:** Walmart has faced allegations of monitoring employees for union activity, using surveillance cameras and undercover operatives to identify and target union organizers.[175]
- **Anti-Union Training:** The company provides anti-union training for managers, instructing them on how to detect and counter unionization efforts.[176] These sessions often emphasize the risks of unionization, such as potential store closures, job losses, or reduced operational flexibility.
- **Closure of Unionized Stores:** Walmart has, on occasion, closed stores or departments where workers successfully organized. For example, in 2005, the company shut down a store in Quebec, Canada, after employees voted to unionize, citing financial concerns.[177] Labor advocates, however, have argued that such closures are intended to intimidate workers and deter future union efforts.

---

175. Greenhouse, S. (2012, July 2). Walmart Workers Try the Nonunion Route. *The New York Times.* Retrieved from https://www.nytimes.com/2012/07/03/business/at-walmart-there-is-no-union-but-organized-protests.html

176. Olson, E. (2013). Walmart in the US and Walmart Abroad: The Corporate Empire's Approach to Labor Rights. *Business and Human Rights Journal, 8*(1), 1-28.

177. Lichtenstein, N. (2013). *The Retail Revolution: How Wal-Mart Created a Brave New World of Business.* Picador.

- **Legal Challenges:** Walmart frequently employs legal measures to challenge unionization efforts, including disputing the legitimacy of union elections or certifications of union representation.[178]

These tactics reflect Walmart's commitment to maintaining its union-free workforce, though they continue to fuel debates over labor rights and the balance of power between employers and employees.

The Impact of Union Resistance on Workers

Walmart's anti-union stance significantly impacts workers' ability to advocate for better wages, benefits, and conditions, leaving them with limited leverage against exploitation.[179] The absence of union representation reinforces the view of Walmart employees as disposable, treated as interchangeable labor with little regard for individual needs or contributions. Without collective bargaining, workers often feel powerless and disenfranchised, lacking agency in their workplace.[180]

The Broader Impact on Local Economies and Employee Well-Being

Walmart, as the world's largest retailer, wields an enormous influence not just over its workers but also over local economies, industries, and society at large. Its business model, centered on low prices achieved through aggressive cost-cutting measures, has sparked both praise and criticism. While some see Walmart as a driver of economic activity and accessibility, others highlight the significant

---

178. Greenhouse, S. (2012, July 2). Walmart Workers Try the Nonunion Route. *The New York Times*. Retrieved from https://www.nytimes.com/2012/07/03/business/at-walmart-there-is-no-union-but-organized-protests.html

179. Cappelli, P. (1999). *The New Deal at Work: Managing the Market-Driven Workforce.* Harvard Business School Press.

180. Lichtenstein, N. (2013). *The Retail Revolution: How Wal-Mart Created a Brave New World of Business.* Picador.

social and economic costs of its practices. The effects extend far beyond its immediate workforce, influencing wage standards, local businesses, public resources, and employee well-being, making Walmart a focal point in broader debates about labor rights, corporate responsibility, and economic equity.

The Impact on Local Economies

Walmart's presence can stimulate economic activity by creating jobs and offering low-cost goods, benefiting cost-conscious consumers, particularly in low-income communities. However, the negative impacts often outweigh these benefits. Walmart's low-wage and part-time employment model drives down wage standards across the retail sector, forcing competitors to cut costs and wages to remain viable.[181] Furthermore, the company's dominance can erode local economies by driving small businesses out of operation, leading to job losses and reduced economic diversity.[182]

The burden of Walmart's cost-cutting practices extends to taxpayers, as many employees rely on public assistance to meet basic needs.[183] This effectively shifts the cost of supporting its workforce to public resources, subsidizing Walmart's labor practices at the expense of communities.

Impact on Employee Well-Being

Walmart's labor model has far-reaching consequences for employee well-being and economic security. Workers face challenges such as low wages, unpredictable schedules, and limited access to benefits like health insurance or retirement plans, leaving them vulnerable to financial hardship. This insecurity can contribute to

---

181. Jacobs, K., Graham-Squire, D., & Luce, S. (2013). Living Wage Policies and Big-Box Retail: How a Higher Wage Standard Would Impact Walmart Workers and Shoppers. *UC Berkeley Labor Center.*

182. Neumark, D., Zhang, J., & Ciccarella, S. (2008). The Effects of Walmart on Local Labor Markets. *Journal of Urban Economics, 63*(2), 405-430.

183. Jacobs, K., Graham-Squire, D., & Luce, S. (2013). Living Wage Policies and Big-Box Retail: How a Higher Wage Standard Would Impact Walmart Workers and Shoppers. *UC Berkeley Labor Center.*

physical and mental health problems, reduced life expectancy, and higher rates of chronic illness.[184]

For part-time employees, the lack of benefits such as paid leave further compounds their difficulties, preventing long-term financial stability and perpetuating cycles of poverty.[185] Beyond individual employees, Walmart's practices influence labor standards across the retail industry, contributing to declining labor rights, weakened protections, and increasing economic inequality.[186] By prioritizing profit over worker well-being, Walmart's labor practices reflect broader systemic issues in the retail sector, raising critical questions about the balance between corporate success and social responsibility.

Addressing the Challenges of Disposable Employment at Walmart

Given the significant economic and social implications of Walmart's labor practices, it is essential to explore potential solutions to address these challenges. These solutions may include policy interventions, changes in corporate governance, and efforts to strengthen worker protections and support systems.

Policy Interventions and Labor Market Reforms

Policy interventions and labor market reforms can play a crucial role in addressing the challenges of disposable employment at Walmart. Governments can implement policies that promote fair wages, job security, and access to benefits for all workers, regardless of their employment status.[187] This may include measures

---

184. Benach, J., Vives, A., Amable, M., Vanroelen, C., Tarafa, G., & Muntaner, C. (2014). Precarious Employment: Understanding an Emerging Social Determinant of Health. *Annual Review of Public Health, 35*, 229-253.

185. Olson, E. (2013). Walmart in the US and Walmart Abroad: The Corporate Empire's Approach to Labor Rights. *Business and Human Rights Journal, 8*(1), 1-28.

186. Lichtenstein, N. (2013). *The Retail Revolution: How Wal-Mart Created a Brave New World of Business.* Picador.

187. Baccaro, L., & Howell, C. (2011). A Common Neoliberal Trajectory: The Transformation of Industrial Relations in Advanced Capitalism. *Politics & Society, 39*(4), 521-563.

such as raising the minimum wage, expanding access to health insurance and retirement benefits, and strengthening labor rights and protections.

Labor market reforms that promote more stable and secure employment arrangements, such as the regulation of part-time work and the protection of workers' rights to unionize, can help reduce the prevalence of disposable employment. Governments can also invest in workforce development programs that provide training and education opportunities for workers, helping them transition to more stable and higher-paying jobs.[188]

Changes in Corporate Governance and Business Practices

Changes in corporate governance and business practices are also essential to addressing the challenges of disposable employment at Walmart. The company can adopt more inclusive and sustainable business practices that prioritize the long-term well-being of its employees, customers, and communities.[189] This may include investing in employee development, providing opportunities for career advancement, and fostering a supportive and inclusive work environment.

Walmart can adopt stakeholder-oriented governance models that consider the interests of all stakeholders, not just shareholders.[190] This approach can help create more equitable and sustainable business practices that benefit workers, organizations, and society as a whole.

---

188. Kalleberg, A. L. (2011). *Good Jobs, Bad Jobs: The Rise of Polarized and Precarious Employment Systems in the United States, 1970s-2000s.* Russell Sage Foundation.

189. Freeman, R. E. (2010). *Strategic Management: A Stakeholder Approach.* Cambridge University Press.

190. Lazonick, W. (2014). Profits Without Prosperity. *Harvard Business Review, 92*(9), 46-55.

Strengthening Worker Protections and Support Systems

Strengthening worker protections is vital to addressing the negative impacts of Walmart's disposable employment model. Ensuring fair wages, benefits, and job security for all workers, regardless of employment status, is a crucial step. Governments can play a key role by implementing and enforcing stronger labor laws to protect workers from exploitation and uphold their dignity.[191]

Rebuilding labor unions and supporting collective bargaining rights can empower workers to advocate for improved wages and working conditions. Unions are particularly critical for low-wage and precarious jobs, where employees often lack leverage against employers.[192]

Walmart's reliance on low wages, part-time work, and resistance to unionization highlights the broader challenges of disposable employment. These practices fuel economic insecurity, deepen social inequality, and weaken labor protections. Addressing these issues requires comprehensive efforts, including policy reforms, corporate accountability, and stronger worker support systems. By prioritizing worker well-being, governments and businesses can foster a more equitable and sustainable economy that benefits everyone.

---

191. Baccaro, L., & Howell, C. (2011). A Common Neoliberal Trajectory: The Transformation of Industrial Relations in Advanced Capitalism. *Politics & Society, 39*(4), 521-563.

192. Kalleberg, A. L. (2011). *Good Jobs, Bad Jobs: The Rise of Polarized and Precarious Employment Systems in the United States, 1970s-2000s.* Russell Sage Foundation.

Addressing the Challenges of Disposable Employment

Given the significant implications of disposable employment, it is essential to explore potential solutions to address the challenges it presents. These solutions may include policy interventions, changes in corporate governance, and efforts to strengthen worker protections and labor rights.

Policy Interventions and Labor Market Reforms

Policy interventions and labor market reforms can play a crucial role in addressing the challenges of disposable employment. Governments can implement policies that promote job security, fair wages, and access to benefits for all workers, regardless of their employment status.[193] This may include measures such as raising the minimum wage, expanding access to health insurance and retirement benefits, and strengthening labor rights and protections.

In addition, labor market reforms that promote more stable and secure employment arrangements, such as the regulation of temporary and contract work, can help reduce the prevalence of disposable employment. Governments can also invest in workforce development programs that provide training and education opportunities for workers, helping them transition to more stable and higher-paying jobs.[194]

Changes in Corporate Governance

Changes in corporate governance can also help address the challenges of disposable employment. Companies can adopt more inclusive and sustainable business practices that prioritize the long-term well-being of their employees, customers, and communities. This may include investing

---

193. Baccaro, L., & Howell, C. (2011). A Common Neoliberal Trajectory: The Transformation of Industrial Relations in Advanced Capitalism. *Politics & Society*, 39(4), 521-563.

194. Kalleberg, A. L. (2011). *Good Jobs, Bad Jobs: The Rise of Polarized and Precarious Employment Systems in the United States, 1970s-2000s.* Russell Sage Foundation.

in employee development, providing opportunities for career advancement, and fostering a supportive and inclusive work environment.[195]

Businesses can also implement stakeholder-oriented governance models, which take into account the interests of all parties involved, not just shareholders. This approach can help create more equitable and sustainable business practices that benefit workers, organizations, and society as a whole.[196]

Strengthening Worker Protections and Labor Rights

Strengthening worker protections and labor rights is crucial to addressing the challenges posed by disposable employment. Governments can enact stronger labor laws to ensure all workers, regardless of employment status, have access to fair wages, benefits, and job security, safeguarding them from exploitation and fostering dignity in the workplace.[197] Rebuilding labor unions and expanding collective bargaining rights further empower workers to negotiate for improved wages, benefits, and conditions, particularly for those in precarious jobs.[198]

Disposable employment practices, driven by globalization, technological advancements, and profit-focused business models, have led to job insecurity, low wages, limited growth opportunities, and high turnover, with widespread consequences for workers and society. Addressing these issues requires policy reforms, corporate responsibility, and strengthened worker protections to build a more equitable and sustainable economy that prioritizes the well-being and stability of its workforce.

---

195. Freeman, R. E. (2010). *Strategic Management: A Stakeholder Approach*. Cambridge University Press.

196. Lazonick, W. (2014). Profits Without Prosperity. *Harvard Business Review*, 92(9), 46-55.

197. Baccaro, L., & Howell, C. (2011). A Common Neoliberal Trajectory: The Transformation of Industrial Relations in Advanced Capitalism. *Politics & Society*, 39(4), 521-563.

198. Kalleberg, A. L. (2011). *Good Jobs, Bad Jobs: The Rise of Polarized and Precarious Employment Systems in the United States, 1970s-2000s*. Russell Sage Foundation.

The Emergence of the Disposable Workforce

The concept of the disposable workforce refers to employment practices that prioritize flexibility and cost-efficiency over long-term employment relationships. In such a workforce, employees are often hired on a temporary, part-time, or contract basis, with little assurance of continued employment.[199] This trend has been driven by several factors, including globalization, technological advancements, and changes in corporate governance that emphasize short-term profits and shareholder value over long-term stability and employee welfare.

Factors Contributing to the Disposable Workforce

The rise of the disposable workforce is rooted in key developments from the late 20th and early 21st centuries. Globalization, which gained momentum in the 1980s and 1990s, spurred increased competition and job outsourcing to countries with lower labor costs, prompting companies in developed economies to adopt more flexible labor practices.[200] Technological advancements, particularly in automation and digital platforms, further fueled this shift.

Automation reduced the need for permanent employees, while digital platforms promoted the gig economy, where workers are hired for individual tasks without job security.[201] Additionally, changes in corporate governance, with a focus on shareholder value, have led to cost-cutting measures like layoffs, outsourcing, and reliance on temporary labor, eroding job security and treating workers as disposable assets.[202]

---

199. Kalleberg, A. L. (2009). Precarious Work, Insecure Workers: Employment Relations in Transition. *American Sociological Review*, 74(1), 1-22.

200. Levy, D. L. (2005). Offshoring in the New Global Political Economy. *Journal of Management Studies*, 42(3), 685-693.

201. Brynjolfsson, E., & McAfee, A. (2014). *The Second Machine Age: Work, Progress, and Prosperity in a Time of Brilliant Technologies*. W.W. Norton & Company.

202. Lazonick, W. (2014). Profits Without Prosperity. *Harvard Business Review*, 92(9), 46-55.

The Costs of a Disposable Workforce: Instability and Impact

The evolution of the global workforce has seen a significant shift towards more precarious forms of employment, characterized by high turnover, job security, and an increasing sense of disposability among workers. This shift has led to a range of negative economic and social effects, not only for the employees directly affected but also for organizations and society at large.

High Turnover Rates and Their Economic Impact

One of the most immediate economic impacts of a disposable workforce is high employee turnover, particularly in industries that depend heavily on temporary, part-time, or contract workers. These employees often leave their positions in search of better opportunities or due to the inherent lack of job security.[203] This constant churn of workers creates significant challenges for organizations.

High turnover requires businesses to invest substantial resources into recruiting, hiring, and training new employees. These costs can be particularly burdensome in industries that demand specialized skills or expertise. According to the Society for Human Resource Management (SHRM), replacing an employee can cost anywhere from 50% to 200% of their annual salary, depending on the position's level.[204] Frequent turnover also weakens institutional expertise and knowledge. As experienced employees leave, they take their valuable insights and skills with them, leading to decreased productivity, lower-quality work, and a steeper learning curve for incoming staff.[205]

---

203. Kalleberg, A. L. (2011). *Good Jobs, Bad Jobs: The Rise of Polarized and Precarious Employment Systems in the United States, 1970s-2000s*. Russell Sage Foundation.

204. SHRM. (2017). Employee Turnover: Understanding and Reducing Turnover Costs. Society for Human Resource Management. Retrieved from https://www.shrm.org/resourcesandtools/tools-and-samples/toolkits/pages/understanding-and-reducing-turnover-costs.aspx

205. Katz, L. F., & Krueger, A. B. (2016). The Rise and Nature of Alternative Work Arrangements in the United States, 1995-2015. *National Bureau of Economic Research*. https://doi.org/10.3386/w22667

The effects of high turnover also extend to employee morale and engagement. Workers who witness their colleagues leaving in large numbers often experience a sense of instability and uncertainty. This atmosphere can undermine motivation and productivity, as remaining employees struggle with the emotional toll of constant change and the added workload left behind by departing team members.[206]

The Cost of Lack of Job Security

The economic consequences of disposable employment practices are profound, affecting both workplace performance and broader consumer behavior. Job insecurity diminishes productivity and innovation as employees disengage and avoid risks.[207] Probst (2003) links job insecurity to reduced organizational commitment, absenteeism, and presenteeism, all of which negatively impact workplace outcomes.[208, 209] Furthermore, workers reduce their discretionary spending in response to financial uncertainty, which lowers demand for goods and services and impedes economic growth.[210]

Impacts on Long-Term Organizational Success

While disposable employment practices may provide short-term cost savings, they often undermine long-term organizational success. Companies that prioritize immediate profits over the welfare of their employees may

---

206. Cappelli, P. (1999). *The New Deal at Work: Managing the Market-Driven Workforce.* Harvard Business School Press.

207. Benach, J., Vives, A., Amable, M., Vanroelen, C., Tarafa, G., & Muntaner, C. (2014). Precarious Employment: Understanding an Emerging Social Determinant of Health. *Annual Review of Public Health*, 35, 229-253.

208. Probst, T. M. (2003). Development and validation of the job security index and the job security satisfaction scale: A classical test theory and IRT approach. *Journal of Occupational and Organizational Psychology*, 76(4), 451-467.

209. Bockerman, P., & Ilmakunnas, P. (2009). Job disamenities, job satisfaction, quit intentions, and actual separations: Putting the pieces together. *Industrial Relations*, 48(1), 73-96.

210. Lichtenstein, N. (2013). *State of the Union: A Century of American Labor.* Princeton University Press.

struggle to attract and retain top talent, which can lead to decreased performance and reduced competitiveness in the market.[211]

Another significant downside is the decline in innovation and creativity. When employees feel insecure about their jobs, they are less likely to take risks or suggest new ideas, stifling creativity. Research by Amabile et al. (1996) found that job security and a supportive work environment are crucial elements for fostering innovation, which disposable employment models tend to undermine.[212]

Companies that treat workers as disposable assets risk damaging their reputation and brand loyalty. In today's socially conscious marketplace, consumers increasingly gravitate toward companies that demonstrate ethical labor practices and prioritize employee welfare.[213] Organizations that fail to meet these expectations may face public backlash, leading to a decline in customer trust and loyalty.

Social Effects of a Disposable Workforce

The rise of a disposable workforce has far-reaching social implications, affecting not only the individuals directly involved but also the broader society. The psychological and emotional toll of disposable employment practices can lead to increased stress, anxiety, anger, and apathy among workers, which in turn can have negative effects on social cohesion and stability.

Psychological Impacts of Job Insecurity and High Turnover

Job insecurity and high turnover rates can lead to heightened stress, anxiety, anger, and apathy, negatively impacting both individual well-being and organizational performance. Employees often experience stress

211. Cappelli, P. (1999). *The New Deal at Work: Managing the Market-Driven Workforce.* Harvard Business School Press.

212. Amabile, T. M., Conti, R., Coon, H., Lazenby, J., & Herron, M. (1996). Assessing the work environment for creativity. *Academy of Management Journal*, 39(5), 1154-1184.

213. Freeman, R. E. (2010). *Strategic Management: A Stakeholder Approach.* Cambridge University Press.

and anxiety from the fear of job loss, manifesting physically through headaches, fatigue, and sleep disturbances, and emotionally as irritability, depression, and anxiety disorders.[214]

Feelings of disposableness can also breed resentment and anger toward employers, which lowers engagement, motivation, and productivity while raising conflict at work.[215] Over time, these strains may lead to apathy and disengagement, further decreasing productivity and work quality, and increasing absenteeism and presenteeism, creating a damaging cycle for both individuals and organizations.[216]

Social Consequences of Disposable Employment

The social consequences of disposable employment stretch far beyond the workplace, impacting families, communities, and society at large. The instability and uncertainty inherent in disposable employment can create a range of negative outcomes, from increasing inequality to fueling social unrest and ultimately eroding overall quality of life.

One of the most significant social repercussions is the growing inequality driven by disposable employment. As workers in precarious jobs tend to earn lower wages and lack access to essential benefits such as healthcare, retirement plans, and paid leave, the gap between the wealthy and the poor widens.[217]

This disparity exacerbates existing social and economic inequalities, leading to greater stratification in society.

Economic insecurity caused by disposable employment can also foster social unrest. When large groups of individuals feel economically

---

214. Benach, J., Vives, A., Amable, M., Vanroelen, C., Tarafa, G., & Muntaner, C. (2014). Precarious Employment: Understanding an Emerging Social Determinant of Health. *Annual Review of Public Health*, 35, 229-253.

215. Probst, T. M. (2003). Development and validation of the job security index and the job security satisfaction scale: A classical test theory and IRT approach. *Journal of Occupational and Organizational Psychology*, 76(4), 451-467.

216. Cappelli, P. (1999). *The New Deal at Work: Managing the Market-Driven Workforce.* Harvard Business School Press.

217. Standing, G. (2011). *The Precariat: The New Dangerous Class.* Bloomsbury Academic.

powerless or unfairly treated, it can breed frustration and resentment, leading to increased social tension and even public protests or violent acts.[218]

Moreover, disposable employment undermines social cohesion. In communities where job insecurity is prevalent, trust and social capital tend to decline. The lack of stable, well-compensated work can discourage civic engagement and collective action, weakening the social fabric and fostering a sense of isolation among individuals who feel alienated from society.[219]

Effects on Community and Family Well-Being

At the family level, the stress caused by job insecurity and financial instability can create significant tension. As parents struggle with uncertainty and low wages, family dynamics often suffer, leading to increased conflict and dysfunction. This strain can manifest in higher rates of divorce, domestic violence, and mental health issues among family members.[220]

Children in families impacted by disposable employment are particularly vulnerable. Economic hardship and parental stress can reduce the quality of parenting, leading to less involvement in children's lives, fewer educational opportunities, and higher rates of emotional and behavioral problems.[221] The long-term effects on children growing up in such environments can have far-reaching consequences for their own future stability.

At the community level, areas with high levels of disposable employment often face a decline in overall well-being. Economic insecurity leads to reduced investment in public services and infrastructure, weakening

---

218. Wilkinson, R. G., & Pickett, K. (2010). *The Spirit Level: Why Equality is Better for Everyone*. Penguin Books.

219. Putnam, R. D. (2000). *Bowling Alone: The Collapse and Revival of American Community*. Simon & Schuster.

220. Conger, R. D., Conger, K. J., Elder, G. H., Lorenz, F. O., Simons, R. L., & Whitbeck, L. B. (1990). Linking economic hardship to marital quality and instability. *Journal of Marriage and the Family*, 643-656.

221. McLoyd, V. C. (1998). Socioeconomic disadvantage and child development. *American Psychologist*, 53(2), 185.

community development efforts. As a result, communities may experience deteriorating quality of life, increasing poverty, rising crime rates, and a breakdown in social cohesion.[222] The vicious cycle of economic instability fuels broader social disintegration, impacting the community's ability to thrive.

Addressing the Negative Effects of a Disposable Workforce

Given the significant economic and social impacts of a disposable workforce, it is essential to explore potential solutions to address these challenges. These solutions may include policy interventions, changes in corporate governance, and efforts to strengthen worker protections and support systems.

Policy Interventions and Labor Market Reforms

Policy interventions and labor market reforms can play a crucial role in addressing the negative effects of a disposable workforce. Governments can implement policies that promote job security, fair wages, and access to benefits for all workers, regardless of their employment status. This may include measures such as raising the minimum wage, expanding access to health insurance and retirement benefits, and strengthening labor rights and protections.[223]

Labor market reforms that promote more stable and secure employment arrangements, such as the regulation of temporary and contract work, can help reduce the prevalence of disposable employment. Governments can also invest in workforce development programs that provide training and education opportunities for workers, helping them transition to more stable and higher-paying jobs.[224]

---

222. Wilson, W. J. (1996). *When Work Disappears: The World of the New Urban Poor.* Knopf.

223. Baccaro, L., & Howell, C. (2011). A Common Neoliberal Trajectory: The Transformation of Industrial Relations in Advanced Capitalism. *Politics & Society*, 39(4), 521-563.

224. Kalleberg, A. L. (2011). *Good Jobs, Bad Jobs: The Rise of Polarized and Precarious Employment Systems in the United States, 1970s-2000s.* Russell Sage Foundation.

Changes in Corporate Governance and Business Practices

Changes in corporate governance and business practices are also essential to addressing the negative effects of a disposable workforce. Companies can adopt more inclusive and sustainable business practices that prioritize the long-term well-being of their employees, customers, and communities.[225] This may include investing in employee development, providing opportunities for career advancement, and fostering a supportive and inclusive work environment.

Companies can adopt stakeholder-oriented governance models that consider the interests of all stakeholders, not just shareholders. This approach can help create more equitable and sustainable business practices that benefit workers, organizations, and society as a whole.[226] rise of a disposable workforce, characterized by high turnover, lack of job security, and the perception of workers as easily replaceable, has significant economic and social implications. The negative effects of these employment practices extend beyond the workplace, affecting individual well-being, organizational performance, and broader social cohesion and stability.

Addressing the challenges of a disposable workforce requires a multifaceted approach that includes policy interventions, changes in corporate governance, and efforts to strengthen worker protections and support systems. By prioritizing the well-being and security of workers, organizations and governments can help create a more equitable and sustainable economy that benefits all members of society.

225. Freeman, R. E. (2010). *Strategic Management: A Stakeholder Approach*. Cambridge University Press.

226. Lazonick, W. (2014). Profits Without Prosperity. *Harvard Business Review*, 92(9), 46-55.

KEY TAKEAWAYS

- **The Rise of Disposable Employment**, The shift toward a "disposable workforce" has been driven by globalization, automation, and shareholder-focused corporate governance. Companies prioritize short-term profits over employee stability, leading to a surge in contract, gig, and temporary employment.
- **High Turnover and Job Insecurity**, Workers in disposable roles face persistent job instability, with no guarantees of long-term employment. This leads to constant workforce churn, diminishing company productivity, eroding institutional knowledge, and negatively impacting employee well-being.
- **Financial and Career Struggles for Workers**, Disposable employees earn lower wages, often lack benefits like healthcare or retirement plans, and have few opportunities for advancement. These conditions exacerbate income inequality, trapping workers in cycles of financial insecurity.
- **Broader Social and Economic Consequences**, The rise of disposable employment worsens economic disparity, weakens community stability, and fuels stress-related health issues. It also burdens social safety nets as more workers struggle with financial insecurity.
- **Potential Solutions for Workforce Stability**, Addressing disposable employment requires stronger labor protections, policy interventions (such as regulating contract work and raising minimum wages), and corporate governance changes that prioritize employees as long-term assets rather than short-term costs.

Chapter 6

Technology at Work, Innovation Without Losing the Human Touch

Technology is changing the way we work faster than ever before. Industries are being flipped on their heads, efficiency is through the roof, and new kinds of jobs are popping up everywhere. But there's a downside that's hard to ignore. With automation and artificial intelligence (AI) taking over more tasks, people are starting to question what it means for real human work, and whether our roles in the workplace are losing their value.

The Rise of Automation and AI in the Workplace

Automation uses machines, robots, and advanced computer systems to take over tasks once performed by humans. These tasks can be as simple as repetitive assembly line duties in factories or as sophisticated as analyzing data, managing customer interactions, and even making decisions.[227] By handling these responsibilities, automation has unlocked tremendous productivity for businesses, with machines often outpacing human workers in speed, accuracy, and consistency.

However, the gains in efficiency come with significant drawbacks. The rise of automation has displaced millions of workers across numerous

227. Brynjolfsson, E., & McAfee, A. (2014). *The Second Machine Age: Work, Progress, and Prosperity in a Time of Brilliant Technologies.* W.W. Norton & Company.

industries. Manufacturing, for instance, has seen a steep decline in factory jobs due to machines taking over critical processes like welding, painting, and assembling products.[228] This shift in labor has drastically altered the economic landscape for workers in these roles.

The disruption caused by automation isn't confined to blue-collar jobs. In retail, self-checkout kiosks and automated inventory systems have reduced the need for cashiers and stock clerks. Similarly, the transportation industry faces upheaval as autonomous vehicles loom, threatening the livelihoods of millions of drivers. Meanwhile, white-collar jobs are feeling the squeeze as well. AI-driven tools now handle tasks such as legal research, financial modeling, and customer service, shrinking opportunities for human workers in traditionally stable fields.[229]

AI and the Transformation of Work

The workplace is being reshaped by artificial intelligence (AI), which encompasses technologies such as machine learning, natural language processing, and intelligent automation. Unlike traditional automation, which focuses on performing predetermined tasks, AI adds a new level of capability by learning, adapting, and making decisions, enabling it to handle more complex and cognitive responsibilities.

One of AI's greatest strengths lies in processing massive amounts of data, uncovering patterns, and making predictions at a speed and accuracy far beyond human ability. Industries such as finance, healthcare, and marketing have been quick to adopt AI-powered tools to streamline operations, customize customer interactions, and even diagnose complex medical conditions.[230] While these advances promise improved efficiency and effectiveness, they also spark unease over the potential loss of skilled jobs and the diminishing value placed on human expertise.

---

228. Acemoglu, D., & Restrepo, P. (2018). *Artificial Intelligence, Automation, and Work. National Bureau of Economic Research.* https://doi.org/10.3386/w24196

229. Frey, C. B., & Osborne, M. A. (2017). *The Future of Employment: How Susceptible Are Jobs to Computerization? Technological Forecasting and Social Change*, 114, 254-280.

230. Kaplan, J. (2015). *Humans Need Not Apply: A Guide to Wealth and Work in the Age of Artificial Intelligence.* Yale University Press.

AI's influence extends beyond traditional workplaces into the gig economy, where algorithms now pair workers with tasks based on skills and availability. These platforms bring flexibility and new earning possibilities, but they come with significant downsides. Workers often find themselves treated as interchangeable, facing precarious job conditions, limited security, and little control over their schedules or work environment.[231]

Dehumanization of Work

In ways that were previously only found in science fiction, the swift advancement of technology, especially automation and artificial intelligence, is changing the nature of work. While these advancements promise efficiency and innovation, they also spark deep concerns about the dehumanization of work. This shift involves reducing human labor to inputs in a system where efficiency and cost-effectiveness overshadow the value of individuality, creativity, and dignity.

The implications are far-reaching, from eroding job quality and personal fulfillment to sidelining human creativity and expertise. As machines increasingly take over roles once considered uniquely human, questions arise about the future of work and the place of people in a system increasingly run by algorithms and automation.

Erosion of Job Quality and Meaningful Work

One of the most pressing consequences of the dehumanization of work is the decline in job quality. As automation and AI take over repetitive tasks, many remaining roles lack autonomy, creativity, or a sense of purpose. Workers often find themselves relegated to monitoring machines, following algorithm-driven instructions, or performing monotonous tasks.[232] This setup frequently leads to disengagement and alienation, with employees feeling like mere tools rather than valued contributors.

---

231. Rosenblat, A. (2018). *Uberland: How Algorithms are Rewriting the Rules of Work.* University of California Press.

232. Bainbridge, W. S. (1983). *The Impact of Technology on Work: The Future of Human Labor. American Journal of Sociology,* 88(5), 939-964.

The gig economy exemplifies this trend. Workers here are often treated as "human cogs" in sprawling automated systems. Algorithms match them with tasks based solely on efficiency and cost-effectiveness, ignoring their well-being or aspirations. This approach can leave workers feeling undervalued, with little opportunity for growth or meaningful engagement.[233] The rise of precarious employment arrangements, characterized by low wages and insecure contracts, compounds these challenges. Technology enables companies to outsource work globally, favoring short-term, unstable gig jobs over traditional employment relationships that provide benefits and stability.[234]

A prime example of this is Tesla, where the push for automation and rapid production has led to significant safety concerns, high employee turnover, and allegations of union-busting.

---

233. Scholz, T. (2016). *Uberworked and Underpaid: How Workers Are Disrupting the Digital Economy.* Polity Press.

234. Kalleberg, A. L. (2011). *Good Jobs, Bad Jobs: The Rise of Polarized and Precarious Employment Systems in the United States, 1970s-2000s.* Russell Sage Foundation.

Teslas's Dehumanization of Work

Tesla, the electric vehicle and clean energy company, has rapidly ascended to become one of the most prominent and valuable companies in the world. Known for its innovation in electric vehicles, autonomous driving technology, and sustainable energy solutions, Tesla has also faced significant controversy regarding its labor practices.

The company has been accused of dehumanizing work by prioritizing high production targets over employee safety, engaging in union-busting tactics, and placing immense strain on its workforce. This case study explores the dehumanization of work at Tesla, focusing on controversies surrounding employee safety, production pressures, and allegations of union-busting, and examines the broader implications for workers and the industry.

Controversies Around Employee Safety and Production Pressures

Tesla's rise to prominence has been accompanied by a relentless focus on achieving ambitious production goals, particularly in the manufacturing of its electric vehicles.But because of this emphasis, there are now serious worries about worker safety and wellbeing.

The Push for Higher Production Targets

Tesla's production targets have been a central aspect of its strategy, particularly as it sought to ramp up production of the Model 3, its first mass-market electric vehicle. CEO Elon Musk set ambitious goals for the company, aiming to produce 5,000 Model 3 vehicles per week by mid-2018. This push for rapid scaling led to what

Musk described as "production hell," where the company faced significant challenges in meeting these targets.[235]

At Tesla's factories, especially the Fremont, California, facility, the pressure to reach these production goals directly affected the working conditions. Reports from workers and investigations by journalists revealed that employees were often required to work long hours, including mandatory overtime, to keep up with the production demands. In some cases, workers reported working 12-hour shifts, six or seven days a week, with little time for rest or recovery.[236]

The intense production pressure also led to the use of unorthodox and potentially unsafe manufacturing practices. For example, Tesla implemented an "all-hands-on-deck" approach, where employees from different departments, including office staff, were brought onto the production line to help meet targets. This approach, while aimed at increasing output, raised concerns about the adequacy of training and the potential for accidents and injuries.[237]

Employee Safety Concerns

Significant worries about worker safety have been connected to Tesla's drive for increased production targets. Multiple reports and investigations have highlighted a pattern of workplace injuries, safety violations, and inadequate responses to safety concerns at Tesla's factories.

A 2017 investigation by Reveal from The Center for Investigative Reporting found that Tesla's injury rate at its Fremont plant was higher than the industry average. The investigation revealed that the company had underreported workplace injuries and that employees faced unsafe working conditions, including exposure

235. Hull, D. (2018, July 2). Tesla Hits Model 3 Production Goal by Working Around the Clock. *Bloomberg*. Retrieved from https://www.bloomberg.com/news/articles/2018-07-02/tesla-hits-model-3-production-goal-by-working-around-the-clock

236. Higgins, T. (2018, April 12). Tesla Factory Workers Reveal Pain, Injury and Stress: 'Everything Feels Like the Future but Us.' *The Guardian*. Retrieved from https://www.theguardian.com/technology/2018/apr/12/tesla-workers-pain-injury-stress-production-goals

237. *Ibid.*

to dangerous machinery, high heat, and hazardous materials. Workers reported being pressured to continue working even after sustaining injuries, with some claiming that their injuries were downplayed or not properly documented by the company's medical staff.[238]

The investigation also found that Tesla had a pattern of prioritizing production over safety. Former safety professionals at the company claimed that safety protocols were often ignored or overridden to meet production goals. For example, Tesla removed safety signs and labels from the factory floor, reportedly because they were deemed aesthetically unpleasing, and workers were not provided with adequate training or personal protective equipment.[239]

Workers felt that the company's objectives came before their own well-being as a result of the emphasis on production at the expense of safety.[240] This culture of dehumanization, where employees were seen as disposable assets in the pursuit of higher production, contributed to a high rate of workplace injuries and dissatisfaction among the workforce.

The Impact on Worker Well-Being

Employee well-being has been significantly impacted by Tesla's combination of hazardous working conditions and high production pressures. Many employees reported experiencing stress, fatigue, and physical strain due to the long hours and demanding work environment.[241] The lack of adequate rest breaks, combined with the pressure to meet production targets, led to a decline in morale and job satisfaction among workers.

---

238. Levy, A. (2017, May 18). Tesla Factory's Safety Issues Tied to Its Push for Production. *Reveal from The Center for Investigative Reporting*. Retrieved from https://www.revealnews.org/article/tesla-factorys-safety-issues-tied-to-its-push-for-production/

239. *Ibid.*

240. *Ibid.*

241. Higgins, T. (2018, April 12). Tesla Factory Workers Reveal Pain, Injury and Stress: 'Everything Feels Like the Future but Us.' *The Guardian*. Retrieved from https://www.theguardian.com/technology/2018/apr/12/tesla-workers-pain-injury-stress-production-goals

The physical toll of working at Tesla's factories was compounded by the psychological stress of working in an environment where safety concerns were often ignored or downplayed. Workers reported feeling that their safety and well-being were not valued by the company, leading to a sense of alienation and disillusionment.[242] This sense of dehumanization, where workers were treated as mere cogs in the production machine, contributed to a culture of burnout and high turnover.

Allegations of Union-Busting and Worker Strain

Concerns about employee safety and production pressures, Tesla has faced allegations of union-busting and creating a hostile environment for workers who seek to organize or advocate for better working conditions.

Unionization Efforts and Tesla's Response

Tesla's Fremont plant, where the majority of the company's vehicles are manufactured, has been the focal point of unionization efforts by workers seeking to improve wages, benefits, and working conditions. The United Auto Workers (UAW) union has been actively involved in these efforts, aiming to represent Tesla workers and negotiate on their behalf.[243]

However, Tesla has been accused of engaging in aggressive union-busting tactics to prevent workers from organizing. These tactics have included surveillance of pro-union employees, threats of retaliation, and efforts to undermine union support. In one instance in 2017, workers at the Fremont plant reported that Tesla had placed security personnel on the factory floor to monitor

---

242. Levy, A. (2017, May 18). Tesla Factory's Safety Issues Tied to Its Push for Production. *Reveal from The Center for Investigative Reporting*. Retrieved from https://www.revealnews.org/article/tesla-factorys-safety-issues-tied-to-its-push-for-production/

243. Feiner, L. (2019, September 27). Tesla's Elon Musk Violated Labor Law with Tweet, NLRB Judge Rules. *CNBC*. Retrieved from https://www.cnbc.com/2019/09/27/tesla-ceo-elon-musk-violated-labor-law-with-tweet-nlrb-judge-rules.html

union activity and that pro-union employees were subjected to harassment and intimidation.[244]

Elon Musk, the CEO of Tesla, has also been accused of making anti-union remarks and taking other acts that deter unionization. In 2018, Musk tweeted that workers who chose to unionize would give up their stock options, a statement that was widely interpreted as a threat to discourage union activity. The tweet led to a complaint filed with the National Labor Relations Board (NLRB), which ruled that Musk's tweet violated U.S. labor laws by interfering with workers' rights to organize.[245]

The Strain on Workers

The allegations of union-busting at Tesla have exacerbated the strain on workers, many of whom are already dealing with the challenges of high production pressures and unsafe working conditions.[246] The lack of a union to represent workers' interests means that employees have limited leverage to negotiate for better wages, benefits, and working conditions, leaving them vulnerable to exploitation and mistreatment.

According to reports, Tesla's factories have a culture of fear and retaliation, which adds to the stress on employees. Employees who speak out about safety concerns or advocate for unionization have reported being disciplined, demoted, or even terminated. This culture of fear creates a chilling effect, where workers are afraid to voice their concerns or push for changes, further entrenching the dehumanization of work at Tesla.[247]

---

244. Levy, A. (2017, May 18). Tesla Factory's Safety Issues Tied to Its Push for Production. *Reveal from The Center for Investigative Reporting*. Retrieved from https://www.revealnews.org/article/tesla-factorys-safety-issues-tied-to-its-push-for-production/

245. Feiner, L. (2019, September 27). Tesla's Elon Musk Violated Labor Law with Tweet, NLRB Judge Rules. *CNBC*. Retrieved from https://www.cnbc.com/2019/09/27/tesla-ceo-elon-musk-violated-labor-law-with-tweet-nlrb-judge-rules.html

246. Higgins, T. (2018, April 12). Tesla Factory Workers Reveal Pain, Injury and Stress: 'Everything Feels Like the Future but Us.' *The Guardian*. Retrieved from https://www.theguardian.com/technology/2018/apr/12/tesla-workers-pain-injury-stress-production-goals

247. Levy, A. (2017, May 18). Tesla Factory's Safety Issues Tied to Its Push for Production. *Reveal from The Center for Investigative Reporting*. Retrieved from https://www.revealnews.org/article/tesla-factorys-safety-issues-tied-to-its-push-for-production/

The lack of union representation also contributes to a sense of powerlessness among workers, who feel that they have little control over their working conditions or the direction of the company.[248] This sense of powerlessness, combined with the physical and psychological strain of the job, can lead to a decline in morale and an increase in turnover, as workers seek out more stable and supportive employment opportunities.

Legal and Moral Consequences

Considering Tesla's reputation as a progressive and socially conscious company, the claims of union-busting at the company have serious ethical and legal ramifications. The NLRB's ruling against Musk's tweet and other labor practices highlights the legal risks associated with anti-union activity, including potential fines, penalties, and reputational damage.[249]

Ethically, Tesla's approach to labor relations raises questions about the company's commitment to its workers and its values. While Tesla has positioned itself as a leader in sustainability and innovation, its labor practices suggest a disconnect between its public image and its treatment of employees.[250] The allegations of union-busting and the dehumanization of work at Tesla undermine the company's credibility as a socially responsible employer and raise concerns about the broader impact of its business practices on workers and society.

Wider Effects on Employees and the Sector

Tesla's labor practices have drawn attention to the challenges faced by workers in the automotive industry, particularly as companies increasingly rely on automation and advanced manufacturing

---

248. Feiner, L. (2019, September 27). Tesla's Elon Musk Violated Labor Law with Tweet, NLRB Judge Rules. *CNBC*. Retrieved from https://www.cnbc.com/2019/09/27/tesla-ceo-elon-musk-violated-labor-law-with-tweet-nlrb-judge-rules.html

249. *Ibid.*

250. Levy, A. (2017, May 18). Tesla Factory's Safety Issues Tied to Its Push for Production. *Reveal from The Center for Investigative Reporting*. Retrieved from https://www.revealnews.org/article/tesla-factorys-safety-issues-tied-to-its-push-for-production/

techniques to improve efficiency and meet production targets.[251] The push for higher productivity, combined with the use of automation, can lead to a devaluation of human labor, where workers are seen as interchangeable and disposable.

The focus on production at the expense of worker safety and well-being is not unique to Tesla but is indicative of broader trends in the industry. As companies face increasing pressure to compete in a global market, there is a risk that workers' rights and protections will be eroded in the pursuit of higher profits and greater efficiency.[252] This trend raises important questions about the role of labor in the modern economy and the need for stronger protections and representation for workers.

Future of Work and the Role of Unions

Tesla employees' struggles also serve as a reminder of how crucial unions are to defending employees' rights and giving them a voice at work.[253] As companies like Tesla push the boundaries of innovation and automation, there is a growing need for labor representation that can advocate for fair wages, safe working conditions, and job security in an increasingly automated and technology-driven world.

In the face of corporate power and technological change, workers' capacity to organize and fight for their rights will determine the nature of work in the automotive sector and beyond.[254] Unions and labor organizations will play a critical role in ensuring that workers are treated with dignity and respect and that their contributions are valued in a rapidly evolving economy.

---

251. Brynjolfsson, E., & McAfee, A. (2014). *The Second Machine Age: Work, Progress, and Prosperity in a Time of Brilliant Technologies*. W.W. Norton & Company.

252. Kaplan, J. (2015). *Humans Need Not Apply: A Guide to Wealth and Work in the Age of Artificial Intelligence*. Yale University Press.

253. Kalleberg, A. L. (2011). *Good Jobs, Bad Jobs: The Rise of Polarized and Precarious Employment Systems in the United States, 1970s-2000s*. Russell Sage Foundation.

254. Feiner, L. (2019, September 27). Tesla's Elon Musk Violated Labor Law with Tweet, NLRB Judge Rules. *CNBC*. Retrieved from https://www.cnbc.com/2019/09/27/tesla-ceo-elon-musk-violated-labor-law-with-tweet-nlrb-judge-rules.html

Ethical Responsibility of Companies

Tesla's approach to labor relations raises important ethical questions about the responsibility of companies to their workers. As a leading company in the automotive industry and a symbol of innovation, Tesla has a responsibility to set an example for how companies should treat their employees.[255] This includes ensuring that workers have a safe and supportive work environment, fair wages, and the right to organize and advocate for their interests.

The dehumanization of work at Tesla and the allegations of union-busting suggest that the company has not fully lived up to its ethical responsibilities. As Tesla continues to grow and expand its influence, it will be essential for the company to address these issues and demonstrate a commitment to the well-being of its workers.[256] This will not only improve the lives of Tesla employees but also set a positive example for the broader industry and society.

In light of technological advancement and intense production pressures, the Tesla case serves as a reminder of the difficulties and unfavorable effects that come with the dehumanization of labor. The company's focus on meeting ambitious production targets, combined with allegations of unsafe working conditions and union-busting, has led to significant strain on its workforce and raised important questions about the role of labor in the modern economy.

Stronger worker protections, the ability to organize and demand better working conditions, and a dedication from businesses like Tesla to put their employees' welfare first are all necessary components of a multifaceted strategy to address these issues. By addressing these issues, Tesla and other companies can help create a more equitable and sustainable future for workers in the automotive industry and beyond.

---

255. Kaplan, J. (2015). *Humans Need Not Apply: A Guide to Wealth and Work in the Age of Artificial Intelligence*. Yale University Press.

256. Levy, A. (2017, May 18). Tesla Factory's Safety Issues Tied to Its Push for Production. *Reveal from The Center for Investigative Reporting*. Retrieved from https://www.revealnews.org/article/tesla-factorys-safety-issues-tied-to-its-push-for-production/

Displacement of Human Creativity and Expertise

The growing integration of AI and automation into the workplace is raising serious concerns about the displacement of human creativity and expertise. While machines excel at routine tasks, they are increasingly taking on roles that require cognitive skills such as problem-solving, decision-making, and innovative thinking.[257] Industries like journalism, marketing, and finance now rely on AI-driven tools to analyze data, generate reports, and create content with minimal human oversight. Although these technologies enhance efficiency, they risk diminishing the value of human expertise, as tasks once considered uniquely human are increasingly handed over to machines.[258]

This shift is especially troubling in professions where judgment, intuition, and empathy are critical. In healthcare, for instance, AI systems are used to diagnose medical conditions and recommend treatments, raising ethical questions about their role in patient care. While machines can provide precise analysis, they lack the emotional intelligence and nuanced understanding that human caregivers bring to their work.[259] Such developments highlight the tension between technological innovation and the need to preserve human elements in industries that demand both expertise and empathy.

Loss of Human Connection and Social Capital

The dehumanization of work extends beyond the displacement of human labor and creativity; it also impacts the social fabric of the workplace. As technology mediates more interactions among workers, customers, and employers, relational aspects such as collaboration, mentorship,

257. Kaplan, J. (2015). *Humans Need Not Apply: A Guide to Wealth and Work in the Age of Artificial Intelligence.* Yale University Press.

258. Frey, C. B., & Osborne, M. A. (2017). *The Future of Employment: How Susceptible Are Jobs to Computerization? Technological Forecasting and Social Change*, 114, 254-280.

259. Topol, E. (2019). *Deep Medicine: How Artificial Intelligence Can Make Healthcare Human Again.* Basic Books.

and camaraderie are at risk of being eroded.[260] Automated systems and digital platforms increasingly isolate workers from their colleagues and customers, reducing interactions to impersonal transactions. This isolation fosters a sense of disconnection, stripping work of its relational value and leaving workers with fewer opportunities to build meaningful relationships or engage in collaborative efforts.[261]

The loss of social capital, the networks, trust, and shared norms that support collaboration and group action, is also reflected in the disappearance of traditional workplace communities.[262] As workers become more dispersed and disconnected, the erosion of these social bonds exacerbates the alienation and depersonalization of work, compounding the challenges posed by automation and technological advancements.

Nowhere is the dehumanizing effect of mass production and technological efficiency more evident than in the case of Foxconn, a global electronics manufacturer whose factory conditions have drawn intense scrutiny. The relentless push for productivity, coupled with extreme working conditions, has led to dire consequences for workers, including widespread reports of mental and physical strain, and, in some tragic cases, suicide.

---

260. Putnam, R. D. (2000). *Bowling Alone: The Collapse and Revival of American Community.* Simon & Schuster.

261. Rosenblat, A. (2018). *Uberland: How Algorithms are Rewriting the Rules of Work.* University of California Press.

262. Putnam, R. D. (2000). *Bowling Alone: The Collapse and Revival of American Community.* Simon & Schuster.

Human Tolls of Foxconn's Practices

Foxconn, one of the world's largest electronics manufacturers, is best known as a key supplier for Apple, producing iPhones and other Apple products at massive scales. However, the company has been the subject of intense scrutiny and criticism due to its labor practices, particularly concerning the dehumanization of work. The relentless focus on mass production, coupled with poor working conditions, has led to significant negative impacts on employee health and safety.

An important note is the company's response to a series of employee suicides and the subsequent public outcry, which highlights the broader issues of worker exploitation and the ethical responsibilities of multinational corporations. This case study examines the dehumanization of work at Foxconn, focusing on the impact of mass production on employee health and safety and the company's response to suicides and public outcry.

Mass Production's Effect on Employee Safety and Health

Foxconn operates massive factories in China, where it employs hundreds of thousands of workers to meet the global demand for electronics. The company's focus on efficiency and productivity has come at the expense of employee health and safety, leading to widespread concerns about the dehumanization of its workforce.

The Scale and Intensity of Production

Some of Foxconn's factories employ over 200,000 people, and they are built to function at extraordinary scales. The largest of these, often referred to as "Foxconn City," is located in Shenzhen,

China, and covers a vast area with dormitories, cafeterias, and even its own television network. These factories operate around the clock, with workers often putting in long hours to meet the stringent production targets set by companies like Apple.[263]

The intensity of production at Foxconn is driven by the need to meet tight deadlines and deliver large quantities of products within short time frames. Workers are often required to work 12-hour shifts, six or seven days a week, with limited breaks and little time for rest.[264] The repetitive nature of the tasks, combined with the pressure to maintain high levels of productivity, can lead to physical and mental exhaustion.

Foxconn's production process's focus on efficiency and speed has also been connected to a culture that views employees as interchangeable components of a huge machine. This dehumanization of labor is evident in the way workers are expected to perform monotonous tasks for hours on end, with little consideration given to their well-being or job satisfaction.[265] The result is a workforce that is physically and mentally strained, with high levels of stress and burnout.

Health and Safety Concerns

The intense working conditions at Foxconn have led to numerous health and safety concerns. Workers are often exposed to hazardous conditions, including poor ventilation, exposure to toxic chemicals, and inadequate safety measures.[266] These conditions have been linked to a range of health problems, including respiratory issues, musculoskeletal disorders, and chronic fatigue.

---

263. Chan, J., Pun, N., & Selden, M. (2013). The Politics of Global Production: Apple, Foxconn and China's New Working Class. *New Technology, Work and Employment*, 28(2), 100-115.

264. Pun, N., Chan, J., & Selden, M. (2016). Apple, Foxconn, and Chinese Workers' Struggles from a Global Labor Perspective. *Inter-Asia Cultural Studies*, 17(2), 166-185.

265. Smith, C. (2013). Foxconned Labor as the Dark Side of the Apple Story. *Economic and Labour Relations Review*, 24(2), 231-248.

266. Chan, J., Pun, N., & Selden, M. (2013). The Politics of Global Production: Apple, Foxconn and China's New Working Class. *New Technology, Work and Employment*, 28(2), 100-115.

One of the most notable incidents highlighting the dangers of Foxconn's working environment occurred in 2011, when an explosion at a factory in Chengdu, China, killed three workers and injured several others. The explosion was caused by the accumulation of aluminum dust, a byproduct of the polishing process for iPad cases. Investigations revealed that the factory had failed to implement proper safety measures, despite warnings from employees about the dangers of dust accumulation.[267]

Foxconn employees' mental health has been a major concern in addition to the physical health risks. The high-pressure environment, long working hours, and isolation from family and friends have contributed to widespread reports of stress, depression, and anxiety among workers.[268] The company's dormitory-style living arrangements, where workers are housed in cramped quarters with little privacy, further exacerbate these issues.

Suicide Reactions and Public Outcry

The harsh working conditions at Foxconn gained international attention in 2010 when a series of worker suicides brought the company's labor practices under intense scrutiny. The suicides sparked a global outcry, leading to widespread criticism of Foxconn and its clients, particularly Apple.

The Wave of Suicides

In 2010, Foxconn experienced a wave of employee suicides, with 14 workers taking their own lives at the company's Shenzhen factory. Most of the victims were young migrant workers, aged 18 to 25, who had come to the city from rural areas in search of employment.[269] The suicides were a stark indicator of the extreme pressure and despair felt by many of Foxconn's employees.

---

267. Barboza, D. (2011, May 20). Explosion at Apple Supplier in China Kills 2 Workers. *The New York Times*. Retrieved from https://www.nytimes.com/2011/05/21/technology/21foxconn.html

268. Pun, N., Chan, J., & Selden, M. (2016). Apple, Foxconn, and Chinese Workers' Struggles from a Global Labor Perspective. *Inter-Asia Cultural Studies*, 17(2), 166-185.

269. Chan, J., Pun, N., & Selden, M. (2013). The Politics of Global Production: Apple, Foxconn and China's New Working Class. *New Technology, Work and Employment*, 28(2), 100-115.

The suicides were attributed to a combination of factors, including the oppressive working conditions, lack of social support, and the intense stress associated with the job. Workers at Foxconn reported feeling isolated and alienated, with little opportunity for social interaction or emotional support.[270] The repetitive and monotonous nature of the work, combined with the high expectations and strict management practices, created an environment where many employees felt hopeless and trapped.

The public response to the suicides was swift and intense. Media outlets around the world reported on the conditions at Foxconn, and human rights organizations condemned the company's labor practices. The suicides also sparked protests in China, where activists called for better working conditions and greater protections for workers.[271]

Foxconn's Response

In response to the suicides and the subsequent public outcry, Foxconn implemented a series of measures aimed at improving working conditions and addressing the mental health of its employees. These measures included increasing wages, reducing working hours, and providing mental health counseling for workers.[272] The company also installed safety nets around its dormitory buildings to prevent workers from jumping to their deaths, a move that was widely criticized as a superficial solution to a deeper problem.

Foxconn's response to the suicides was seen by many as an attempt to deflect criticism rather than address the underlying issues. While the company made some improvements to working conditions, many of the fundamental problems, such as the high-pressure environment and the lack of worker autonomy, remained

270. Smith, C. (2013). Foxconned Labor as the Dark Side of the Apple Story. *Economic and Labour Relations Review*, 24(2), 231-248.

271. Barboza, D. (2011, May 20). Explosion at Apple Supplier in China Kills 2 Workers. *The New York Times*. Retrieved from https://www.nytimes.com/2011/05/21/technology/21foxconn.html

272. Chan, J., Pun, N., & Selden, M. (2013). The Politics of Global Production: Apple, Foxconn and China's New Working Class. *New Technology, Work and Employment*, 28(2), 100-115.

unaddressed.[273] Critics argued that Foxconn's measures were insufficient and that the company needed to take more meaningful steps to improve the well-being of its workers.

Despite Foxconn's actions, Apple was under a lot of pressure to resolve the issue. As Foxconn's largest client, Apple was criticized for its role in enabling the company's labor practices. In response, Apple conducted audits of Foxconn's factories and worked with the company to implement changes.[274] However, Apple's efforts were also met with skepticism, as many observers questioned the effectiveness of the audits and the company's commitment to enforcing labor standards.

The Suicides' Wider Repercussions

Both the business and the larger electronics sector were significantly impacted by the Foxconn suicides. The incident highlighted the human cost of mass production and the pressure to deliver products quickly and cheaply in a globalized market.[275] It also raised important questions about the responsibilities of multinational corporations in ensuring the welfare of workers in their supply chains.

The public outcry following the suicides forced Foxconn and other electronics manufacturers to confront the ethical consequences of their labor practices. It also led to increased scrutiny of working conditions in the electronics industry, with consumers, activists, and governments calling for greater transparency and accountability.[276] The incident underscored the need for stronger labor protections and more robust enforcement of labor standards in global supply chains.

---

273. Pun, N., Chan, J., & Selden, M. (2016). Apple, Foxconn, and Chinese Workers' Struggles from a Global Labor Perspective. *Inter-Asia Cultural Studies*, 17(2), 166-185.

274. Smith, C. (2013). Foxconned Labor as the Dark Side of the Apple Story. *Economic and Labour Relations Review*, 24(2), 231-248.

275. Chan, J., Pun, N., & Selden, M. (2013). The Politics of Global Production: Apple, Foxconn and China's New Working Class. *New Technology, Work and Employment*, 28(2), 100-115.

276. Barboza, D. (2011, May 20). Explosion at Apple Supplier in China Kills 2 Workers. *The New York Times*. Retrieved from https://www.nytimes.com/2011/05/21/technology/21foxconn.html

Greater Effects on Worldwide Supply Chains

The case of Foxconn is emblematic of broader issues in global supply chains, where the drive for efficiency and cost-cutting often comes at the expense of worker well-being. The dehumanization of work at Foxconn reflects the challenges faced by workers in many industries, particularly in developing countries where labor laws and protections are often weak or poorly enforced.

Roles of Multinational Corporations

Multinational corporations, such as Apple, play a significant role in shaping labor practices in global supply chains. As the primary clients of companies like Foxconn, these corporations have significant influence over working conditions, wages, and labor standards.[277] However, the pursuit of low production costs and high profit margins can create incentives for suppliers to cut corners on safety and worker welfare.

Multinational firms must be held more accountable for the conditions in their supply chains, as the Foxconn case makes clear. This includes conducting thorough audits, ensuring compliance with labor standards, and working with suppliers to improve working conditions.[278] It also requires a commitment to transparency and accountability, with companies disclosing information about their supply chains and the steps they are taking to address labor issues.

Challenge of Enforcing Labor Standards

One of the key challenges in addressing the dehumanization of work in global supply chains is the enforcement of labor standards. While many countries have laws and regulations designed to protect workers, these are often poorly enforced, particularly in developing countries where labor inspections are infrequent and penalties

---

277. Smith, C. (2013). Foxconned Labor as the Dark Side of the Apple Story. *Economic and Labour Relations Review*, 24(2), 231-248.

278. Chan, J., Pun, N., & Selden, M. (2013). The Politics of Global Production: Apple, Foxconn and China's New Working Class. *New Technology, Work and Employment*, 28(2), 100-115.

for violations are weak.[279] This creates an environment where companies can exploit workers with little fear of repercussions.

The Foxconn case illustrates the limitations of relying on audits and self-regulation to enforce labor standards. Despite numerous audits and inspections by Apple and other clients, the underlying issues at Foxconn persisted.[280] This suggests that more robust enforcement mechanisms are needed, including stronger legal frameworks, independent inspections, and greater involvement of workers in monitoring and reporting labor violations.

Importance of Worker Representation and Rights

The dehumanization of work at Foxconn also highlights the importance of worker representation and rights in improving working conditions. In many global supply chains, workers have little voice in the decisions that affect their lives and attempts to organize or form unions are often met with resistance or repression. This lack of representation leaves workers vulnerable to exploitation and abuse.[281]

Empowering workers through unions, worker councils, or other forms of representation is essential to addressing the dehumanization of work. This includes ensuring that workers have the right to organize, bargain collectively, and participate in decision-making processes.[282] It also requires a commitment from multinational corporations and governments to support and protect workers' rights, both in law and in practice.

The dehumanization of work at Foxconn, characterized by unsafe working conditions, intense production pressures, and a lack of

279. Pun, N., Chan, J., & Selden, M. (2016). Apple, Foxconn, and Chinese Workers' Struggles from a Global Labor Perspective. *Inter-Asia Cultural Studies*, 17(2), 166-185.

280. Smith, C. (2013). Foxconned Labor as the Dark Side of the Apple Story. *Economic and Labour Relations Review*, 24(2), 231-248.

281. Chan, J., Pun, N., & Selden, M. (2013). The Politics of Global Production: Apple, Foxconn and China's New Working Class. *New Technology, Work and Employment*, 28(2), 100-115.

282. Pun, N., Chan, J., & Selden, M. (2016). Apple, Foxconn, and Chinese Workers' Struggles from a Global Labor Perspective. *Inter-Asia Cultural Studies*, 17(2), 166-185.

worker autonomy, has had severe consequences for employee health and well-being. The wave of suicides at

Foxconn brought these issues to the forefront, sparking a global outcry and forcing both the company and its clients to confront the ethical implications of their labor practices.

Addressing the dehumanization of work in global supply chains requires a multifaceted approach, including stronger labor protections and greater transparency and accountability from multinational corporations and increased representation and rights for workers. By taking these steps, companies, and governments can help ensure that workers are treated with dignity and respect and that the benefits of globalization are shared more equitably across society.

Impact on the Value of Human Labor

The rise of technology in the workplace has significant implications for the value of human labor. As machines and AI take over more tasks, the demand for certain types of human labor is declining, leading to a shift in the labor market and a revaluation of the skills and capabilities that are considered valuable.

Decline of Routine and Manual Jobs

The rise of automation and AI has triggered a sharp decline in routine and manual jobs, particularly in sectors like manufacturing, retail, and transportation. Machines now perform tasks such as assembly line work, data entry, and driving with greater efficiency, leading to reduced demand for workers in these roles. As a result, job losses and wage stagnation have become pressing concerns.[283] This shift disproportionately affects low-skilled workers, who face the greatest risk of displacement. With fewer opportunities available, many are forced to compete for low-wage, low-skill jobs, further eroding job quality across the board.[284]

283. Acemoglu, D., & Restrepo, P. (2018). *Artificial Intelligence, Automation, and Work. National Bureau of Economic Research.* https://doi.org/10.3386/w24196

284. Autor, D. H. (2015). *Why Are There Still So Many Jobs? The History and Future of Workplace Automation.* Journal of Economic Perspectives, 29(3), 3-30.

This trend is also driving labor market polarization, with high-wage, high-skill jobs in fields like technology, finance, and healthcare clustering at the top, while low-wage roles dominate the bottom. The resulting gap exacerbates income inequality, creating a stark divide between the "haves" and "have-nots" and intensifying socioeconomic challenges in an increasingly automated world.[285]

As automation continues to replace low-wage, routine jobs, the fast-food industry has become a prime battleground for the fight over labor rights and fair wages. This trend is exemplified at the popular world-wide chain McDonald's, where rising labor costs and the push for higher wages have led the company to aggressively pursue automation, fundamentally reshaping the fast-food workforce.

---

285. Autor, D. H. (2015). *Why Are There Still So Many Jobs? The History and Future of Workplace Automation.* Journal of Economic Perspectives, 29(3), 3-30.

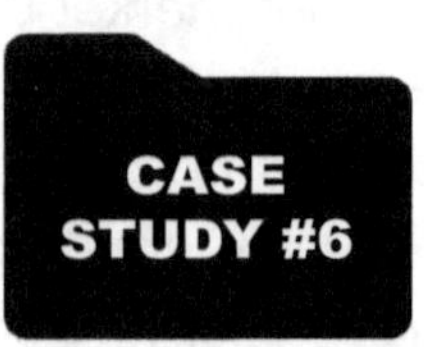

Taking Out the Human Element at McDonald's

McDonald's, one of the world's largest and most recognizable fast-food chains, has been at the forefront of debates surrounding labor practices and the dehumanization of work. The company's business model, which relies heavily on low-wage, entry-level jobs, has been criticized for its treatment of workers, particularly in terms of wages and working conditions.

Over the years, McDonald's has faced mounting pressure from workers and labor advocates demanding a living wage. In response, the company has implemented various strategies, including wage adjustments and the increased use of automation to reduce labor costs. This case study explores the fight for a living wage at McDonald's, the company's response, and the implications of automation on the workforce.

Fight for a Living Wage

With McDonald's frequently at the forefront of these initiatives, the fight for a living wage has been a major component of labor activism in the fast-food sector. Workers and advocates argue that the wages paid by McDonald's are insufficient to meet basic living expenses, leading to a widespread call for wage increases and better working conditions.

Origins and Growth of the Fight for $15

The Fight for $15 movement began in 2012 when fast-food workers in New York City organized a one-day strike demanding a $15 minimum wage and the right to unionize.[286] This movement

286. Rolf, D. (2016). *The Fight for $15: The Right Wage for a Working America*. New Press.

quickly gained momentum, spreading to other cities across the United States and drawing attention to the low wages and poor working conditions prevalent in the fast-food industry, including at McDonald's.

A fundamental standard of living cannot be maintained on the wages paid by corporations such as McDonald's, according to the movement's main contention. The federal minimum wage in the United States, which many McDonald's workers earn or come close to, has not kept pace with inflation and the rising cost of living, particularly in urban areas. As a result, many McDonald's employees rely on public assistance programs such as food stamps and Medicaid to make ends meet. A 2013 study by the University of California, Berkeley, found that more than half of fast-food workers, including those at McDonald's, were enrolled in one or more public assistance programs, costing U.S. taxpayers an estimated $7 billion annually.[287]

The Fight for $15 is not only about increasing wages; it is also about challenging the broader dehumanization of work in the fast-food industry. Workers argue that the low wages, lack of benefits, and precarious nature of their employment reflect a system that treats them as disposable and undervalues their labor.[288] The movement calls for higher wages, better working conditions, and the right to unionize, all of which are seen as essential to ensuring that workers are treated with dignity and respect.

McDonald's Response to the Fight for $15

In response to the growing pressure from the Fight for $15 movement and increasing public scrutiny, McDonald's has taken several steps to address the demands of its workers. In 2015, McDonald's announced that it would raise the wages of employees at company-owned restaurants to at least $1 above the local

287. Jacobs, K., Perry, I., & MacGillvary, J. (2015). *The High Public Cost of Low Wages*. UC Berkeley Center for Labor Research and Education. Retrieved from https://laborcenter.berkeley.edu/the-high-public-cost-of-low-wages/

288. Rolf, D. (2016). *The Fight for $15: The Right Wage for a Working America*. New Press.

minimum wage.[289] The company also offered paid time off for employees who had worked for more than a year.

However, this wage increase applied only to employees at company-owned stores, which make up a small percentage of McDonald's locations. The vast majority of McDonald's restaurants are operated by franchisees, who set their own wages and are not bound by the company's wage policies.[290] Many franchised employees did not receive pay increases as a result, which caused ongoing discontent and criticism from labor activists.

McDonald's has also faced criticism for its attempts to deflect responsibility for low wages onto its franchisees. The company has argued that it does not have control over the wages set by independent franchise owners, despite the significant influence it exerts over franchise operations through strict contractual agreements and business practices.[291] Critics argue that McDonald's could do more to ensure that all of its workers, including those at franchised locations, are paid a living wage.

Through public relations campaigns and corporate social responsibility programs, McDonald's has tried to enhance its reputation. The company has promoted itself as a responsible employer that provides opportunities for career advancement and invests in employee training and development.[292] However, these efforts have been met with skepticism by workers and labor activists, who argue that McDonald's has not done enough to address the systemic issues of low wages and poor working conditions in its restaurants.

---

289. Jacobs, K., Perry, I., & MacGillvary, J. (2015). *The High Public Cost of Low Wages*. UC Berkeley Center for Labor Research and Education. Retrieved from https://laborcenter.berkeley.edu/the-high-public-cost-of-low-wages/

290. Jacobs, K., Perry, I., & MacGillvary, J. (2015). *The High Public Cost of Low Wages*. UC Berkeley Center for Labor Research and Education. Retrieved from https://laborcenter.berkeley.edu/the-high-public-cost-of-low-wages/

291. Rolf, D. (2016). *The Fight for $15: The Right Wage for a Working America*. New Press.

292. *Ibid.*

The Impact and Ongoing Challenges

The Fight for $15 movement has had a significant impact on the broader debate over wages and labor rights in the fast-food industry. The movement has brought national attention to the issue of low wages and has led to wage increases in several states and cities across the United States. For example, California, New York, and several other states have passed legislation raising the minimum wage to $15 per hour, a direct result of the pressure exerted by the Fight for $15 movement.[293]

The movement has also influenced public opinion, with a majority of Americans now supporting a $15 minimum wage.[294] This shift in public sentiment has put pressure on companies like McDonald's to address the demands of workers and to take meaningful action to improve wages and working conditions.

However, the fight for a living wage is far from over. Many fast-food workers, including those at McDonald's, continue to struggle with low pay, job insecurity, and a lack of benefits. The movement has highlighted the broader issues of inequality and worker exploitation in the fast-food industry and underscored the need for continued advocacy and activism to ensure that all workers are treated with dignity and respect.

Using Automation to Reduce Labor Costs

In response to the pressures of rising labor costs and the demand for higher wages, McDonald's has increasingly turned to automation as a way to reduce its reliance on human labor and cut operating expenses. The use of technology to streamline operations and replace workers has raised significant concerns about the dehumanization of work in the fast-food industry.

---

293. Jacobs, K., Perry, I., & MacGillvary, J. (2015). *The High Public Cost of Low Wages*. UC Berkeley Center for Labor Research and Education. Retrieved from https://laborcenter.berkeley.edu/the-high-public-cost-of-low-wages/

294. *Ibid.*

Implementation of Self-Service Kiosks

One of the most visible examples of McDonald's use of automation is the implementation of self-service kiosks in its restaurants. These kiosks allow customers to place orders and pay for their meals without interacting with a cashier.[295] The kiosks are designed to increase efficiency, reduce wait times, and minimize errors in order processing.

As part of a larger plan to update its eateries and attract tech-savvy customers, McDonald's installed self-service kiosks. However, it has also been driven by the desire to reduce labor costs. By replacing cashiers with kiosks, McDonald's can cut down on the number of employees needed to operate each restaurant, thereby reducing payroll expenses.[296]

The use of kiosks has raised concerns about the impact on workers, particularly in the context of the Fight for $15 movement. Critics argue that McDonald's is using automation as a way to avoid paying higher wages and providing benefits to its employees.[297] By automating tasks that were previously performed by human workers, McDonald's is reducing the number of jobs available, particularly for low-wage, entry-level workers who rely on these positions as a source of income.

Expansion of Automation in McDonald's Operations

Self-service kiosks at McDonald's have explored other forms of automation to streamline its operations and reduce labor costs. This includes the use of robotic kitchen equipment, such as automated fryers and drink dispensers, which can prepare food and beverages with minimal human intervention. These

295. Barrett, E. (2017, November 7). McDonald's $1 Billion Bet on Kiosks. *Fortune*. Retrieved from https://fortune.com/2017/11/07/mcdonalds-kiosks-fast-food-automation/

296. *Ibid.*

297. Rosenblat, A. (2018). *Uberland: How Algorithms are Rewriting the Rules of Work.* University of California Press.

technologies are designed to increase efficiency, reduce waste, and improve consistency in food preparation.[298]

McDonald's has also invested in digital ordering and delivery platforms, which allow customers to place orders through mobile apps or online platforms. These systems reduce the need for human interaction and can be integrated with automated kitchen equipment to create a more seamless and efficient operation. The use of technology to manage orders and deliveries has been particularly important during the COVID-19 pandemic, as it has allowed McDonald's to continue serving customers while minimizing contact between employees and customers.[299]

The expansion of automation in McDonald's operations raises important questions about the future of work in the fast-food industry. As technology continues to advance, the potential for further automation of tasks currently performed by human workers is significant.[300] This could lead to a reduction in the number of jobs available in the industry, particularly for low-wage workers who are most vulnerable to displacement by automation.

The Impact of Automation on Workers

For its employees, McDonald's growing automation has important ramifications. While automation can improve efficiency and reduce costs, it also has the potential to dehumanize work by replacing human workers with machines and reducing the value of human labor.

One of the primary concerns is the potential for job loss. As McDonald's continues to automate tasks such as order-taking, food preparation, and payment processing, the number of jobs available for cashiers, kitchen staff, and other entry-level positions is likely to decrease. This could lead to significant job losses in

298. Fitzgerald, M. (2019, March 18). McDonald's Pushes Automation to the Front Lines. *Wall Street Journal.* Retrieved from https://www.wsj.com/articles/mcdonalds-pushes-automation-to-the-front-lines-11552998805

299. *Ibid.*

300. Rosenblat, A. (2018). *Uberland: How Algorithms are Rewriting the Rules of Work.* University of California Press.

the fast-food industry, particularly for workers who lack the skills or opportunities to transition to other forms of employment.[301]

As more tasks are automated, the remaining jobs may become more monotonous and less meaningful, with workers relegated to monitoring machines or performing tasks that require little skill or creativity.[302] This can lead to a decline in job satisfaction and a sense of alienation among workers, who may feel that their contributions are undervalued or that they are being replaced by machines.

Low-wage workers, who are more likely to be displaced by automation, may struggle to find new employment opportunities, particularly in industries where automation is rapidly expanding. This can lead to increased economic insecurity and a widening gap between those who have the skills to thrive in a technology-driven economy and those who do not.[303]

Wider Repercussions on the Fast-Food Sector

The dehumanization of work at McDonald's, characterized by the fight for a living wage and the increasing use of automation, has broader implications for the fast-food industry and the future of work. These issues raise important questions about the role of technology in the workplace, the value of human labor, and the need for policies that protect workers' rights and ensure fair wages.

Technology's Place at Work

The use of automation at McDonald's reflects a broader trend in the fast-food industry and other sectors, where technology is increasingly being used to streamline operations and reduce labor

---

301. Fitzgerald, M. (2019, March 18). McDonald's Pushes Automation to the Front Lines. *Wall Street Journal*. Retrieved from https://www.wsj.com/articles/mcdonalds-pushes-automation-to-the-front-lines-11552998805

302. Rosenblat, A. (2018). *Uberland: How Algorithms are Rewriting the Rules of Work*. University of California Press.

303. Brynjolfsson, E., & McAfee, A. (2014). *The Second Machine Age: Work, Progress, and Prosperity in a Time of Brilliant Technologies*. W.W. Norton & Company.

costs.[304] While automation can improve efficiency and reduce costs, it also has the potential to displace workers and reduce the value of human labor.

As technology continues to advance, the potential for further automation in the fast-food industry is significant. This raises important questions about the future of work and the role of human labor in a technology-driven economy.[305]

Policymakers, businesses, and labor organizations must work together to ensure that the benefits of automation are shared equitably and that workers are not left behind in the transition to a more automated economy.

The Value of Human Labor

The fight for a living wage at McDonald's highlights the broader issue of how human labor is valued in the fast-food industry. Despite the essential role that fast-food workers play in the economy, they are often paid low wages and receive few benefits, leading to widespread economic insecurity and a lack of opportunities for advancement.[306]

The dehumanization of work in the fast-food industry is reflected in the way that workers are treated as disposable and replaceable.[307] This devaluation of human labor has significant implications for workers' well-being and for the broader economy, as low wages and poor working conditions contribute to inequality and social instability.

To address these issues, it is essential to recognize the value of human labor and to ensure that all workers are paid fair wages and treated with dignity and respect. This includes advocating for

304. Brynjolfsson, E., & McAfee, A. (2014). *The Second Machine Age: Work, Progress, and Prosperity in a Time of Brilliant Technologies*. W.W. Norton & Company.

305. Rosenblat, A. (2018). *Uberland: How Algorithms are Rewriting the Rules of Work*. University of California Press.

306. Rolf, D. (2016). *The Fight for $15: The Right Wage for a Working America*. New Press.

307. Jacobs, K., Perry, I., & MacGillvary, J. (2015). *The High Public Cost of Low Wages*. UC Berkeley Center for Labor Research and Education. Retrieved from https://laborcenter.berkeley.edu/the-high-public-cost-of-low-wages/

higher wages, better working conditions, and greater protections for workers in the fast-food industry and beyond.[308]

Need for Policies that Protect Workers

Policies that safeguard workers' rights and guarantee equitable pay and working conditions are necessary, as demonstrated by the difficulties McDonald's employees face. Raising the minimum wage, strengthening labor protections, and ensuring that workers have the right to organize and bargain collectively.[309]

These labor protections, there is also a need for policies that address the impact of automation on the workforce.[310] This includes investing in education and training programs that help workers develop the skills needed to thrive in a technology-driven economy, as well as providing support for workers who are displaced by automation.

The case of McDonald's highlights the dehumanization of work in the fast-food industry, characterized by the fight for a living wage and the increasing use of automation to reduce labor. costs. These issues raise important questions about the value of human labor, the role of technology in the workplace, and the need for policies that protect workers' rights and ensure fair wages.

Addressing these challenges requires a multifaceted approach, including advocating for higher wages, improving working conditions, and ensuring that the benefits of automation are shared equitably. By recognizing the value of human labor and ensuring that all workers are treated with dignity and respect, we can create a more equitable and sustainable economy that benefits all members of society.

---

308. Rolf, D. (2016). *The Fight for $15: The Right Wage for a Working America*. New Press.

309. Jacobs, K., Perry, I., & MacGillvary, J. (2015). *The High Public Cost of Low Wages*. UC Berkeley Center for Labor Research and Education. Retrieved from https://laborcenter.berkeley.edu/the-high-public-cost-of-low-wages/

310. Brynjolfsson, E., & McAfee, A. (2014). *The Second Machine Age: Work, Progress, and Prosperity in a Time of Brilliant Technologies*. W.W. Norton & Company.

Revaluation of Cognitive and Interpersonal Skills

While automation and AI are displacing many routine and manual jobs, they are simultaneously generating new opportunities for workers equipped with cognitive and interpersonal skills. As machines handle repetitive tasks, attributes like problem-solving, creativity, critical thinking, and emotional intelligence are becoming increasingly valuable in the knowledge economy, where such skills remain difficult to automate and highly sought after.[311]

Industries such as healthcare, education, and management are seeing growing demand for workers who can analyze complex information, make sound decisions, and communicate effectively. Similarly, creative sectors value individuals capable of generating innovative ideas and adapting to evolving challenges.[312] However, this shift also underscores concerns about rising inequality in the labor market.

Workers with advanced cognitive and interpersonal abilities often secure higher wages and greater job stability, while those lacking these skills face diminished prospects. This trend shows that the critical role of education and training in equipping the workforce for future demands, ensuring more equitable access to the opportunities emerging in an increasingly automated world.[313]

Erosion of the Social Contract

The rise of technology in the workplace is also contributing to the erosion of the social contract between employers and workers, a set of expectations and obligations that have traditionally governed the employment relationship.[314] As companies increasingly rely on automation and AI to perform tasks, the traditional employer-employee relationship is being

311. Brynjolfsson, E., & McAfee, A. (2014). *The Second Machine Age: Work, Progress, and Prosperity in a Time of Brilliant Technologies.* W.W. Norton & Company.

312. Autor, D. H. (2015). *Why Are There Still So Many Jobs? The History and Future of Workplace Automation.* Journal of Economic Perspectives, 29(3), 3-30.

313. Kaplan, J. (2015). *Humans Need Not Apply: A Guide to Wealth and Work in the Age of Artificial Intelligence.* Yale University Press.

314. Kalleberg, A. L. (2011). *Good Jobs, Bad Jobs: The Rise of Polarized and Precarious Employment Systems in the United States, 1970s-2000s.* Russell Sage Foundation.

replaced by more transactional, short-term arrangements, leading to a decline in job security, benefits, and worker protections.

The erosion of the social contract is particularly evident in the gig economy, where workers are often classified as independent contractors rather than employees and are therefore excluded from many of the protections and benefits that have traditionally been associated with full-time employment. This shift is leading to increased economic insecurity for workers, as they are left to navigate the challenges of the modern labor market without the support of traditional employment relationships.[315]

The erosion of the social contract also has broader implications for society, as the decline of stable, secure employment contributes to increased inequality, social fragmentation, and a weakening of the social fabric.[316] As the traditional pillars of the social contract, such as job security, benefits, and worker protections, are eroded, there is a growing need for new forms of social support and protection that can address the challenges of the modern labor market.

Broader Social and Economic Consequences

The increasing dehumanization of work and the erosion of the value of human labor have far-reaching social and economic consequences that extend well beyond individual workplaces. These changes are reshaping the dynamics of the labor market, fueling inequality, and undermining collective well-being.

While technology offers unprecedented opportunities for innovation and efficiency, its unchecked integration into work environments is creating a chasm between economic winners and losers. The benefits of automation and AI often concentrate among a privileged few, exacerbating disparities in income, job security, and career prospects. At the same time, workers at the lower end of the labor spectrum face dwindling opportunities and

315. Rosenblat, A. (2018). *Uberland: How Algorithms are Rewriting the Rules of Work.* University of California Press.

316. Kalleberg, A. L. (2011). *Good Jobs, Bad Jobs: The Rise of Polarized and Precarious Employment Systems in the United States, 1970s-2000s.* Russell Sage Foundation.

precarious employment, intensifying economic instability and social disconnection.

Social Mobility and Inequality's Effects

The rise of technology in the workplace is exacerbating inequality and hindering social mobility by disproportionately rewarding highly skilled, highly paid workers while marginalizing others. Automation and AI primarily benefit a small group of specialists and professionals, concentrating wealth and job stability in the hands of a select few.[317] Meanwhile, the majority of workers experience stagnant or declining wages, insecure employment, and diminished opportunities for advancement.

This labor market polarization has created a widening divide between the winners and losers of the technological revolution. Those at the top enjoy increased income, secure jobs, and access to advancement, while workers at the bottom are relegated to low-wage, precarious roles with little hope for upward mobility.[318] This growing inequality not only threatens economic stability but also weakens social cohesion and democratic ideals. Concentrated wealth and power undermine fairness and equal opportunity, eroding trust in societal systems and amplifying calls for systemic change.[319]

Decline in Well-Being and Quality of Life

As work becomes increasingly dehumanized, the repercussions on individual and collective well-being are stark. Many workers face heightened stress, anxiety, and a sense of powerlessness in response to the rapid technological changes disrupting the labor market. This has led to the rise of precarious employment characterized by low wages, insecure contracts, and limited access to benefits. Workers in these roles experience economic insecurity, making it difficult to plan for the future or protect

317. Autor, D. H. (2015). *Why Are There Still So Many Jobs? The History and Future of Workplace Automation.* Journal of Economic Perspectives, 29(3), 3-30.

318. Acemoglu, D., & Restrepo, P. (2018). *Artificial Intelligence, Automation, and Work. National Bureau of Economic Research.* https://doi.org/10.3386/w24196

319. Piketty, T. (2014). *Capital in the Twenty-First Century.* Harvard University Press.

themselves from financial hardship.[320] Such insecurity has been linked to a host of negative health outcomes, including chronic illnesses, reduced life expectancy, and deteriorating mental health.

The loss of meaningful work further compounds these challenges. As jobs become less engaging and more transactional, many workers report feeling alienated and undervalued, with little control over their roles or working conditions. This disconnect diminishes job satisfaction, reduces motivation, and negatively impacts overall quality of life.[321] Addressing these issues requires rethinking the balance between technological progress and preserving the dignity, creativity, and value of human labor to foster a more equitable and humane future.

Need for New Social and Economic Models

The dehumanization of work and the diminishing value of human labor underscore the urgent need for new social and economic frameworks to address the evolving challenges of the modern labor market. As automation and AI continue to reshape the nature of work, it is crucial to rethink the role of employment in society, create robust systems of social support and protection, and ensure that the benefits of technological advancements are more equitably distributed. This vision requires a fundamental shift in how we view work, workers, and the broader economy.[322]

One promising solution is the implementation of Universal Basic Income (UBI), a concept that proposes providing all citizens with a guaranteed income, regardless of their employment status. UBI offers a potential safety net for workers displaced by automation, providing economic security while allowing individuals the freedom to pursue education, training, or creative endeavors without the constant pressure to secure traditional jobs. By decoupling income from traditional employment, UBI

---

320. Benach, J., Vives, A., Amable, M., Vanroelen, C., Tarafa, G., & Muntaner, C. (2014). *Precarious Employment: Understanding an Emerging Social Determinant of Health. Annual Review of Public Health*, 35, 229-253.

321. Bainbridge, W. S. (1983). *The Impact of Technology on Work: The Future of Human Labor. American Journal of Sociology,* 88(5), 939-964.

322. Brynjolfsson, E., & McAfee, A. (2014). *The Second Machine Age: Work, Progress, and Prosperity in a Time of Brilliant Technologies.* W.W. Norton & Company.

could mitigate the economic instability caused by automation and reduce inequality in the labor market.

Another solution lies in the development of new forms of labor organization and worker representation. As the workforce increasingly shifts toward non-traditional employment models, such as the gig economy, there is a pressing need to create digital platforms, cooperatives, or unions that can advocate for workers' rights. These new structures could empower workers to have a voice in the workplace, ensuring fair treatment, improved working conditions, and better wages. This shift would contribute to restoring dignity and respect in the labor market, counteracting the isolation and fragmentation that often accompany the rise of automation.[323]

Ultimately, the rise of technology in the workplace presents a transformative challenge, one that threatens not only jobs but also social cohesion and individual well-being. To mitigate the negative consequences of these shifts, society must adopt innovative models that prioritize the dignity of work and ensure that the benefits of technological progress are shared more inclusively. By embracing these new frameworks, we can build an economy that serves all members of society, fostering greater equity, social stability, and a higher quality of life for everyone.

---

323. Scholz, T. (2016). *Uberworked and Underpaid: How Workers Are Disrupting the Digital Economy.* Polity Press.

KEY TAKEAWAYS

Automation and AI Are Reshaping the Workforce
Technology is rapidly transforming industries by replacing human labor with machines and AI. While this increases efficiency and productivity, it also eliminates jobs across sectors, from factory work to white-collar professions like legal research and finance.

Job Quality and Worker Satisfaction Are Declining
As automation takes over, many remaining jobs lack autonomy and creativity, reducing workers to machine monitors or gig workers with little security. The gig economy, for example, often treats workers as interchangeable and disregards their well-being.

Real-World Cases Highlight the Human Cost of Automation
Companies like Tesla, Foxconn, and McDonald's demonstrate how automation prioritizes efficiency over worker welfare. Tesla's high-pressure production goals have led to safety concerns and high turnover. Foxconn's mass-production system has resulted in worker exploitation and mental health crises. McDonald's has replaced workers with kiosks, eliminating entry-level jobs.

Technology Is Widening Economic Inequality
AI and automation create a polarized labor market, where high-paying jobs go to highly skilled professionals while low-wage workers face job insecurity. This exacerbates income inequality and reduces opportunities for social mobility, leading to greater economic instability.

Urgent Need for New Social and Economic Models
The rise of automation calls for stronger worker protections, upskilling initiatives, and innovative policies like Universal Basic Income (UBI) to ensure economic security. Companies must balance technological progress with ethical labor practices to prevent widespread worker exploitation.

Chapter 7

The Human Cost, Stress, Burnout, and Workplace Well-Being

Over the past few decades, technological advancements, globalization, and shifting economic dynamics have all contributed to significant changes in the modern workplace. While these changes have brought about increased efficiency, flexibility, and connectivity, they have also introduced new challenges, particularly concerning the psychological well-being of employees. Employees have suffered significant psychological harm as a result of job insecurity, pressure to perform, the breakdown of work-life balance, and the demands of a quickly evolving workplace.

Workplace Stress and Its Causes

Workplace stress is one of the most significant psychological challenges faced by employees in today's work environment. Stress is a response to the demands and pressures of work that exceed an individual's ability to cope effectively. While some level of stress can be motivating, chronic stress can have detrimental effects on both physical and mental health.

High Workloads and Time Pressures

One of the primary contributors to workplace stress is the increasing workload and time pressures that many employees face. The expectation to do more with less, whether due to organizational downsizing, budget cuts, or increased competition, has led to higher workloads for employees.[324] Many workers find themselves juggling multiple tasks, working long hours, and facing tight deadlines, all of which contribute to elevated stress levels.

The proliferation of technology has further exacerbated these pressures. The advent of smartphones, email, and instant messaging has blurred the boundaries between work and personal life, making it difficult for employees to disconnect and recharge. The expectation to be constantly available and responsive has created an "always-on" culture, where employees feel compelled to check and respond to work-related communications even outside of regular working hours.[325]

Lack of Control and Autonomy

Another significant source of workplace stress is the lack of control and autonomy that employees experience in their jobs. Autonomy refers to the degree of freedom and independence employees have in making decisions about their work.[326] When employees feel that they have little control over their tasks, schedules, or working conditions, it can lead to feelings of helplessness and frustration, contributing to stress.

In many modern workplaces, employees are subject to strict monitoring and micromanagement, often driven by the need to meet performance metrics and productivity targets. The use of surveillance technologies, such as tracking software and performance monitoring tools, can create a sense of being constantly watched and evaluated, leading to heightened stress and anxiety.[327] This lack of autonomy and control can be particularly pronounced in low-wage, high-pressure jobs, where employees have little say in how their work is organized or carried out.

---

324. Schaufeli, W. B. (2017). Applying the Job Demands-Resources Model: A 'How To' Guide to Measuring and Tackling Work Engagement and Burnout. *Organizational Dynamics*, 46(2), 120-132.

325. Schieman, S., & Young, M. (2010). The Demands of Work and the Mental Health Benefits of Work-to-Family Resources: The Emotional Costs of Managing the Demands of Work and Family. *Journal of Health and Social Behavior*, 51(3), 308-323.

326. Karasek, R. A., & Theorell, T. (1990). *Healthy Work: Stress, Productivity, and the Reconstruction of Working Life*. Basic Books.

327. Rosenblat, A. (2018). *Uberland: How Algorithms are Rewriting the Rules of Work*. University of California Press.

Job Insecurity and Financial Uncertainty

Job insecurity, defined as the perceived threat of losing one's job, is another major contributor to workplace stress. In an increasingly competitive and volatile economy, many employees face uncertainty about the stability of their employment.[328] This insecurity can stem from factors such as organizational restructuring, outsourcing, automation, or economic downturns.

The fear of job loss can lead to chronic stress, as employees worry about their financial stability, career prospects, and ability to support themselves and their families. This stress is often compounded by the reality that finding new employment, particularly in certain industries or age groups, can be challenging. Because of this, job insecurity can have serious psychological repercussions, such as anxiety, depression, and a decline in job satisfaction.[329]

Burnout: The Consequence of Chronic Workplace Stress

Burnout is a psychological condition characterized by emotional exhaustion, depersonalization, and a reduced sense of personal accomplishment. It is often the result of prolonged exposure to workplace stress and is particularly prevalent in high-stress professions such as healthcare, education, and social work. However, burnout can occur in any work environment where employees experience chronic stress, high demands, and insufficient support.

Emotional Exhaustion

Emotional exhaustion is a core component of burnout and refers to the feeling of being emotionally drained and depleted of energy.[330] Employees experiencing emotional exhaustion often feel overwhelmed by the demands

---

328. De Witte, H. (2005). Job Insecurity: Review of the International Literature on Definitions, Prevalence, Antecedents and Consequences. *SA Journal of Industrial Psychology*, 31(4), 1-6.

329. Brynjolfsson, E., & McAfee, A. (2014). *The Second Machine Age: Work, Progress, and Prosperity in a Time of Brilliant Technologies*. W.W. Norton & Company.

330. Maslach, C., & Leiter, M. P. (2016). *Burnout: A Brief History and How to Build Better Workplaces*. Wiley.

of their job and may struggle to find the motivation or energy to continue performing their tasks.

The causes of emotional exhaustion are multifaceted and can include factors such as excessive workload, lack of support from supervisors or colleagues, and the emotional demands of dealing with difficult clients or patients.[331] Over time, emotional exhaustion can lead to a range of negative outcomes, including decreased job performance, increased absenteeism, and a higher likelihood of leaving the organization.

Depersonalization and Cynicism

Cynicism, or depersonalization, is another important component of burnout. It involves a sense of detachment from one's work and a negative, cynical attitude toward one's job, colleagues, or clients.[332] Employees experiencing depersonalization may begin to see their work as meaningless or unfulfilling and may distance themselves emotionally from their tasks and the people they interact with.

Depersonalization can be a coping mechanism for dealing with the overwhelming demands of work, but it often leads to further disengagement and dissatisfaction.[333] Employees who become cynical about their work are less likely to invest effort or take pride in their job, which can negatively impact their performance and relationships with colleagues and clients.

Reduced Personal Accomplishment

The third dimension of burnout is a reduced sense of personal accomplishment, where employees feel that their work is not meaningful or that they are not making a positive contribution. This can lead to feelings of incompetence, low self-esteem, and a lack of motivation.[334] Employees experiencing this aspect of burnout may feel that their efforts go unrecognized or that they are unable to achieve their professional goals. This

331. *Ibid.*

332. *Ibid.*

333. *Ibid.*

334. Maslach, C., & Leiter, M. P. (2016). *Burnout: A Brief History and How to Build Better Workplaces*. Wiley.

sense of ineffectiveness can be particularly demoralizing and may lead to a desire to leave the job or even the profession altogether.[335]

Nike's workplace challenges highlight how high-pressure environments, excessive workloads, and managerial shortcomings can drive employee dissatisfaction and burnout, leading to significant internal upheaval.

---

335. *Ibid.*

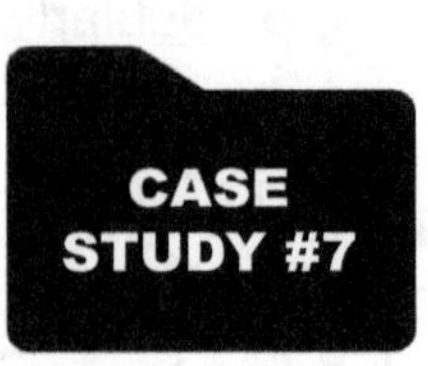

Psychological Impact on Nike Employees

Nike is one of the world's most iconic and successful sportswear brands, and has built its reputation on innovation, athletic excellence, and a dynamic corporate culture. However, beneath this successful exterior, Nike has faced significant scrutiny over its workplace environment, particularly concerning allegations of a hostile work environment for women.

These allegations have raised serious concerns about the psychological toll on employees, the impact of Nike's internal culture on morale, and the broader implications for workplace equality and well-being. This case study explores these issues, focusing on the specific challenges faced by women at Nike, the internal culture's impact on employee morale, and the company's response to these allegations.

Allegations of a Hostile Work Environment for Women

Nike has been the subject of numerous allegations regarding a hostile work environment, particularly for women. These allegations have included claims of gender discrimination, sexual harassment, and a pervasive "boys' club" culture that marginalizes female employees.

Gender Discrimination and Pay Disparities

One of the key issues highlighted in the allegations against Nike is gender discrimination, particularly in terms of pay disparities and promotion opportunities. Several women at Nike have reported that they were paid less than their male counterparts for similar roles and responsibilities.[336] They also claimed that they were passed over for promotions in favor of less qualified male colleagues, reinforcing a culture of gender inequality within the company.

These disparities in pay and promotion opportunities contribute to a sense of marginalization and injustice among female employees. The perception that their contributions are undervalued and that they are not given the same opportunities as their male counterparts can lead to feelings of frustration, demoralization, and helplessness.[337] Over time, these feelings can erode job satisfaction and contribute to a negative work environment.

Sexual Harassment and the "Boys' Club" Culture

Several women at Nike have alleged that they were subjected to sexual harassment and inappropriate behavior by male colleagues and supervisors. These allegations have included unwanted advances, inappropriate comments, and a general culture of disrespect toward women. The "boys' club" culture at Nike, characterized by an informal network of male employees who hold significant power and influence within the company, has been cited as a key factor in perpetuating these behaviors.[338]

The prevalence of sexual harassment in the workplace can have severe psychological consequences for the victims. Women who are subjected to harassment may experience anxiety, depression, and a loss of self-esteem.[339] They may also feel isolated and unsupported, particularly if they believe that reporting the harassment will lead

---

336. Reyes, E. (2018, April 19). Nike Forced Out Several Top Executives Amid Misconduct Allegations. *The Wall Street Journal*. Retrieved from https://www.wsj.com/articles/nike-forced-out-several-top-executives-amid-misconduct-allegations-1524172800

337. Parker, K. (2018). The Gender Discrimination Lawsuit at Nike: A Step Toward Equity in Corporate America. *Harvard Business Review*, 96(4), 72-83.

338. Sorkin, A. (2018, April 25). The "Boys' Club" at Nike: How Women Are Pushing Back Against Workplace Inequality. *The New York Times*. Retrieved from https://www.nytimes.com/2018/04/25/business/nike-women-inequality.html

339. Reyes, E. (2018, April 19). Nike Forced Out Several Top Executives Amid Misconduct Allegations. *The Wall Street Journal*. Retrieved from https://www.wsj.com/articles/nike-forced-out-several-top-executives-amid-misconduct-allegations-1524172800

to retaliation or if they perceive that the company's leadership is not committed to addressing the issue.

Nike's "boys' club" culture has also come under fire for fostering an atmosphere in which women are marginalized in important decision-making and networking opportunities. This exclusion can limit their opportunities for career advancement and contribute to a sense of alienation and disempowerment.[340] The impact of this culture on women's career trajectories can be profound, leading to diminished job satisfaction and a higher likelihood of turnover.

Discrimination and Harassment's Effect on Workers' Well-Being

Female employees may experience severe psychological harm as a result of the combined effects of sexual harassment, pay inequalities, and gender discrimination. These experiences can lead to chronic stress, burnout, and a range of mental health issues, including anxiety, depression, and post-traumatic stress disorder (PTSD).[341] The fear of harassment or retaliation can also create a constant state of vigilance and anxiety, further exacerbating the psychological impact.

The hostile work environment at Nike has had a particularly damaging effect on employee morale and well-being. Women who feel marginalized and unsupported are less likely to be engaged in their work and may struggle to maintain motivation and job satisfaction. The stress and emotional toll of working in such an environment can also lead to physical health problems, including headaches, insomnia, and digestive issues.[342]

---

340. Sorkin, A. (2018, April 25). The "Boys' Club" at Nike: How Women Are Pushing Back Against Workplace Inequality. *The New York Times*. Retrieved from https://www.nytimes.com/2018/04/25/business/nike-women-inequality.html

341. Parker, K. (2018). The Gender Discrimination Lawsuit at Nike: A Step Toward Equity in Corporate America. *Harvard Business Review*, 96(4), 72-83.

342. Reyes, E. (2018, April 19). Nike Forced Out Several Top Executives Amid Misconduct Allegations. *The Wall Street Journal*. Retrieved from https://www.wsj.com/articles/nike-forced-out-several-top-executives-amid-misconduct-allegations-1524172800

How Internal Culture Affects Employee Morale

The internal culture at Nike has played a significant role in shaping employee morale and well-being. While Nike promotes itself as a forward-thinking and inclusive company, the reality for many employees, particularly women, has been markedly different. The internal culture, characterized by competitiveness, a lack of accountability, and the aforementioned "boys' club" mentality, has had profound effects on employee morale.

The Culture of Competitiveness and Pressure to Perform

Nike's internal culture is highly competitive, with a strong emphasis on performance and results. While this drive for excellence can foster innovation and achievement, it can also create an environment where employees feel constant pressure to meet high expectations. This pressure can be particularly intense for women, who may feel that they need to work harder and achieve more to gain the same recognition and opportunities as their male counterparts.[343]

The relentless focus on performance can lead to a work environment where employees feel overworked, stressed, and burned out. The pressure to constantly perform at a high level can contribute to feelings of inadequacy and self-doubt, particularly in an environment where gender discrimination and harassment are prevalent.[344] This stress can have a negative impact on mental health and overall well-being, leading to a decline in employee morale and job satisfaction.

Lack of Accountability and Support

Another significant issue within Nike's internal culture is the perceived lack of accountability and support for employees who experience discrimination or harassment. Several employees

343. Parker, K. (2018). The Gender Discrimination Lawsuit at Nike: A Step Toward Equity in Corporate America. *Harvard Business Review*, 96(4), 72-83.

344. *Ibid.*

have reported that when they raised concerns about inappropriate behavior or unfair treatment, their complaints were dismissed or ignored by management. This lack of accountability creates an environment where harassment and discrimination can flourish, as employees may feel that there are no consequences for such behavior.[345]

The lack of support for employees who experience discrimination or harassment can also contribute to a culture of silence and fear. Employees who do not feel safe reporting issues or who believe that their concerns will not be taken seriously are less likely to come forward, allowing the toxic culture to persist.[346] This lack of trust in the company's leadership can lead to a decline in employee morale and a sense of disillusionment with the organization.

The "Boys' Club" Mentality and Its Effect on Inclusion

Nike's "boys' club" mentality has posed a serious obstacle to fostering a welcoming and encouraging workplace.[347] This culture, which privileges male employees and excludes women from key professional networks and decision-making processes, has had a detrimental effect on employee morale, particularly for women and minority employees.

Women who feel excluded from important conversations and opportunities for career advancement are more likely to feel alienated and disengaged from their work. This exclusion can also lead to a sense of frustration and resentment, as employees may feel that their contributions are not valued or recognized. The

345. Reyes, E. (2018, April 19). Nike Forced Out Several Top Executives Amid Misconduct Allegations. *The Wall Street Journal*. Retrieved from https://www.wsj.com/articles/nike-forced-out-several-top-executives-amid-misconduct-allegations-1524172800

346. Sorkin, A. (2018, April 25). The "Boys' Club" at Nike: How Women Are Pushing Back Against Workplace Inequality. *The New York Times*. Retrieved from https://www.nytimes.com/2018/04/25/business/nike-women-inequality.html

347. *Ibid.*

impact of this exclusion on morale can be profound, leading to a decline in job satisfaction and a higher likelihood of turnover.[348]

Nike's Reaction to Public Disclosures

The public revelations of the toxic workplace culture at Nike, particularly for women, have had significant implications for the company. These revelations have prompted widespread criticism and calls for accountability, leading Nike to take several steps to address the issues and improve its workplace culture.

The 2018 Internal Review and Leadership Changes

In 2018, Nike conducted an internal review of its workplace culture following numerous complaints of discrimination and harassment.[349] This review led to the departure of several high-ranking executives who were implicated in the allegations, including Nike's brand president, Trevor Edwards, who was widely seen as a key figure in perpetuating the toxic culture.

The leadership changes were a significant step for Nike, signaling the company's recognition of the seriousness of the issues and its commitment to addressing them. However, these changes also highlighted the extent of the problem and the need for a comprehensive overhaul of the company's culture to create a more inclusive and supportive environment for all employees.[350]

Putting New Initiatives and Policies into Practice

In response to the revelations, Nike also implemented several new policies and initiatives aimed at improving workplace culture

348. Reyes, E. (2018, April 19). Nike Forced Out Several Top Executives Amid Misconduct Allegations. *The Wall Street Journal*. Retrieved from https://www.wsj.com/articles/nike-forced-out-several-top-executives-amid-misconduct-allegations-1524172800

349. *Ibid.*

350. Reyes, E. (2018, April 19). Nike Forced Out Several Top Executives Amid Misconduct Allegations. *The Wall Street Journal*. Retrieved from https://www.wsj.com/articles/nike-forced-out-several-top-executives-amid-misconduct-allegations-1524172800

and addressing issues of discrimination and harassment. These included revising the company's code of conduct, increasing diversity and inclusion training, and establishing clearer procedures for reporting and addressing complaints.[351]

Nike also committed to increasing transparency and accountability within the organization.[352] This included regular reporting on diversity metrics, holding leadership accountable for fostering an inclusive work environment, and providing employees with more resources and support to address issues of discrimination and harassment.

While these initiatives were a positive step forward, many critics argued that they were not enough to fully address the deep-rooted issues within Nike's culture. The effectiveness of these measures in creating lasting change and improving employee morale remains a subject of debate, particularly given the long-standing nature of the problems.[353]

The Effect on Nike's Image and Employee Confidence

Nike's reputation has suffered greatly as a result of the public disclosures of the company's toxic workplace culture. The allegations of discrimination and harassment, particularly in a company that has built its brand on values of empowerment and inclusivity, have led to widespread criticism from consumers, advocacy groups, and the media.[354] The damage to Nike's reputation has also raised questions about the company's commitment to its values and its ability to create a safe and inclusive work environment.

The revelations have also had an impact on employee trust in the company. Employees who feel that the company's leadership is

---

351. Parker, K. (2018). The Gender Discrimination Lawsuit at Nike: A Step Toward Equity in Corporate America. *Harvard Business Review*, 96(4), 72-83.

352. *Ibid.*

353. Sorkin, A. (2018, April 25). The "Boys' Club" at Nike: How Women Are Pushing Back Against Workplace Inequality. *The New York Times*. Retrieved from https://www.nytimes.com/2018/04/25/business/nike-women-inequality.html

354. Parker, K. (2018). The Gender Discrimination Lawsuit at Nike: A Step Toward Equity in Corporate America. *Harvard Business Review*, 96(4), 72-83.

not genuinely committed to addressing the issues or who believe that the changes are merely cosmetic may struggle to trust the organization's leadership. This lack of trust can contribute to ongoing morale issues and a sense of disillusionment with the company.[355]

The Wider Repercussions for the Business Sector

The case of Nike is not unique, as many large corporations face similar challenges in addressing issues of discrimination, harassment, and toxic workplace cultures. The broader implications of the Nike case highlight the importance of creating inclusive and supportive work environments and the need for systemic change to address these issues across the corporate world.

Leadership's Crucial Role in Creating Workplace Culture

A company's workplace culture is greatly influenced by its leadership. Leaders who are committed to creating an inclusive and respectful work environment can set the tone for the entire organization and ensure that all employees feel valued and supported.[356] Conversely, leaders who ignore or perpetuate toxic behaviors can contribute to a culture of discrimination and harassment that negatively impacts employee morale and well-being.

The Nike case emphasizes how crucial it is for leaders to be held accountable and how businesses must be proactive in addressing harassment and discrimination.[357] This includes holding leaders accountable for their actions, providing training and resources to support inclusive leadership, and fostering a culture of transparency and accountability.

---

355. Sorkin, A. (2018, April 25). The "Boys' Club" at Nike: How Women Are Pushing Back Against Workplace Inequality. *The New York Times*. Retrieved from https://www.nytimes.com/2018/04/25/business/nike-women-inequality.html

356. Good, M. (2021). *Corporate Culture and Leadership Accountability: Preventing Toxic Workplace Environments*. Wiley.

357. *Ibid.*

The Role of Corporate Policies and Practices

Corporate policies and practices play a critical role in preventing and addressing issues of discrimination and harassment in the workplace. Companies must have clear and comprehensive policies in place that define unacceptable behavior, provide procedures for reporting and investigating complaints, and protect employees from retaliation.[358] These policies should be regularly reviewed and updated to ensure they are effective and aligned with best practices.

The case of Nike highlights the importance of having strong corporate policies and practices in place to address issues of discrimination and harassment. Companies must also ensure that these policies are consistently enforced and that employees have access to the resources and support they need to address issues when they arise.[359]

Cultural Change Is Necessary

Creating a truly inclusive and supportive work environment requires more than just policies and leadership accountability; it requires a cultural transformation. Companies must actively work to create a culture that values diversity, inclusion, and respect for all employees. This includes promoting diverse leadership, providing opportunities for all employees to succeed, and fostering an environment where everyone feels safe and supported.[360]

The case of Nike demonstrates the challenges of achieving cultural transformation in large, established organizations.[10] However, it also highlights the importance of making this transformation a priority to create a more positive and productive work environment for all employees.

---

358. *Ibid.*

359. Good, M. (2021). *Corporate Culture and Leadership Accountability: Preventing Toxic Workplace Environments*. Wiley.

360. Schreier, J. (2020). *Press Reset: Ruin and Recovery in the Video Game Industry*. Hachette Book Group.

In order to create inclusive and encouraging work environments, the Nike case's wider ramifications emphasize the significance of strong corporate policies, leadership accountability, and cultural change. By prioritizing the well-being of their employees and fostering a culture of respect and inclusion, companies can create a more positive and productive work environment that benefits both employees and the organization as a whole.

The Impact of Job Insecurity on Psychological Well-Being

Job insecurity is a significant stressor that can have profound effects on an employee's psychological well-being. As mentioned earlier, job insecurity is characterized by the fear of losing one's job or experiencing significant changes in job conditions, such as reduced hours, pay cuts, or changes in responsibilities.

Anxiety and Depression

One of the most common psychological responses to job insecurity is anxiety. Employees who are uncertain about their job's future may experience constant worry, nervousness, and unease. This anxiety can be all-consuming, making it difficult for employees to focus on their work or enjoy their personal lives.[361] Over time, chronic anxiety can lead to more severe mental health issues, such as generalized anxiety disorder or panic attacks.

As well as anxiety, job insecurity can also lead to depression. The constant fear of job loss, coupled with feelings of helplessness and a lack of control over one's future, can lead to symptoms of depression, such as sadness, hopelessness, and a loss of interest in activities once enjoyed. Depression can have a devastating impact on an individual's quality of life and can impair their ability to function effectively both at work and in their personal life.[362]

361. De Witte, H. (2005). Job Insecurity: Review of the International Literature on Definitions, Prevalence, Antecedents and Consequences. *SA Journal of Industrial Psychology*, 31(4), 1-6.

362. Brynjolfsson, E., & McAfee, A. (2014). *The Second Machine Age: Work, Progress, and Prosperity in a Time of Brilliant Technologies*. W.W. Norton & Company.

Decreased Job Satisfaction and Commitment

Job insecurity can also lead to decreased job satisfaction and organizational commitment. When employees feel that their job is at risk, they may become less satisfied with their work and less committed to their employer. This can result in decreased motivation, lower productivity, and an increased likelihood of turnover.[363] The relationship between job insecurity and job satisfaction is complex, as employees may feel a sense of loyalty or obligation to their employer, even in the face of uncertainty. However, prolonged job insecurity is likely to erode this commitment, leading to a decline in job satisfaction and a sense of disengagement from the organization.[364]

Coping Mechanisms and Resilience

Employees who experience job insecurity may develop various coping mechanisms to manage their stress and anxiety. These coping strategies can be adaptive, such as seeking social support, developing new skills, or finding alternative sources of income.[365] However, they can also be maladaptive, such as substance abuse, withdrawal, or avoidance behaviors.

Resilience, or the ability to adapt to and recover from adversity, plays a crucial role in determining how employees respond to job insecurity. Employees with high levels of resilience are more likely to cope effectively with uncertainty and maintain their psychological well-being.[366] In contrast, those with lower resilience may struggle to manage their stress and may be more vulnerable to the negative effects of job insecurity.

---

363. Ashford, S. J., Lee, C., & Bobko, P. (1989). Content, Causes, and Consequences of Job Insecurity: A Theory-Based Measure and Substantive Test. *Academy of Management Journal*, 32(4), 803-829.

364. *Ibid.*

365. De Witte, H. (2005). Job Insecurity: Review of the International Literature on Definitions, Prevalence, Antecedents and Consequences. *SA Journal of Industrial Psychology*, 31(4), 1-6.

366. Brynjolfsson, E., & McAfee, A. (2014). *The Second Machine Age: Work, Progress, and Prosperity in a Time of Brilliant Technologies*. W.W. Norton & Company.

The Role of Technology in Exacerbating Psychological Strain

Technology has transformed the modern workplace, bringing both opportunities and challenges. While technology has improved efficiency and enabled new ways of working, it has also contributed to the psychological strain experienced by employees.

The "Always-On" Culture

One of the most significant ways technology has impacted employee well-being is through the creation of an "always-on" culture. With the widespread use of smartphones, email, and instant messaging, employees are often expected to be available and responsive outside of regular working hours.[367] This blurring of boundaries between work and personal life can lead to increased stress, as employees feel pressured to stay connected and respond to work-related communications, even during their free time.

The inability to disconnect from work can prevent employees from fully relaxing and recovering, leading to burnout and decreased overall well-being. The constant connectivity enabled by technology can also contribute to feelings of being overwhelmed, as employees struggle to keep up with the demands of work while balancing their personal lives.[368]

Surveillance and Monitoring

Another way technology has contributed to psychological strain in the workplace is through increased surveillance and monitoring. Many organizations use technology to track employee performance, monitor productivity, and enforce compliance with company policies.[369] While

---

367. Schieman, S., & Young, M. (2010). The Demands of Work and the Mental Health Benefits of Work-to-Family Resources: The Emotional Costs of Managing the Demands of Work and Family. *Journal of Health and Social Behavior*, 51(3), 308-323.

368. Schieman, S., & Young, M. (2010). The Demands of Work and the Mental Health Benefits of Work-to-Family Resources: The Emotional Costs of Managing the Demands of Work and Family. *Journal of Health and Social Behavior*, 51(3), 308-323.

369. Rosenblat, A. (2018). *Uberland: How Algorithms are Rewriting the Rules of Work*. University of California Press.

these practices can improve efficiency and accountability, they can also create a sense of constant scrutiny and pressure.

Employees who feel that they are being constantly monitored may experience heightened stress and anxiety, as they worry about making mistakes or failing to meet expectations.[370] This can lead to a decline in job satisfaction and a sense of being devalued as a human being, as employees may feel that they are being treated as mere cogs in a machine rather than as individuals with unique skills and contributions.

Job Automation and the Fear of Obsolescence

The increasing use of automation and artificial intelligence (AI) in the workplace has also contributed to the psychological toll on employees. As more tasks are automated, many workers fear that their jobs may become obsolete, leading to anxiety about job security and future employment prospects.[371] The fear of job loss due to automation can lead to feelings of helplessness and a lack of control over one's future.

This fear is particularly pronounced in industries where automation is rapidly expanding, such as manufacturing, retail, and customer service.[372] Employees in these industries may feel that their skills are becoming outdated and that they are at risk of being replaced by machines.

The Broader Implications for Organizations and Society

The psychological toll on employees has significant implications for organizations and society as a whole. Addressing these challenges requires a concerted effort to improve workplace conditions, support employee well-being, and create a more sustainable work environment.

---

370. *Ibid.*

371. Maslach, C., & Leiter, M. P. (2016). *Burnout: A Brief History and How to Build Better Workplaces.* Wiley.

372. *Ibid.*

Organizational Costs

The psychological strain experienced by employees can have significant costs for organizations. Stress, burnout, and job insecurity can lead to decreased productivity, increased absenteeism, and higher turnover rates.[373] These factors can negatively impact an organization's bottom line, as they result in lost productivity, increased recruitment and training costs, and a decline in overall employee morale.

A particularly stark example of these consequences can be seen in the case of Activision Blizzard, where allegations of workplace toxicity, harassment, and discrimination not only harmed employee well-being but also led to widespread turmoil within the company.

---

373. *Ibid.*

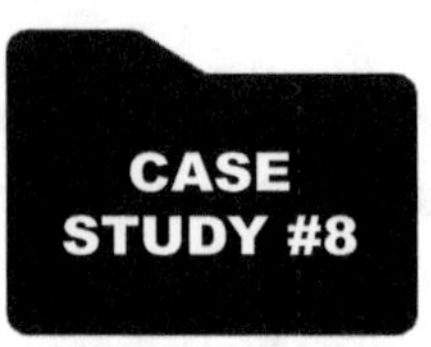

Activision Blizzard's Toxic Workplace Culture

Activision Blizzard's workplace culture has been characterized as toxic, especially for minority and femal=e employees. This toxic environment has been characterized by systemic discrimination, harassment, and a lack of accountability, all of which have contributed to significant psychological stress for employees.

Systemic Discrimination and Harassment

One of the most significant aspects of the toxic culture at Activision Blizzard is the systemic discrimination and harassment that many employees, particularly women, have reported. According to a lawsuit filed by the California Department of Fair Employment and Housing (DFEH) in July 2021, female employees at Activision Blizzard were subjected to a pervasive "frat boy" culture where they were routinely harassed and discriminated against.[374]

The lawsuit detailed numerous instances of sexual harassment, including inappropriate comments, groping, and advances made by male colleagues. Female employees also reported being passed over for promotions, receiving lower pay than their male counterparts, and being excluded from key meetings and decision-making processes.[375] This environment created a culture of fear

374. Makuch, E. (2021, July 21). California Sues Activision Blizzard Over 'Frat Boy' Culture, Harassment, And Discrimination. *GameSpot*. Retrieved from https://www.gamespot.com/articles/california-sues-activision-blizzard-over-frat-boy-culture-harassment-and-discrimination/1100-6494007/

375. Makuch, E. (2021, July 21). California Sues Activision Blizzard Over 'Frat Boy' Culture, Harassment, And Discrimination. *GameSpot*. Retrieved from https://www.gamespot.com/articles/california-sues-activision-blizzard-over-frat-boy-culture-harassment-and-discrimination/1100-6494007/

and intimidation, where victims of harassment felt unable to speak out or seek justice without risking retaliation.

Employee Well-Being Affected

Employees' mental health has been significantly impacted by Activision Blizzard's toxic workplace culture. This constant exposure to harassment, discrimination, and a hostile work environment can lead to severe stress, anxiety, and depression. Many employees reported feeling powerless and demoralized, with some describing the workplace as "soul-crushing" and "emotionally draining."[376]

The fear of retaliation and the lack of trust in the company's leadership further exacerbated the psychological toll on employees. Victims of harassment often felt isolated and unsupported, with little recourse to address their grievances. This environment of fear and intimidation can lead to long-term mental health issues, including post-traumatic stress disorder (PTSD), burnout, and a sense of hopelessness.[377]

The Broader Implications of a Toxic Culture

Beyond the direct effects on specific employees, Activision Blizzard's toxic culture has wider ramifications. A toxic work environment can lead to high turnover rates, decreased productivity, and a decline in overall morale.[378] Employees who feel unsafe, undervalued, or unsupported are less likely to be engaged in their work, which can negatively impact the company's performance and creativity.

Moreover, a toxic culture can have a ripple effect throughout the organization, contributing to the erosion of trust, collaboration, and innovation. When employees are constantly on guard and fearful of harassment or discrimination, they are less likely to take risks,

376. *Ibid.*

377. Macdonald, K., & Saravanan, C. (2021, August 11). The Fallout from Activision Blizzard's Toxic Culture. *Wired*. Retrieved from https://www.wired.com/story/activision-blizzard-toxic-culture-fallout/

378. Sutton, R. I. (2007). *The No Asshole Rule: Building a Civilized Workplace and Surviving One That Isn't*. Business Plus.

share ideas, or collaborate effectively with their colleagues.[379] This can stifle creativity and innovation, which are critical components of success in the video game industry.

Public Revelations and the Company's Response

Calls for accountability and widespread condemnation have resulted from Activision Blizzard's toxic workplace culture being made public. The company's response to these allegations has been closely scrutinized, with many questioning whether enough has been done to address the issues and protect employees.

Coverage of the California DFEH Lawsuit in the Media

An important step in exposing Activision Blizzard's toxic culture was the lawsuit the California DFEH filed in July 2021. The lawsuit alleged that the company had failed to address widespread harassment and discrimination and had actively ignored or covered up incidents of misconduct.[380] The lawsuit also accused the company of fostering a hostile work environment that disproportionately affected female and minority employees.

Widespread awareness of Activision Blizzard's problems was raised by the lawsuit's aftermath media coverage. Numerous former and current employees came forward with their own stories of harassment and discrimination, further corroborating the allegations in the lawsuit.[381] The revelations led to protests, walkouts, and calls for the resignation of key executives, including CEO Bobby Kotick.

---

379. *Ibid.*

380. Makuch, E. (2021, July 21). California Sues Activision Blizzard Over 'Frat Boy' Culture, Harassment, And Discrimination. *GameSpot*. Retrieved from https://www.gamespot.com/articles/california-sues-activision-blizzard-over-frat-boy-culture-harassment-and-discrimination/1100-6494007/

381. Macdonald, K., & Saravanan, C. (2021, August 11). The Fallout from Activision Blizzard's Toxic Culture. *Wired*. Retrieved from https://www.wired.com/story/activision-blizzard-toxic-culture-fallout/

Activision Blizzard's Initial Response

In response to the lawsuit and the public outcry, Activision Blizzard initially issued statements that were widely criticized as dismissive and defensive.[382] The company's initial response downplayed the severity of the allegations and denied any wrongdoing, which further fueled anger among employees and the public.

The company's leadership faced significant backlash for their handling of the situation, with many employees accusing them of failing to take the issues seriously and of fostering the very culture of discrimination and harassment that was being criticized.[383] The initial response was seen as a missed opportunity to acknowledge the problems and commit to meaningful change.

Employee Walkouts and Continued Pressure

Employee activism increased as a result of Activision Blizzard's leadership's poor response. In July 2021, hundreds of employees staged a walkout to protest the company's handling of the allegations and to demand accountability and change.[384] The walkout was a significant moment in the history of the company, as it highlighted the deep frustration and anger among the workforce.

Many people in the gaming industry, advocacy organizations, and gamers themselves supported the walkout. The pressure on Activision Blizzard continued to mount, with calls for the resignation of key executives and for the company to undergo a comprehensive overhaul of its workplace practices.[7385]

---

382. Makuch, E. (2021, July 21). California Sues Activision Blizzard Over 'Frat Boy' Culture, Harassment, And Discrimination. *GameSpot*. Retrieved from https://www.gamespot.com/articles/california-sues-activision-blizzard-over-frat-boy-culture-harassment-and-discrimination/1100-6494007/

383. Makuch, E. (2021, July 21). California Sues Activision Blizzard Over 'Frat Boy' Culture, Harassment, And Discrimination. *GameSpot*. Retrieved from https://www.gamespot.com/articles/california-sues-activision-blizzard-over-frat-boy-culture-harassment-and-discrimination/1100-6494007/

384. Macdonald, K., & Saravanan, C. (2021, August 11). The Fallout from Activision Blizzard's Toxic Culture. *Wired*. Retrieved from https://www.wired.com/story/activision-blizzard-toxic-culture-fallout/

385. *Ibid.*

Subsequent Actions by Activision Blizzard

In response to the continued pressure, Activision Blizzard eventually took more concrete steps to address the issues. The company announced the departure of several high-profile executives who were implicated in the allegations and pledged to make changes to its workplace culture. This included hiring a new head of human resources, creating a diversity and inclusion task force, and implementing new policies aimed at preventing harassment and discrimination.[386]

Additionally, Activision Blizzard announced that it would be conducting an internal review of its policies and practices, as well as working with an external law firm to investigate the allegations. The company also pledged to increase transparency and accountability, including regular reports on its progress in addressing the issues.[387]

While these actions were seen as a step in the right direction, many critics argued that they were not enough to address the deep-rooted problems within the company.[388] The ongoing legal battles, employee dissatisfaction, and public scrutiny suggested that more significant changes were needed to rebuild trust and create a safe and inclusive workplace.

The Effects on Activision Blizzard Over Time

In the long run, Activision Blizzard has been significantly impacted by the public disclosures and the company's response. The company's reputation has been severely damaged, with many gamers, industry professionals, and advocacy groups calling for boycotts and increased scrutiny of its practices.[389] The legal and financial repercussions of the lawsuit, as well as the potential loss

386. Good, M. (2021). *Corporate Culture and Leadership Accountability: Preventing Toxic Workplace Environments*. Wiley.

387. *Ibid.*

388. *Ibid.*

389. *Ibid.*

of talent due to high turnover and low morale, have also created challenges for the company's future.

Broader discussions concerning workplace culture in the video game industry and beyond have also been spurred by the Activision Blizzard case. The issues of harassment, discrimination, and toxic work environments are not unique to Activision Blizzard but are prevalent across many industries.[390] The public outcry and the response to the Activision Blizzard case have highlighted the need for systemic change to protect employees and ensure a safe and respectful workplace.

Consequences for the Video Game Industry

The toxic workplace culture at Activision Blizzard and the subsequent public revelations have had significant implications for the broader video game industry. The case has brought attention to the pervasive issues of harassment, discrimination, and poor working conditions that exist across the industry.

How Commonly Toxic Work Cultures Are in the Gaming Sector

Activision Blizzard's problems are not unique; rather, they are a reflection of larger patterns in the video game business. Many game development studios have been criticized for fostering toxic work environments, where employees are subjected to long hours, intense pressure, and a culture of harassment and discrimination. The "crunch" culture, where employees are expected to work excessive hours to meet deadlines, is particularly prevalent in the industry and contributes to burnout, stress, and poor mental health.[391] Another long-standing problem in the gaming industry is the lack of diversity and inclusion; women and minority employees

390. Macdonald, K., & Saravanan, C. (2021, August 11). The Fallout from Activision Blizzard's Toxic Culture. *Wired*. Retrieved from https://www.wired.com/story/activision-blizzard-toxic-culture-fallout/

391. Schreier, J. (2020). *Press Reset: Ruin and Recovery in the Video Game Industry*. Hachette Book Group.

frequently face major obstacles to advancement and are the targets of discriminatory practices.[392] The revelations from the Activision Blizzard case have highlighted the need for the industry to address these systemic issues and to create a more inclusive and supportive work environment.

Industry Leadership's Function in Promoting Change

Workplace culture in the video game industry is greatly influenced by the leadership of the companies involved. The actions and attitudes of executives and managers set the tone for how employees are treated and what behaviors are tolerated.[393] The failures of leadership at Activision Blizzard have underscored the importance of accountability and the need for leaders to take a proactive approach to addressing issues of harassment and discrimination.

To drive meaningful change, industry leaders must commit to creating a culture of respect, inclusion, and transparency.[394] This includes implementing robust policies and procedures to prevent harassment and discrimination, providing training and resources for employees, and fostering an environment where employees feel safe to speak out and report misconduct.

Advocacy and Employee Activism's Role

The Activision Blizzard case has also highlighted the importance of advocacy and employee activism in driving change.[395] The walkouts, protests, and public statements made by employees have played a critical role in bringing attention to the issues and holding the company accountable. The support from industry groups,

---

392. Schreier, J. (2020). *Press Reset: Ruin and Recovery in the Video Game Industry*. Hachette Book Group.

393. Good, M. (2021). *Corporate Culture and Leadership Accountability: Preventing Toxic Workplace Environments*. Wiley.

394. *Ibid.*

395. Macdonald, K., & Saravanan, C. (2021, August 11). The Fallout from Activision Blizzard's Toxic Culture. *Wired*. Retrieved from https://www.wired.com/story/activision-blizzard-toxic-culture-fallout/

advocacy organizations, and the broader gaming community has also been instrumental in pushing for change.

The case demonstrates the power of collective action and the importance of employees having a voice in their workplace. The continued pressure from employees and advocates is essential to ensuring that companies take meaningful steps to address issues of harassment and discrimination and to create a more equitable and inclusive work environment.[396]

The Path to Creating a Safe and Inclusive Workplace

The case of Activision Blizzard has highlighted the need for systemic change to address the toxic workplace culture and to protect the well-being of employees. Creating a safe and inclusive workplace requires a comprehensive approach that involves leadership, policy changes, and cultural transformation.

Leadership Accountability and Transparency

One of the key steps in creating a safe and inclusive workplace is ensuring leadership accountability and transparency. Company leaders must take responsibility for the culture of their organization and be committed to addressing issues of harassment and discrimination. This includes being transparent about the actions being taken to address these issues and regularly reporting on progress.[397]

Leaders must also be held accountable for their actions and decisions. This includes removing or disciplining executives and managers who have been implicated in misconduct or who have failed to address issues within their teams.[398] By demonstrating

396. *Ibid.*

397. Sutton, R. I. (2007). *The No Asshole Rule: Building a Civilized Workplace and Surviving One That Isn't*. Business Plus.

398. *Ibid.*

a commitment to accountability, companies can begin to rebuild trust and create a culture of respect and inclusion.

Comprehensive Policies and Procedures

Implementing comprehensive policies and procedures is essential to preventing harassment and discrimination in the workplace. These policies should include clear definitions of unacceptable behavior, procedures for reporting and investigating complaints, and protections against retaliation for those who come forward.[399]

Companies should also provide regular training for employees and managers on these policies, as well as on topics such as diversity, inclusion, and unconscious bias.[400] By educating employees and fostering a culture of awareness, companies can help prevent incidents of harassment and discrimination and create a more inclusive work environment.

Fostering a Culture of Inclusion and Support

Creating a safe and inclusive workplace requires more than just policies and procedures; it also requires a cultural shift.

Companies must actively work to create an environment where all employees feel valued, respected, and supported.[401] This includes promoting diversity and inclusion at all levels of the organization, providing resources for employee well-being, and encouraging open communication and collaboration.

Companies should also create spaces for employees to connect, share experiences, and support one another. Employee resource groups, mentorship programs, and other initiatives can help foster a sense of community and belonging, particularly for underrepresented groups. By prioritizing employee well-being

---

399. Good, M. (2021). *Corporate Culture and Leadership Accountability: Preventing Toxic Workplace Environments*. Wiley.

400. *Ibid.*

401. Schreier, J. (2020). *Press Reset: Ruin and Recovery in the Video Game Industry*. Hachette Book Group.

and creating a supportive culture, companies can reduce the psychological toll on employees and improve overall morale and productivity.[402]

The case of Activision Blizzard serves as a stark reminder of the psychological toll that a toxic workplace culture can take on employees. The systemic harassment, discrimination, and hostile work environment at the company have had severe consequences for employee well-being, leading to stress, anxiety, and long-term mental health issues. The public revelations of these issues have prompted widespread condemnation and calls for change, both within the company and across the broader video game industry.

Addressing the toxic culture at Activision Blizzard and similar companies requires a comprehensive approach that includes leadership accountability, robust policies and procedures, and a cultural shift towards inclusion and support. By taking these steps, companies can create a safer and more equitable work environment that prioritizes the well-being of employees and fosters innovation, creativity, and success.

These direct costs, organizations that fail to address the psychological well-being of their employees may also face reputational risks. Companies that are perceived as neglecting their employees' mental health and well-being may struggle to attract and retain top talent, as well as face backlash from consumers and stakeholders.[403]

Social and Economic Consequences

The psychological toll on employees also has broader social and economic consequences. Mental health issues, such as anxiety and depression, are associated with significant healthcare costs and can contribute to a decline in overall public health.[404] The stress and strain experienced

402. *Ibid.*

403. Maslach, C., & Leiter, M. P. (2016). *Burnout: A Brief History and How to Build Better Workplaces.* Wiley..

404. De Witte, H. (2005). Job Insecurity: Review of the International Literature on Definitions, Prevalence, Antecedents and Consequences. *SA Journal of Industrial Psychology*, 31(4), 1-6.

by employees can also lead to a range of social issues, including family conflict, substance abuse, and decreased community engagement.

Economic insecurity is associated with job insecurity, and the fear of automation can exacerbate inequality and social instability. Employees who are unable to find stable and secure employment may struggle to support themselves and their families, leading to increased reliance on social safety nets and a decline in overall economic mobility.[405]

The Need for Supportive Work Environments

To address the psychological toll on employees, organizations must create supportive work environments that prioritize employee well-being. This includes implementing policies that promote work-life balance, such as flexible working arrangements and the right to disconnect from work outside of regular hours.[406]

Organizations should also provide employees with the resources and support they need to manage stress and maintain their mental health. This can include access to mental health services, stress management programs, and employee assistance programs. Organizations should foster a culture of autonomy and control, where employees feel empowered to make decisions about their work and have a sense of ownership over their tasks.[407]

The psychological toll on employees in modern work environments is a significant issue that requires urgent attention. The pressures of high workloads, job insecurity, and the demands of technology-driven work practices have contributed to increased stress, burnout, and mental health issues among workers.[408] These challenges have broader implications

---

405. Karasek, R. A., & Theorell, T. (1990). *Healthy Work: Stress, Productivity, and the Reconstruction of Working Life*. Basic Books.

406. Schieman, S., & Young, M. (2010). The Demands of Work and the Mental Health Benefits of Work-to-Family Resources: The Emotional Costs of Managing the Demands of Work and Family. *Journal of Health and Social Behavior*, 51(3), 308-323.

407. Karasek, R. A., & Theorell, T. (1990). *Healthy Work: Stress, Productivity, and the Reconstruction of Working Life*. Basic Books.

408. Cheng, G. H. L., & Chan, D. K. S. (2008). Who Suffers More from Job Insecurity? A Meta-Analytic Review. *Applied Psychology*, 57(2), 272-303.

for organizations and society, highlighting the need for supportive work environments that prioritize employee well-being.

One industry that exemplifies the relentless pressure of high workloads and efficiency demands is the service sector, where frontline workers must juggle speed, customer satisfaction, and performance metrics. Few workplaces illustrate this dynamic more clearly than Starbucks, where baristas must navigate a relentless cycle of efficiency, customer satisfaction, and performance expectations.

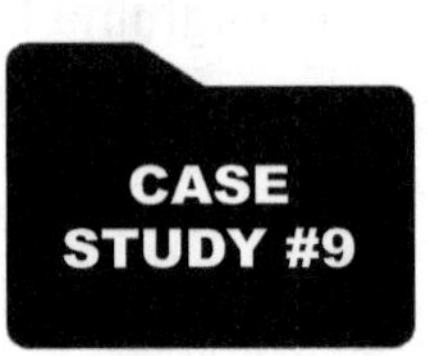

The Hidden Struggles of Starbucks Employees

Starbucks, a global coffeehouse chain, is often celebrated for its commitment to quality, customer service, and the creation of a welcoming "third place" environment between home and work. However, beneath this polished exterior, the company's labor practices have been the subject of increasing scrutiny.

Baristas, the frontline workers of Starbucks, face significant pressures to meet demanding efficiency standards while providing high levels of customer service. This case study explores the psychological toll these pressures take on Starbucks employees, focusing on the demands for relentless efficiency, the impact on employee well-being, and the broader implications for the service industry.

The Role of Baristas and the Demands for Efficiency

Starbucks baristas play a crucial role in the company's business model. They are responsible for preparing and serving coffee, managing customer orders, maintaining the cleanliness of the store, and ensuring a positive customer experience. However, the expectations placed on baristas are high, and the demand for efficiency is relentless.

A Fast-Paced Work Environment

Starbucks operates in a highly competitive industry where speed and efficiency are critical to success. The company prides itself on delivering consistent, high-quality coffee quickly, regardless of the location or time of day. To achieve this, baristas are required to work in a fast-paced environment, often handling multiple tasks simultaneously.[409] This can include taking orders, preparing drinks, processing payments, and cleaning the workspace, all while interacting with customers in a friendly and professional manner.

The pressure to maintain a rapid pace is exacerbated during peak hours, such as morning rushes or lunchtime, when the volume of customers can be overwhelming. Baristas are expected to keep the line moving and minimize wait times, often leading to a frenetic work environment where mistakes are not tolerated.[410] This high-pressure atmosphere can be stressful for employees, particularly those who are new to the job or who struggle to keep up with the pace.

The Emphasis on Customer Satisfaction

Starbucks places a strong emphasis on customer satisfaction. Baristas are expected to provide personalized service, remembering regular customers' names and preferred orders and creating a welcoming environment.[411] This customer-centric approach is central to Starbucks' brand identity, but it also adds to the pressure on baristas to perform consistently at a high level.

When paired with the fast-paced nature of the work, the need for individualized service can be emotionally draining. Baristas must manage the expectations of diverse customers, including those who may be impatient, demanding, or difficult to please. The need to maintain a positive demeanor, even in the face of

---

409. Thompson, D. (2011). The Starbucks Experience: The Impact of Corporate Culture on Employee Well-Being. *Work and Occupations*, 38(3), 357-383.Good, O. (2021, November 16). Activision Blizzard Announces Leadership Changes Amid Ongoing Harassment Lawsuit. *Polygon*. Retrieved from https://www.polygon.com/22784732/activision-blizzard-leadership-changes-harassment-lawsuit

410. Rosenbaum, D. (2015). *The Hard Grind: The Reality of Working at Starbucks*. Labor Relations Journal, 18(2), 55-72.

411. Thompson, D. (2011). The Starbucks Experience: The Impact of Corporate Culture on Employee Well-Being. *Work and Occupations*, 38(3), 357-383.Good, O. (2021, November 16). Activision Blizzard Announces Leadership Changes Amid Ongoing Harassment Lawsuit. *Polygon*. Retrieved from https://www.polygon.com/22784732/activision-blizzard-leadership-changes-harassment-lawsuit

challenging interactions, can contribute to emotional exhaustion and stress.[412]

Efficiency Goals and Metrics' Effect

Like many big businesses, Starbucks tracks and assesses worker productivity using performance metrics. These metrics can include the speed of service, accuracy of orders, and customer feedback scores.[413] While these metrics are intended to ensure consistent service quality, they can also create additional pressure on baristas to meet or exceed targets.

A work environment where employees feel continuously assessed and judged based on their performance can result from the emphasis on metrics. This can result in anxiety and stress, as baristas may worry about making mistakes or failing to meet the company's standards.[414] The pressure to perform can be particularly intense for those working in high-traffic locations, where the volume of customers and the speed of service are closely monitored.

Baristas' Psychological Cost

The relentless demands for efficiency and customer satisfaction at Starbucks can take a significant psychological toll on baristas. The combination of physical exhaustion, emotional labor, and job insecurity can lead to a range of mental health issues, including stress, burnout, and anxiety.

Stress and Physical Exhaustion

Working at Starbucks can be physically taxing due to its fast-paced environment, particularly during peak hours. Baristas are often required to stand for long periods, perform repetitive motions, and handle heavy workloads with minimal breaks. The physical

412. Rosenbaum, D. (2015). *The Hard Grind: The Reality of Working at Starbucks*. Labor Relations Journal, 18(2), 55-72.

413. López, M. J., & Sells, E. (2019). Metrics and Stress: The Psychological Impact of Performance Monitoring in the Service Industry. *Journal of Business Ethics*, 160(3), 617-629.

414. *Ibid.*

demands of the job, combined with the pressure to maintain a rapid pace, can lead to physical exhaustion and stress.[415]

Chronic stress can have serious consequences for employees' physical and mental health. It can lead to sleep disturbances, headaches, muscle tension, and other physical symptoms.[416] Over time, chronic stress can also contribute to more serious health issues, such as hypertension, heart disease, and weakened immune function.

Emotional Labor and Burnout

One of the most significant psychological challenges faced by Starbucks baristas is the emotional labor required to maintain a positive and friendly demeanor while interacting with customers. Emotional labor refers to the process of managing and regulating one's emotions to meet the expectations of a job role.[417] In the service industry, employees are often required to display positive emotions, such as friendliness and enthusiasm, even when they may not genuinely feel that way.

The constant need to engage in emotional labor can be draining and can contribute to burnout, a state of emotional, physical, and mental exhaustion caused by prolonged stress. Burnout is characterized by symptoms such as fatigue, cynicism, and a reduced sense of personal accomplishment.[418] Baristas experiencing burnout may feel disconnected from their work, lose interest in their job, and struggle to maintain the level of performance expected by the company.

---

415. Thompson, D. (2011). The Starbucks Experience: The Impact of Corporate Culture on Employee Well-Being. *Work and Occupations*, 38(3), 357-383.Good, O. (2021, November 16). Activision Blizzard Announces Leadership Changes Amid Ongoing Harassment Lawsuit. *Polygon*. Retrieved from https://www.polygon.com/22784732/activision-blizzard-leadership-changes-harassment-lawsuit

416. López, M. J., & Sells, E. (2019). Metrics and Stress: The Psychological Impact of Performance Monitoring in the Service Industry. *Journal of Business Ethics*, 160(3), 617-629.

417. Hochschild, A. R. (1983). *The Managed Heart: Commercialization of Human Feeling*. University of California Press.

418. Maslach, C., & Leiter, M. P. (2016). *Burnout: A Brief History and How to Build Better Workplaces*. Wiley.

Job Insecurity and Financial Stress

Many Starbucks baristas work part-time, often with unpredictable schedules and limited job security. The practice of "clopening" (closing the store late at night and then opening it early the next morning) and fluctuating hours can make it difficult for employees to achieve a healthy work-life balance.[419] The uncertainty of income and the lack of benefits, such as health insurance or paid time off, can contribute to financial stress and anxiety.

Job insecurity and financial stress can have significant psychological impacts, leading to feelings of helplessness, anxiety, and depression. Baristas who are unsure about their future with the company may feel a lack of control over their lives, which can further exacerbate stress and contribute to a negative work environment.[420]

Starbucks' Corporate Culture and Its Impact on Employees

Starbucks has cultivated a corporate culture that emphasizes community, customer service, and ethical business practices. However, the company's emphasis on efficiency and performance metrics can sometimes conflict with its stated values, leading to tensions that affect employees' psychological well-being.

The Discrepancy Between Corporate Values and Workplace Reality

Starbucks promotes itself as a socially responsible company that values its employees, whom it refers to as "partners."[421] The company offers various benefits, including stock options, tuition reimbursement, and opportunities for career advancement.

---

419. Rosenbaum, D. (2015). *The Hard Grind: The Reality of Working at Starbucks.* Labor Relations Journal, 18(2), 55-72.

420. *Ibid.*

421. Thompson, D. (2011). The Starbucks Experience: The Impact of Corporate Culture on Employee Well-Being. *Work and Occupations*, 38(3), 357-383.Good, O. (2021, November 16). Activision Blizzard Announces Leadership Changes Amid Ongoing Harassment Lawsuit. *Polygon.* Retrieved from https://www.polygon.com/22784732/activision-blizzard-leadership-changes-harassment-lawsuit

However, there is often a discrepancy between the company's public image and the day-to-day experiences of its employees.

Baristas may feel pressure to uphold the company's values while also meeting the demands for efficiency and customer satisfaction. This tension can create a sense of cognitive dissonance, where employees struggle to reconcile the company's stated values with the reality of their work environment. The disconnect between corporate messaging and workplace reality can lead to frustration, disillusionment, and a decline in morale.[422]

Management's Function in Creating the Workplace

The role of management is crucial in shaping the work environment at Starbucks. Store managers are responsible for enforcing company policies, setting the tone for customer interactions, and ensuring that performance metrics are met.[423] However, the demands placed on managers to achieve efficiency targets can sometimes result in a work environment that prioritizes productivity over employee well-being.

Managers who are under pressure to meet sales and performance goals may adopt a more authoritarian style of leadership, focusing on enforcing rules and pushing employees to work faster. This approach can lead to a work environment where baristas feel micromanaged, undervalued, and stressed.[424] Baristas may experience less psychological strain if their managers put their workers' welfare first, offer assistance, and create a positive work atmosphere.

---

422. Rosenbaum, D. (2015). *The Hard Grind: The Reality of Working at Starbucks.* Labor Relations Journal, 18(2), 55-72.

423. López, M. J., & Sells, E. (2019). Metrics and Stress: The Psychological Impact of Performance Monitoring in the Service Industry. *Journal of Business Ethics*, 160(3), 617-629.

424. *Ibid.*

The Impact of Store Culture on Employee Well-Being

Depending on the location, management, and clientele, Starbucks locations can have quite different cultures. In stores where the culture is supportive and collaborative, baristas may feel more connected to their colleagues and more satisfied with their work.[425] However, in stores where the culture is more competitive or where employees feel isolated, the psychological toll of the job can be more pronounced.

Store culture can also be influenced by the demographics of the employees and customers. For example, stores located in busy urban areas may have a faster pace and higher expectations for efficiency, which can increase stress levels.[426] In contrast, stores in suburban or rural areas may have a more relaxed atmosphere, allowing for more meaningful interactions with customers and less pressure on baristas.

Wider Consequences for the Service Sector

The psychological toll on Starbucks baristas is not unique to the company but reflects broader trends in the service industry. As companies strive for efficiency and customer satisfaction, employees across the industry face similar pressures and challenges. The experiences of Starbucks baristas offer valuable insights into the impact of these trends on worker well-being and the need for systemic changes in the service industry.

425. Thompson, D. (2011). The Starbucks Experience: The Impact of Corporate Culture on Employee Well-Being. *Work and Occupations*, 38(3), 357-383.Good, O. (2021, November 16). Activision Blizzard Announces Leadership Changes Amid Ongoing Harassment Lawsuit. *Polygon*. Retrieved from https://www.polygon.com/22784732/activision-blizzard-leadership-changes-harassment-lawsuit

426. Rosenbaum, D. (2015). *The Hard Grind: The Reality of Working at Starbucks*. Labor Relations Journal, 18(2), 55-72.

The Push for Efficiency in the Service Industry

The service industry, particularly in fast-paced environments like coffee shops, restaurants, and retail stores, is increasingly driven by the need for efficiency. Companies rely on metrics, performance targets, and technology to streamline operations and maximize profitability.[427] While these practices can improve customer service and reduce costs, they often come at the expense of employee well-being.

The push for efficiency can lead to a work environment where employees are treated as interchangeable parts of a machine, rather than as individuals with unique skills and needs. This dehumanization of work can result in increased stress, burnout, and job dissatisfaction, leading to high turnover rates and a decline in service quality.[428]

Why Employee Well-Being Is Important

The psychological well-being of employees is crucial to the long-term success of companies in the service industry. Employees who feel supported, valued, and respected are more likely to be engaged in their work, provide high-quality service, and remain with the company for longer periods.[429] Conversely, employees who experience high levels of stress, burnout, and job dissatisfaction are more likely to leave the company, leading to increased recruitment and training costs.

To address these challenges, companies in the service industry must prioritize employee well-being as part of their business

427. López, M. J., & Sells, E. (2019). Metrics and Stress: The Psychological Impact of Performance Monitoring in the Service Industry. *Journal of Business Ethics*, 160(3), 617-629.

428. Thompson, D. (2011). The Starbucks Experience: The Impact of Corporate Culture on Employee Well-Being. *Work and Occupations*, 38(3), 357-383.Good, O. (2021, November 16). Activision Blizzard Announces Leadership Changes Amid Ongoing Harassment Lawsuit. *Polygon*. Retrieved from https://www.polygon.com/22784732/activision-blizzard-leadership-changes-harassment-lawsuit

429. Maslach, C., & Leiter, M. P. (2016). *Burnout: A Brief History and How to Build Better Workplaces*. Wiley.

strategy. This can include offering competitive wages, providing opportunities for career advancement, ensuring a healthy work-life balance, and fostering a positive and supportive work environment.[430] By investing in the well-being of their employees, companies can improve job satisfaction, reduce turnover, and enhance the overall customer experience.

Systemic Change Is Necessary

The psychological toll on employees in the service industry reflects broader systemic issues that require comprehensive solutions. Addressing these challenges will require collaboration between employers, policymakers, and labor organizations to create a more sustainable and equitable work environment.

Policies that promote fair wages, job security, and employee rights are essential to protecting workers in the service industry. Additionally, companies must recognize the importance of mental health and provide resources and support for employees who may be struggling with stress, burnout, or other psychological challenges. By taking a proactive approach to employee well-being, companies can create a more positive and productive work environment, benefiting both employees and customers.[431]

Employees in the service sector may suffer psychologically as a result of the demands of efficiency and customer satisfaction, as demonstrated by the Starbucks case. Baristas face significant challenges, including physical exhaustion, emotional labor, job insecurity, and the constant pressure to meet performance targets. These challenges can lead to stress, burnout, and a decline in overall well-being, with broader implications for the service industry as a whole.

Addressing the psychological toll on employees requires a multifaceted approach, including policies that promote employee well-being, supportive management practices, and a recognition

---

430. *Ibid.*

431. Maslach, C., & Leiter, M. P. (2016). *Burnout: A Brief History and How to Build Better Workplaces*. Wiley.

of the importance of mental health in the workplace. By prioritizing the well-being of their employees, companies like Starbucks can create a more sustainable and equitable work environment, benefiting both workers and the organization as a whole.

Addressing the psychological toll on employees requires a multifaceted approach, including policies that promote work-life balance, access to mental health resources, and efforts to ensure job security in an increasingly automated economy. By prioritizing the mental health and well-being of employees, organizations can create a more sustainable and equitable work environment that benefits both workers and society as a whole.

KEY TAKEAWAYS

- **High Workloads and Lack of Autonomy Contribute to Burnout**
  Employees today face increasing workloads, strict performance targets, and diminishing control over their work. The pressure to meet high expectations while having little autonomy leads to chronic stress, emotional exhaustion, and burnout.

- **Technology Has Created an 'Always-On' Work Culture**
  The rise of smartphones, email, and instant messaging has blurred the boundaries between work and personal life. Many employees feel pressured to remain available outside of regular work hours, leading to increased anxiety, disrupted work-life balance, and a higher risk of mental health issues.

- **Job Insecurity Causes Psychological Distress**
  Economic volatility, automation, and corporate restructuring have made job security increasingly uncertain. Employees who fear job loss experience heightened stress, anxiety, and depression, which can negatively impact job satisfaction and overall well-being.

- **Surveillance and Performance Metrics Amplify Workplace Stress**
  The widespread use of employee monitoring, performance tracking, and rigid productivity metrics has created an environment of constant scrutiny. This leads to heightened workplace anxiety, reduced morale, and a sense of being undervalued or replaceable.

- **Addressing Workplace Mental Health Requires Systemic Change**
  Organizations must implement policies that support mental health, including flexible work arrangements, job security measures, and limits on after-hours communication. Fostering a workplace culture that prioritizes employee well-being benefits both workers and business sustainability.

Chapter 8

From Service to Systems, How Management Replaced Customer Care

Over the past few decades, the relationship between businesses and their customers has shifted dramatically. What once centered on individualized care, prompt attention, and meeting every client's needs has given way to a model driven by efficiency, profit, and the careful management of customer interactions. Globalization, emerging technologies, and relentless pressure to optimize have led many companies to treat customers more like resources than valued individuals. As a result, consumers often feel disconnected and dissatisfied, casting doubt on whether modern business practices truly serve the people they claim to benefit.

The Conventional Approach to Customer Service

Historically, customer service was viewed as a cornerstone of successful business operations. Companies understood that satisfied customers were more likely to become repeat customers, provide positive word-of-mouth referrals, and contribute to long-term business growth. The traditional model of customer service emphasized personalized attention, building relationships, and responding to customer needs with empathy and care.

Personalization and Empathy Are Important

In the traditional customer service model, personalization was key. Companies made an effort to understand their customers' preferences, needs, and concerns, tailoring their services accordingly, an approach that studies have shown helps build trust and loyalty.[432] By ensuring that customers felt genuinely valued and understood, these companies fostered long-term relationships. Empathy played a crucial role as well, with customer service representatives trained to listen actively, address concerns with sincere care, and resolve issues in a manner that left the customer feeling heard and respected.

This focus on personalization and empathy was particularly evident in small businesses and family-owned enterprises, where customer-business relationships often went beyond simple transactions. Such close-knit interactions not only strengthened community ties but also established a mutual respect that benefited both parties.[433] Through consistent, high-quality service and a willingness to engage personally, these businesses created an environment where customers felt like active participants rather than passive consumers.

Building Long-Term Relationships

Another key aspect of the traditional customer service model was the emphasis on building long-term relationships. Companies understood that retaining existing customers was more cost-effective than acquiring new ones and invested in strategies to foster loyalty, such as offering rewards programs, personalized discounts, and consistently exceptional service.[434] This approach helped ensure that customers felt genuinely appreciated and valued throughout their interactions.

In this model, customer feedback was actively sought and used to improve products and services. Businesses recognized that adapting to

---

432. Bitner, M. J., Booms, B. H., & Tetreault, M. S. (1990). The Service Encounter: Diagnosing Favorable and Unfavorable Incidents. *Journal of Marketing*, 54(1), 71-84.

433. Schneider, B., & Bowen, D. E. (1995). Winning the Service Game. *Harvard Business School Press.*

434. Reichheld, F. F., & Schefter, P. (2000). E-Loyalty: Your Secret Weapon on the Web. *Harvard Business Review*, 78(4), 105-113.

customer needs was essential for maintaining a competitive edge and aimed not just to complete transactions but to create positive experiences that inspired repeat patronage and enthusiastic recommendations.[435]

Customer Management Transition

Many businesses now prioritize customer management over customer service in recent decades. This shift has been driven by several factors, including advances in technology, the rise of data analytics, and the increasing pressure to maximize efficiency and profitability. As a result, the traditional model of personalized, relationship-based service has been replaced by a more transactional, data-driven approach that treats customers as resources to be managed.

Data-Driven Customer Management's Ascent

One of the most significant drivers behind the shift from customer service to customer management has been the rise of data analytics and customer relationship management (CRM) systems, which allow companies to collect, analyze, and utilize extensive customer data.[436] By leveraging these tools, businesses can offer targeted marketing and personalized recommendations, potentially enhancing customer experiences. However, this data-driven focus also pushes interactions toward a more impersonal, transactional approach, treating customers less like valued individuals and more like assets to be optimized.

In this customer management framework, organizations frequently segment customers based on purchasing behavior, demographics, or profitability, adjusting their strategies to maximize revenue and minimize costs.[437] High-value customers, for example, may receive special treatment and dedicated support, while those deemed lower-value encounter self-service options or automated systems. Such segmentation often fosters

---

435. Parasuraman, A., Zeithaml, V. A., & Berry, L. L. (1985). A Conceptual Model of Service Quality and Its Implications for Future Research. *Journal of Marketing*, 49(4), 41-50.

436. Peppers, D., & Rogers, M. (1999). *The One to One Manager: Real-World Lessons in Customer Relationship Management*. Currency Doubleday.

437. Mittal, V., Sarkees, M., & Murshed, F. (2008). The Right Way to Manage Your Customer Base. *Harvard Business Review*, 86(7/8), 96-104.

inequality, as certain customers benefit from enhanced care while others struggle with a less attentive environment, all determined by their perceived worth to the company.

Automation and the Decline of Personal Interaction

The shift to customer management has also been marked by the growing reliance on automation in customer interactions, where automated phone systems, chatbots, and self-service portals have become standard tools for managing high volumes of inquiries.[438] By reducing the need for human intervention, companies can boost efficiency and cut costs. However, this streamlined approach often comes at the expense of the personal touch that once defined customer service, leaving customers to navigate impersonal menus and scripted responses.

Customers confronting complex issues can find these automated systems limited and unhelpful, sparking frustration and dissatisfaction.[439] The inability to speak with a real person can make customers feel dehumanized, reinforcing the perception that companies value efficiency over genuine care. This erosion of personal connection may ultimately undermine trust and loyalty, as individuals sense that their concerns and well-being rank lower than an organization's operational priorities.

The Focus on Efficiency and Profitability

Another key factor fueling the shift from customer service to customer management is the escalating focus on efficiency and profitability, a reality evident in many companies that perceive customer interactions as cost centers rather than opportunities for relationship-building.[440] Under relentless pressure to cut costs and boost profits in a competitive global market, businesses often prioritize reducing expenses over nurturing customer satisfaction.

---

438. Zeithaml, V. A., Bitner, M. J., & Gremler, D. D. (2018). *Services Marketing: Integrating Customer Focus Across the Firm*. McGraw-Hill Education.

439. Van Doorn, J., Lemon, K. N., Mittal, V., Nass, S., Pick, D., Pirner, P., & Verhoef, P. C. (2017). Customer Engagement Behavior: Theoretical Foundations a[6]nd Research Directions. *Journal of Service Research*, 13(3), 253-266.

440. Grönroos, C. (2007). *Service Management and Marketing: Customer Management in Service Competition*. Wiley.

Within this customer management framework, the objective frequently involves streamlining interactions to save time and resources.[441] This standardized, one-size-fits-all approach may achieve operational efficiency, but it risks leaving customers feeling like mere numbers instead of valued individuals. As a result, the emphasis on speed and cost-effectiveness can erode the personal connections that once formed the backbone of strong customer relationships.

Repercussions of the Customer Management Transition

The shift from customer service to customer management has significant consequences for both customers and businesses. While the customer management model may offer short-term gains in efficiency and profitability, it can have long-term negative effects on customer satisfaction, loyalty, and brand reputation.

Customer Dissatisfaction and Alienation

One of the most immediate consequences of shifting to customer management is a surge in customer dissatisfaction and alienation. As companies lean more on automation and data-driven strategies, customers may feel their individual needs and preferences are overlooked, provoking frustration when automated systems fail to provide adequate support.[8442] This sense of being ignored or undervalued can erode the personal connection customers once experienced, leaving them disappointed and dissatisfied.

The impersonal nature of customer management also undermines trust and loyalty. When customers sense they are regarded as mere resources rather than valued individuals, their faith in the brand weakens.[3] In response, they are more inclined to seek alternatives that respect their individuality, ultimately raising churn rates and prompting many to

441. *Ibid.*

442. Van Doorn, J., Lemon, K. N., Mittal, V., Nass, S., Pick, D., Pirner, P., & Verhoef, P. C. (2017). Customer Engagement Behavior: Theoretical Foundations a[6]nd Research Directions. *Journal of Service Research*, 13(3), 253-266.

abandon companies that fail to deliver a more authentic, personalized experience.

This growing disconnect between businesses and their customers is not just a theoretical concern, it has played out in real-world scandals that have severely damaged consumer trust. One of the most infamous examples is the Wells Fargo fake accounts scandal, where a once-revered financial institution prioritized sales targets over customer relationships, leading to widespread deception and lasting reputational harm.

Wells Fargo's Contempt for the Customer

Wells Fargo, once celebrated for financial stability and strong customer service, saw its reputation collapse following a 2016 scandal involving the creation of millions of fake customer accounts. Unethical internal practices emerged, shattering customer trust and causing severe reputational harm. Examining this event reveals how such betrayal damaged the bank's image and left lasting scars on customer relationships.

The Fake Accounts Scandal: A Betrayal of Customer Trust

The Wells Fargo scandal centered around the discovery that employees had created millions of unauthorized bank and credit card accounts in customers' names without their knowledge or consent. This practice, which was driven by aggressive sales targets and a toxic corporate culture, represented a profound betrayal of the trust that customers had placed in the bank.

Mechanics of the Scandal

The fake accounts scandal emerged in 2013 when reports indicated that Wells Fargo employees, under intense pressure to meet sales quotas, were opening unauthorized accounts using existing customer information without permission and, at times, charging fees on these fraudulent products. Over time, approximately 3.5 million such accounts were created between 2002 and 2016, revealing a widespread pattern of unethical behavior across the organization.[443]

Unrealistic sales targets and aggressive cross-selling goals drove these practices, as management pushed employees to encourage customers to open multiple checking, savings, and credit card accounts.[444] Fearing disciplinary action, workers resorted to creating fake accounts rather than risk job loss, ultimately prioritizing internal metrics and bonuses over the trust and welfare of their customers.

Ethical Failures and Corporate Culture

Wells Fargo's scandal reflected deeper ethical failures and a profit-driven culture that prioritized targets over customers. Senior leadership, aware of ongoing issues, ignored repeated warnings and complaints, choosing not to intervene.[445] Instead of curbing misconduct, executives tolerated unethical tactics, prompting employees to value sales goals over honesty.[446] This pressure stemmed from top management's refusal to address moral lapses, ultimately leaving workers feeling compelled to commit fraud just to keep their jobs.

CEO John Stumpf and other leaders knew the aggressive sales environment risked fostering wrongdoing.[447] Employee reports were dismissed, making deception seem like self-preservation

443. Cowley, S. (2016, September 8). Wells Fargo Fined $185 Million for Opening Accounts Without Customers' Knowledge. *The New York Times*. Retrieved from https://www.nytimes.com/2016/09/09/business/wells-fargo-fine.html

444. Flitter, E., & Corkery, M. (2016, September 28). Wells Fargo CEO Faces Harsh Criticism in Senate Hearing. *Reuters*. Retrieved from https://www.reuters.com/article/us-wells-fargo-accounts-hearing/wells-fargo-ceo-faces-harsh-criticism-in-senate-hearing-idUSKCN11X2PY

445. Flitter, E., & Corkery, M. (2016, September 28). Wells Fargo CEO Faces Harsh Criticism in Senate Hearing. *Reuters*. Retrieved from https://www.reuters.com/article/us-wells-fargo-accounts-hearing/wells-fargo-ceo-faces-harsh-criticism-in-senate-hearing-idUSKCN11X2PY

446. Corkery, M., & Cowley, S. (2016, October 12). Wells Fargo Struggling in Aftermath of Fraud Scandal. *The New York Times*. Retrieved from https://www.nytimes.com/2016/10/13/business/dealbook/wells-fargo-scandal.html

447. Flitter, E., & Corkery, M. (2016, September 28). Wells Fargo CEO Faces Harsh Criticism in Senate Hearing. *Reuters*. Retrieved from https://www.reuters.com/article/us-wells-fargo-accounts-hearing/wells-fargo-ceo-faces-harsh-criticism-in-senate-hearing-idUSKCN11X2PY

rather than a breach of trust.[448] By emphasizing "selling more" rather than serving customers, the bank created a rift between its public image and its internal practices,[449] a disparity that ultimately undermined Wells Fargo's credibility.

Betrayal of Customer Trust

The creation of fake accounts represented a profound betrayal of trust, as customers expected their bank to safeguard their interests and financial data but instead found Wells Fargo misusing that information to open unauthorized accounts.[450] Rather than receiving honest and transparent services, customers discovered unexpected fees and data manipulation aimed at meeting internal goals instead of fulfilling their needs.

Many customers, unaware of these fabricated accounts, only learned of them after encountering unjustified charges or noticing harm to their credit, realizations that heightened the emotional distress of realizing their trusted bank had deceived them.[451] This breach went beyond ethical lapses and struck at the core of the bank-customer relationship. By prioritizing short-term profits over genuine care, Wells Fargo demonstrated a disregard for its clients' well-being.[452]

Impact on Wells Fargo's Reputation and Customer Relationships

Significant harm was done to Wells Fargo's reputation and long-term customer relationships as a result of the quick and serious

448. Corkery, M., & Cowley, S. (2016, October 12). Wells Fargo Struggling in Aftermath of Fraud Scandal. *The New York Times*. Retrieved from https://www.nytimes.com/2016/10/13/business/dealbook/wells-fargo-scandal.html

449. *Ibid.*

450. Cowley, S. (2016, September 8). Wells Fargo Fined $185 Million for Opening Accounts Without Customers' Knowledge. *The New York Times*. Retrieved from https://www.nytimes.com/2016/09/09/business/wells-fargo-fine.html

451. *Ibid.*

452. Flitter, E., & Corkery, M. (2016, September 28). Wells Fargo CEO Faces Harsh Criticism in Senate Hearing. *Reuters*. Retrieved from https://www.reuters.com/article/us-wells-fargo-accounts-hearing/wells-fargo-ceo-faces-harsh-criticism-in-senate-hearing-idUSKCN11X2PY

fallout from the fake accounts scandal. The scandal not only eroded public trust in the bank but also had broader implications for the financial industry as a whole.

Immediate Consequences and Legal Repercussions

In the aftermath of the scandal, Wells Fargo faced severe legal and regulatory repercussions. Among the penalties, the bank was fined $185 million by the Consumer Financial Protection Bureau, the Office of the Comptroller of the Currency, and the City of Los Angeles, underscoring the gravity of its misconduct.[453] Intended to penalize unethical behavior and compensate victims, these fines severely damaged the bank's image and public standing.

Beyond fines, Wells Fargo contended with lawsuits filed by customers, shareholders, and former employees, all alleging fraudulent practices and violations of consumer protection laws.[454] Such legal battles deepened the bank's reputational crisis, highlighting systemic failures and further eroding trust.

Leadership changes soon followed, as CEO John Stumpf resigned in October 2016 under mounting scrutiny and public outrage.[455] His departure and that of other high-ranking executives marked an attempt to restore credibility and signal accountability while simultaneously underscoring how ingrained the problems had become within Wells Fargo's upper ranks.

---

453. Cowley, S. (2016, September 8). Wells Fargo Fined $185 Million for Opening Accounts Without Customers' Knowledge. *The New York Times*. Retrieved from https://www.nytimes.com/2016/09/09/business/wells-fargo-fine.html

454. Corkery, M., & Cowley, S. (2016, October 12). Wells Fargo Struggling in Aftermath of Fraud Scandal. *The New York Times*. Retrieved from https://www.nytimes.com/2016/10/13/business/dealbook/wells-fargo-scandal.html

455. Flitter, E., & Corkery, M. (2016, September 28). Wells Fargo CEO Faces Harsh Criticism in Senate Hearing. *Reuters*. Retrieved from https://www.reuters.com/article/us-wells-fargo-accounts-hearing/wells-fargo-ceo-faces-harsh-criticism-in-senate-hearing-idUSKCN11X2PY

Erosion of Customer Trust and Loyalty

One long-term consequence of the scandal was the erosion of trust and loyalty, as Wells Fargo, once seen as dependable, came to symbolize corporate greed and unethical behavior. Many customers, feeling betrayed, began to question their relationship with the bank and considered moving their accounts elsewhere.[456] This collapse of trust was especially harmful in the financial sector, where confidence guides customer decisions and can take years to restore once shattered.[457]

In the aftermath, surveys recorded declining satisfaction and loyalty, alongside an increase in account closures and complaints that underscored the severity of the damage.[458] Wells Fargo's once-strong reputation, built on service and reliability, struggled to recover in the wake of the deception, leaving the bank grappling with how to regain credibility among those it had wronged.

Influence on Market Position and Brand Image

Wells Fargo's damaged reputation spread beyond its customer base, reaching the broader public and financial markets as the scandal became a symbol of corporate misconduct and the perils of profit over ethics. The intense media coverage and regulatory scrutiny tarnished the bank's brand[1], weakening its once-strong position.[459] Investors, alarmed by ongoing legal battles and possible customer attrition, saw the stock price drop amid doubts about the bank's future, while the financial impact deepened as customer confidence waned, eroding revenues.

---

456. Corkery, M., & Cowley, S. (2016, October 12). Wells Fargo Struggling in Aftermath of Fraud Scandal. *The New York Times*. Retrieved from https://www.nytimes.com/2016/10/13/business/dealbook/wells-fargo-scandal.html

457. Reichheld, F. F., & Schefter, P. (2000). E-Loyalty: Your Secret Weapon on the Web. *Harvard Business Review*, 78(4), 105-113.

458. Corkery, M., & Cowley, S. (2016, October 12). Wells Fargo Struggling in Aftermath of Fraud Scandal. *The New York Times*. Retrieved from https://www.nytimes.com/2016/10/13/business/dealbook/wells-fargo-scandal.html

459. Flitter, E., & Corkery, M. (2016, September 28). Wells Fargo CEO Faces Harsh Criticism in Senate Hearing. *Reuters*. Retrieved from https://www.reuters.com/article/us-wells-fargo-accounts-hearing/wells-fargo-ceo-faces-harsh-criticism-in-senate-hearing-idUSKCN11X2PY

This crisis extended beyond Wells Fargo, fueling public skepticism about ethical standards in the banking sector and prompting demands for tighter oversight. The situation underscored the importance of maintaining integrity and customer trust, serving as a cautionary example that irresponsible behavior can carry lasting consequences not only for one institution but for the entire industry.[460]

Efforts to Rebuild Trust and Reform Corporate Culture

In the years after the scandal, Wells Fargo introduced measures to rebuild trust and reshape its culture, overhauling sales practices, tightening internal controls, and increasing transparency, which included providing restitution to affected customers.[461] These efforts aimed to improve customer service processes, signaling that the bank sought meaningful change, even as skepticism persisted. One key shift involved eliminating sales quotas for retail banking employees, an attempt to relieve pressure and reduce unethical behavior, and introducing new training programs focused on ethics and genuine service.[462] By adopting this more customer-centric approach, Wells Fargo tried to distance itself from past misconduct and restore faith in its brand.

Still, regaining trust proved difficult. Many customers remained doubtful of the bank's promises, seeing its reputation as deeply scarred by the scandal. Achieving lasting credibility required more than policy revisions; the bank needed to demonstrate consistent ethical conduct and show that customer welfare truly took precedence over short-term gain.[463] Without genuine, sustained

460. Corkery, M., & Cowley, S. (2016, October 12). Wells Fargo Struggling in Aftermath of Fraud Scandal. *The New York Times*. Retrieved from https://www.nytimes.com/2016/10/13/business/dealbook/wells-fargo-scandal.html

461. Wells Fargo. (2018). *Wells Fargo 2018 Annual Report*. Retrieved from https://www.wellsfargo.com/about/investor-relations/annual-reports

462. *Ibid.*

463. Wells Fargo. (2018). *Wells Fargo 2018 Annual Report*. Retrieved from https://www.wellsfargo.com/about/investor-relations/annual-reports

commitment to putting customers first, Wells Fargo's long-term success in repairing its image would remain uncertain.

Lessons Learned and Broader Implications

The Wells Fargo scandal offers several important lessons for businesses, particularly in the financial services industry. It highlights the dangers of prioritizing short-term profits over ethical conduct, the importance of maintaining a customer-centric approach, and the need for strong leadership and accountability.

Dangers of a Profit-Driven Culture

One of the key lessons from the Wells Fargo scandal is the danger of allowing a profit-driven culture to override ethical considerations. The bank's focus on meeting aggressive sales targets led to a culture where unethical behavior was not only tolerated but encouraged.[464] This created an environment where employees felt compelled to engage in fraudulent practices to meet the demands of their managers, ultimately leading to a betrayal of customer trust.

Businesses must recognize that a singular focus on profit can lead to serious ethical lapses and long-term damage to their reputation. It is essential for companies to balance the pursuit of financial goals with a commitment to ethical conduct and customer well-being.[465] This requires strong leadership, clear ethical guidelines, and a corporate culture that prioritizes integrity and accountability.

Importance of Customer-Centric Practices

Wells Fargo's scandal highlights how companies jeopardize trust and loyalty when they fail to prioritize customer interests. By

---

464. Flitter, E., & Corkery, M. (2016, September 28). Wells Fargo CEO Faces Harsh Criticism in Senate Hearing. *Reuters*. Retrieved from https://www.reuters.com/article/us-wells-fargo-accounts-hearing/wells-fargo-ceo-faces-harsh-criticism-in-senate-hearing-idUSKCN11X2PY

465. Corkery, M., & Cowley, S. (2016, October 12). Wells Fargo Struggling in Aftermath of Fraud Scandal. *The New York Times*. Retrieved from https://www.nytimes.com/2016/10/13/business/dealbook/wells-fargo-scandal.html

neglecting transparent, honest services and ethical standards, the bank alienated its clientele, demonstrating that customers expect genuine care rather than mere transactional efficiency.[466]

To preserve strong relationships, businesses must deliver real value, address concerns quickly, and foster transparency and accountability.[467] Emphasizing ethical behavior in every employee interaction, actively seeking feedback, and promptly resolving issues can help restore confidence and ensure that customer well-being remains central to a company's long-term success.

Roles of Leadership and Accountability

Wells Fargo's scandal revealed how weak leadership and minimal accountability undermine ethical standards. Senior executives, despite repeated warnings, tolerated ongoing misconduct[468], prioritizing sales targets over responsibility. Effective leadership means embracing ethics, maintaining transparency, and ensuring everyone is held accountable, steps that help prevent misconduct and safeguard credibility.[469]

Driven by profit-first thinking, Wells Fargo's creation of fake accounts proved that betraying customer trust has grave repercussions. Once-loyal customers were deceived, financially harmed, and left questioning the bank's integrity. Legal penalties, leadership changes, and eroded loyalty demonstrated the high cost of ignoring ethical principles. By rejecting profit-driven cultures, focusing on customer welfare, and upholding ethical leadership, businesses can preserve trust, nurture long-term relationships, and achieve sustainable success.

---

466. Reichheld, F. F., & Schefter, P. (2000). E-Loyalty: Your Secret Weapon on the Web. *Harvard Business Review*, 78(4), 105-113.

467. Zeithaml, V. A., Bitner, M. J., & Gremler, D. D. (2018). *Services Marketing: Integrating Customer Focus Across the Firm*. McGraw-Hill Education

468. Flitter, E., & Corkery, M. (2016, September 28). Wells Fargo CEO Faces Harsh Criticism in Senate Hearing. *Reuters*. Retrieved from https://www.reuters.com/article/us-wells-fargo-accounts-hearing/wells-fargo-ceo-faces-harsh-criticism-in-senate-hearing-idUSKCN11X2PY

469. Sutton, R. I. (2007). *The No Asshole Rule: Building a Civilized Workplace and Surviving One That Isn't*. Business Plus.

The Erosion of Brand Loyalty

Brand loyalty, once a central pillar of business success, now often falters as companies shift from building genuine connections to simply managing customer interactions. In the traditional service model, loyalty thrived on exceptional care and memorable experiences, allowing customers to feel truly valued. Now, however, the focus on efficiency and profitability overshadows these personal touches, reducing loyalty to a product of convenience or price rather than heartfelt engagement.[470] By sidestepping the emotional elements that once formed the backbone of loyal relationships, businesses risk weakening bonds that previously differentiated them in competitive markets.

As customers grow more attuned to the ways their experiences are being managed and optimized, their allegiance to brands that place profit above satisfaction may diminish. By realizing that companies fine-tune their processes more for revenue than for genuine service, customers become less inclined to stick around out of loyalty.[471] This erosion of trust not only hinders repeat purchases and positive word-of-mouth but also undercuts the advocacy role satisfied customers once played. Without the strong foundation of customer loyalty that traditional service methods cultivated, businesses may struggle to maintain their edge and secure long-term success.

Risk of Negative Public Perception

The shift to customer management also exposes companies to the risk of being viewed unfavorably by the public. As customers grow more aware of manipulative tactics and impersonal treatment, they may develop negative opinions about the brand and its priorities.[472] In today's social media landscape, a few dissatisfied customers can swiftly share their experiences with large audiences, amplifying the potential damage.

---

470. Mittal, V., Sarkees, M., & Murshed, F. (2008). The Right Way to Manage Your Customer Base. *Harvard Business Review*, 86(7/8), 96-104.

471. Reichheld, F. F., & Schefter, P. (2000). E-Loyalty: Your Secret Weapon on the Web. *Harvard Business Review*, 78(4), 105-113.

472. Grönroos, C. (2007). *Service Management and Marketing: Customer Management in Service Competition*. Wiley.

Such negative perception can trigger a chain reaction, eroding brand reputation, customer trust, and market share. Companies seen as dismissive or indifferent toward their customers may attract backlash from consumers, advocacy groups, and the media.[473] In turn, this can prompt boycotts, regulatory interventions, or even legal challenges, carrying serious financial and reputational fallout.

Few corporate failures have demonstrated the devastating impact of negligence and disregard for consumer protection as clearly as the Equifax data breach. As one of the largest credit reporting agencies, Equifax was entrusted with safeguarding sensitive personal information, yet its failure to address known security vulnerabilities led to one of the most damaging data breaches in history.

---

473. Van Doorn, J., Lemon, K. N., Mittal, V., Nass, S., Pick, D., Pirner, P., & Verhoef, P. C. (2017). Customer Engagement Behavior: Theoretical Foundations a[6]nd Research Directions. *Journal of Service Research*, 13(3), 253-266.

Equifax's Disdain for the Customer

Equifax, a major global credit reporting agency entrusted with sensitive data from millions of consumers, suffered a massive data breach in 2017 that compromised personal information of about 147 million people. Rather than prioritizing protection, the company's inadequate response exposed glaring security weaknesses and revealed a disturbing disregard for customers' well-being. Examining these failures and their impact on affected individuals underscores the urgent need for stronger accountability and ethical standards within Equifax.

The Equifax Data Breach: A Catastrophic Failure of Security

The Equifax data breach, which began in May 2017 and was discovered in July of the same year, exposed a treasure trove of sensitive personal information, including names, Social Security numbers, birth dates, addresses, and, in some cases, driver's license numbers and credit card information. The breach was catastrophic in both scale and impact, affecting nearly half of the U.S. population and exposing them to the risk of identity theft and financial fraud.

The Causes of the Breach

Equifax's data breach stemmed from multiple cybersecurity failures, including a known Apache Struts vulnerability that was never patched in time, allowing intruders to remain undetected for 76 days.[474] This lapse revealed weak infrastructure, poor patch management,

474. GAO (Government Accountability Office). (2018). *Actions Taken by Equifax and Federal Agencies in Response to the 2017 Breach*. Retrieved from https://www.gao.gov/products/gao-18-559

inadequate network segmentation, and insufficient monitoring, enabling hackers to exfiltrate large amounts of sensitive data undisturbed.[475] As a credit reporting agency entrusted with millions of consumers' information, Equifax's complacency in addressing known vulnerabilities and its lack of urgency reflected a troubling disregard for customers' privacy and security.[476]

Equifax's Response to the Breach

Equifax's reaction to the breach was widely deemed slow and inadequate, as the company waited nearly two months after discovery to disclose it, finally going public on September 7, 2017, without providing sufficient details or guidance.[477] In that time, consumers remained vulnerable to identity theft and fraud. Initial attempts to assist customers were marred by technical glitches on the website created to check exposure, offering inconsistent or incorrect information.[478] Worse, the site's terms of service included language that appeared to waive consumers' rights to join class-action lawsuits, intensifying distrust in Equifax's intentions.

The company's proposal of free credit monitoring services, provided through its own TrustedID product, faced heavy skepticism.[479] Many saw this as profiteering, since enrolling required additional personal data, and limiting the offer to one year seemed inadequate, given the lasting risk from the breach.[480] Beyond these missteps, Equifax's overall response raised serious questions about its commitment to transparency and accountability. By failing to deliver timely, accurate information and seemingly attempting to reduce

---

475. *Ibid.*

476. *Ibid.*

477. Monga, V., & McKinnon, J. D. (2017, September 7). Equifax Hack Leaves Millions Vulnerable to Identity Theft. *The Wall Street Journal*. Retrieved from https://www.wsj.com/articles/equifax-says-hack-left-millions-vulnerable-to-identity-theft-1504803674

478. *Ibid.*

479. Monga, V., & McKinnon, J. D. (2017, September 7). Equifax Hack Leaves Millions Vulnerable to Identity Theft. *The Wall Street Journal*. Retrieved from https://www.wsj.com/articles/equifax-says-hack-left-millions-vulnerable-to-identity-theft-1504803674

480. Hartung, M. (2017, September 12). Equifax Data Breach: What You Need to Know. *Consumer Reports*. Retrieved from https://www.consumerreports.org/consumer-protection/equifax-data-breach-what-you-need-to-know/

legal liability, the company signaled a troubling disregard for the very customers harmed by its security failures.[481]

Scale and Impact of the Breach

Approximately 147 million people's personal information in the United States, Canada, and the United Kingdom was compromised in the historic Equifax data breach. Hackers accessed highly sensitive details that could facilitate identity theft, fraud, and other malicious activities, leaving millions with long-term financial vulnerability.

Affected consumers struggled to secure their personal data, monitoring credit reports and repeatedly freezing or unfreezing credit.[482] Uncertainty and anxiety surged as many remained unsure of their exact exposure and the ways criminals might misuse their information. In the years following, victims reported identity theft and fraud, including unauthorized credit card accounts and falsified tax returns.[483] This turmoil paved the way for phishing scams and other social engineering tactics that capitalized on the confusion and fear sparked by the breach.

Consequences for Customers and the Lack of Accountability

The long-term effects on consumers were profound, as sensitive details like Social Security numbers and birth dates remained valuable to criminals for years and made identity theft an enduring threat.[484] Even after the breach, many found themselves constantly at risk, forced into vigilant, time-consuming efforts to safeguard their finances against ongoing attacks.

Victims placed fraud alerts, froze credit, and monitored their accounts closely, actions that demanded time, expense, and

---

481. *Ibid.*

482. *Ibid.*

483. Hartung, M. (2017, September 12). Equifax Data Breach: What You Need to Know. *Consumer Reports*. Retrieved from https://www.consumerreports.org/consumer-protection/equifax-data-breach-what-you-need-to-know/

484. *Ibid.*

emotional resilience.[485] The psychological burden of knowing their personal data had been compromised added to the stress and anxiety they faced.

Beyond individual harm, this breach eroded trust in the broader financial system. The fact that a major credit reporting agency, supposedly a guardian of consumer data, could be so easily infiltrated raised doubts about other institutions' security as well.[486] In response, consumers called for stronger data protection measures and greater accountability, underscoring the need for more robust safeguards in an increasingly data-driven world.

Lack of Accountability at Equifax

One of the most troubling aspects of the Equifax data breach was the lack of accountability within the company, as few individuals faced meaningful consequences for the failures that enabled the breach. While some executives, including CEO Richard Smith, stepped down, evidence of true responsibility remained scarce, revealing a leadership unwilling to confront its cybersecurity failures.[487]

This absence of accountability appeared even starker when it emerged that top Equifax executives sold nearly $1.8 million in company stock shortly after discovering the breach, yet before informing the public, undermining trust further.[488] Such insider trading suggested leaders prioritized personal financial gain over helping consumers, deepening the perception that those at the top escaped real repercussions.

---

485. *Ibid.*

486. GAO (Government Accountability Office). (2018). *Actions Taken by Equifax and Federal Agencies in Response to the 2017 Breach.* Retrieved from https://www.gao.gov/products/gao-18-559

487. Monga, V., & McKinnon, J. D. (2017, September 7). Equifax Hack Leaves Millions Vulnerable to Identity Theft. *The Wall Street Journal.* Retrieved from https://www.wsj.com/articles/equifax-says-hack-left-millions-vulnerable-to-identity-theft-1504803674

488. Flitter, E. (2017, September 7). Equifax Faces Investigation as Investors Raise Questions. *Reuters.* Retrieved from https://www.reuters.com/article/us-equifax-cyber/executives-reaped-millions-in-stock-sales-after-data-breach-at-equifax-idUSKCN1BR2CB

Limited accountability also shaped Equifax's response to scrutiny and legal challenges. Although the company settled with regulators for up to $700 million, critics argued these penalties were inadequate given the breach's scale and harm.[489] Seen as a minimal consequence, the settlement underscored how Equifax avoided full responsibility for its profound failures.

Wider Effects on Equifax's Industry Trust and Reputation

Equifax's data breach severely damaged its reputation, exposing cybersecurity shortcomings and casting doubt on its commitment to safeguarding personal information. By mishandling the response, the company faced widespread criticism and demands for reform.[490] Negative media coverage, consumer outrage, and regulatory scrutiny followed, while its stock price declined and some clients abandoned the firm, long-term consequences that continue to challenge Equifax's brand.[491]

The incident had broader implications for credit reporting and the financial sector, revealing systemic vulnerabilities as firms handle vast amounts of personal data.[492] In response, stakeholders called for stronger data protection rules, greater transparency, and improved cybersecurity measures to prevent similar failures across the industry.

Regulatory and Legislative Responses

In the wake of the Equifax data breach, there was a renewed focus on the need for stronger data protection regulations and

---

489. FTC (Federal Trade Commission). (2019). *FTC, CFPB, and States Announce Settlement with Equifax over 2017 Data Breach*. Retrieved from https://www.ftc.gov/news-events/press-releases/2019/07/ftc-cfpb-states-announce-settlement-equifax-over-2017-data-breach

490. Flitter, E. (2017, September 7). Equifax Faces Investigation as Investors Raise Questions. *Reuters*. Retrieved from https://www.reuters.com/article/us-equifax-cyber/executives-reaped-millions-in-stock-sales-after-data-breach-at-equifax-idUSKCN1BR2CB

491. *Ibid.*

492. FTC (Federal Trade Commission). (2019). *FTC, CFPB, and States Announce Settlement with Equifax over 2017 Data Breach*. Retrieved from https://www.ftc.gov/news-events/press-releases/2019/07/ftc-cfpb-states-announce-settlement-equifax-over-2017-data-breach

greater accountability for companies that handle sensitive personal information. The breach served as a catalyst for discussions about consumer privacy, data security, and the role of government oversight in protecting consumers from the risks associated with data breaches.[493]

At the federal level, the breach prompted calls for the passage of data protection legislation that would establish clear standards for the collection, storage, and protection of personal information.[494] Lawmakers also called for increased oversight of credit reporting agencies and other companies that handle sensitive data, including the creation of new regulatory bodies or the expansion of the powers of existing agencies like the FTC and CFPB.

Several states introduced or strengthened data breach notification laws in response to the Equifax incident. These laws require companies to notify consumers and regulators promptly in the event of a data breach and to take steps to mitigate the harm caused.[495] The Equifax breach also led to calls for the establishment of national data breach notification standards, which would provide greater consistency and clarity for both consumers and businesses.

Lessons Learned and Broader Implications

The Equifax data breach offers several important lessons for businesses, regulators, and consumers. It underscores the critical importance of data security, the need for accountability within organizations that handle sensitive information, and the broader implications of data breaches for consumer trust and confidence.

---

493. FTC (Federal Trade Commission). (2019). *FTC, CFPB, and States Announce Settlement with Equifax over 2017 Data Breach*. Retrieved from https://www.ftc.gov/news-events/press-releases/2019/07/ftc-cfpb-states-announce-settlement-equifax-over-2017-data-breach

494. GAO (Government Accountability Office). (2018). *Actions Taken by Equifax and Federal Agencies in Response to the 2017 Breach*. Retrieved from https://www.gao.gov/products/gao-18-559

495. *Ibid.*

The Importance of Data Security and Risk Management

One of the key lessons from the Equifax breach is the importance of robust data security and risk management practices. Companies that handle sensitive personal information must prioritize cybersecurity and implement comprehensive strategies to protect their systems from threats.[496] This includes regular patch management, network segmentation, and continuous monitoring of systems for potential vulnerabilities.

Companies need to have clear incident response plans in place. When a breach occurs, companies must act quickly to contain the damage, notify affected consumers, and provide guidance on how to mitigate the risks.[497] The failure to respond effectively to a breach can exacerbate the harm caused and further erode consumer trust.

Need for Accountability and Transparency

The Equifax breach emphasizes the need for accountability and transparency, urging companies to own their failures and communicate openly with consumers and regulators. Providing timely, accurate information and meaningful remedies to affected parties is essential, as is ensuring that those responsible face genuine consequences.[498] By taking these steps, businesses can better protect customers and maintain trust, rather than leaving them vulnerable in the aftermath of a breach.

Within Equifax, the insider trading scandal and the inadequate response revealed a corporate culture that placed profit above

---

496. GAO (Government Accountability Office). (2018). *Actions Taken by Equifax and Federal Agencies in Response to the 2017 Breach*. Retrieved from https://www.gao.gov/products/gao-18-559

497. *Ibid.*

498. FTC (Federal Trade Commission). (2019). *FTC, CFPB, and States Announce Settlement with Equifax over 2017 Data Breach*. Retrieved from https://www.ftc.gov/news-events/press-releases/2019/07/ftc-cfpb-states-announce-settlement-equifax-over-2017-data-breach

ethics.[499] This environment allowed harmful practices to persist, underscoring the importance of fostering integrity and responsibility at every level. When protecting customer data becomes a true priority, and employees and executives alike are held to high ethical standards, the risks of such catastrophic breaches diminish, and trust in the organization is more likely to endure.

Roles of Regulation and Government Oversight

Equifax's breach underscores how regulation and government oversight remain critical, an understanding reinforced by experts who advocate stronger enforcement mechanisms, to protect consumers from data breaches. Rather than leaving companies to police themselves, comprehensive oversight ensures they take necessary steps to safeguard personal data. The incident also reveals the need for national data protection standards, so organizations cannot bypass responsibilities or minimize their obligations.[500]

In response to the breach, renewed discussions emerged about comprehensive data protection legislation in the United States. Such legislation could establish clear standards for data security, breach notification, and consumer rights, providing better protection for individuals and leveling the playing field for businesses that handle sensitive information.[501] By creating uniform rules and expectations, policymakers can help restore trust and ensure that companies respect their customers' privacy.

The Equifax breach represents a profound failure in data security and corporate responsibility, leaving nearly half of the U.S.

---

499. Flitter, E. (2017, September 7). Equifax Faces Investigation as Investors Raise Questions. *Reuters*. Retrieved from https://www.reuters.com/article/us-equifax-cyber/executives-reaped-millions-in-stock-sales-after-data-breach-at-equifax-idUSKCN1BR2CB

500. FTC (Federal Trade Commission). (2019). *FTC, CFPB, and States Announce Settlement with Equifax over 2017 Data Breach*. Retrieved from https://www.ftc.gov/news-events/press-releases/2019/07/ftc-cfpb-states-announce-settlement-equifax-over-2017-data-breach

501. GAO (Government Accountability Office). (2018). *Actions Taken by Equifax and Federal Agencies in Response to the 2017 Breach*. Retrieved from https://www.gao.gov/products/gao-18-559

population vulnerable to identity theft and fraud. Instead of acting swiftly and transparently, Equifax's inadequate response and lack of accountability eroded public trust and caused lasting damage. This lapse was not merely a technical glitch; it was an organizational breakdown that put profit and convenience ahead of the consumers' well-being.

These lessons resonate far beyond Equifax, affecting the entire financial industry and other sectors that rely on personal data. Companies entrusted with sensitive information must prioritize security, cultivate a culture of accountability, and communicate honestly with consumers. Strong regulatory frameworks and vigilant government oversight remain essential as the digital economy expands, reminding all stakeholders that safeguarding consumer information is a responsibility that cannot be ignored.

The consequences of prioritizing profit over service quality are especially evident in the telecommunications industry, where companies frequently face criticism for poor service, hidden fees, and inadequate support. Comcast, in particular, has become a well-known case of customer frustration, with its history of billing disputes, aggressive retention tactics, and persistently low customer satisfaction ratings.

Disrespect for the Consumer by Comcast

Comcast, one of the largest telecommunications and media companies in the United States, has long been criticized for its poor customer service and questionable billing practices. Despite its dominant position in the market, Comcast has consistently ranked among the lowest in customer satisfaction surveys. The company's focus on maximizing profit often comes at the expense of service quality, leading to widespread dissatisfaction among its customers.

The Focus on Profit Over Service Quality

Comcast's business strategy has historically prioritized profit maximization, often at the expense of service quality and customer satisfaction. This approach is evident in the company's aggressive pricing strategies, high fees, and the prioritization of revenue-generating activities over customer support and service improvements.

The Profit-Driven Model

Comcast's profit-driven model prioritizes expanding market share and maximizing revenue, often by bundling cable, internet, and phone services into a single package that restricts customers' ability to switch providers. By locking them into long-term contracts, the company secures a steady revenue stream.[502] Although bundling may sometimes offer discounts, it frequently limits consumer choice and flexibility.

---

502. Bergmayer, J. (2015). *Overcharged and Underserved: How a Decade of Consolidation Has Reduced Competition and Harmed Consumers in the Cable and Broadband Markets*. Public Knowledge.

In order to increase its profitability and inflate bills, Comcast also mainly depends on fees and surcharges, such as those associated with equipment rentals and installation.[503] Because the company provides little clarity about these charges, customers struggle to understand their bills, leading to accusations of predatory practices and growing frustration.

This profit-first approach extends to customer service, where underinvestment results in long wait times and inadequate support.[504] Customers often feel their concerns receive minimal attention, reinforcing the perception that Comcast prioritizes financial gains over genuine care for their needs.

The Consequences of Underinvestment in Service Quality

The underinvestment in service quality has severely impacted Comcast's reputation and customer satisfaction. Despite its expansive market presence, the company consistently performs poorly in customer satisfaction surveys.[505] For instance, the American Customer Satisfaction Index (ACSI) has frequently placed Comcast near the bottom of rankings within the telecommunications sector. Customers often point to issues such as subpar service quality, confusing billing practices, and inadequate responsiveness as key sources of their frustration.

One of the key factors contributing to Comcast's low customer satisfaction is the company's reliance on cost-cutting strategies, particularly outsourcing customer support to third-party providers. This practice often leads to less knowledgeable representatives, who

503. Kang, C. (2015, August 25). Comcast Customer Service Rep Goes Viral After Lengthy Fight to Cancel Service. *The Washington Post*. Retrieved from https://www.washingtonpost.com/news/business/wp/2015/08/25/comcast-customer-service-rep-goes-viral-after-lengthy-fight-to-cancel-service/

504. Temkin Group. (2016). *Customer Experience Ratings for the Telecommunications Industry*. Retrieved from https://experiencematters.wordpress.com/2016/08/03/temkin-customer-experience-ratings-for-the-telecommunications-industry/

505. ACSI (American Customer Satisfaction Index). (2021). *ACSI Telecommunications Report 2021*. Retrieved from https://www.theacsi.org/news-and-resources/reports/telecommunications-report-2021/

struggle to resolve customer issues effectively.[506] Users are irritated by frequent service outages that are caused by the company's emphasis on cutting costs, which has also prevented investment in technology and infrastructure. Comcast's underwhelming response to these issues underscores a recurring theme of prioritizing profits over customer experience.

The emphasis on reducing costs has also led to a high rate of customer churn. Dissatisfied users, many of whom cite slow internet speeds as a persistent issue, increasingly explore alternatives such as streaming services or satellite providers.[507] Despite Comcast's market dominance in some regions, where switching options remain limited, its poor reputation continues to push customers toward other solutions.

High-Profile Cases of Poor Customer Service and Billing Practices

Comcast's focus on profit over service quality has manifested in numerous high-profile cases of poor customer service and questionable billing practices. These cases have further tarnished the company's reputation and underscored the disconnect between its profit-driven approach and the needs of its customers.

Notorious Customer Service Failures

Comcast's customer service failures have become notorious, with several high-profile cases capturing widespread media attention. In 2014, a recording of a customer trying to cancel his service went viral, exposing a grueling conversation with a Comcast

---

506. Kang, C. (2015, August 25). Comcast Customer Service Rep Goes Viral After Lengthy Fight to Cancel Service. *The Washington Post*. Retrieved from https://www.washingtonpost.com/news/business/wp/2015/08/25/comcast-customer-service-rep-goes-viral-after-lengthy-fight-to-cancel-service/

507. Bergmayer, J. (2015). *Overcharged and Underserved: How a Decade of Consolidation Has Reduced Competition and Harmed Consumers in the Cable and Broadband Markets*. Public Knowledge.

representative who refused to process the cancellation.[508] The representative's relentless and aggressive tactics underscored the intense pressure placed on employees to retain customers at all costs, often prioritizing sales goals over customer satisfaction. This incident highlighted the systemic issues within Comcast's customer retention strategies.

Another widely reported case involved a customer who was billed $1,775 for a technician's service call that was initially promised to be free.[509] Despite assurances from Comcast, the customer was later charged and faced resistance when attempting to resolve the issue. Only after the case gained media attention did Comcast reverse the charges. This lack of accountability reinforced the company's reputation for poor customer service, frustrating many of its users.

These high-profile incidents reflect broader systemic problems in Comcast's customer service operations. By prioritizing customer retention and revenue generation, the company often resorts to aggressive sales tactics and neglects accountability, contributing to widespread dissatisfaction among its customer base.[510]

Questionable Billing Practices

Comcast has faced widespread criticism for its billing practices, which many customers describe as opaque, confusing, and predatory. Unexpected charges and fees, including equipment rentals and service calls, are frequent sources of frustration for

---

508. Kang, C. (2015, August 25). Comcast Customer Service Rep Goes Viral After Lengthy Fight to Cancel Service. *The Washington Post*. Retrieved from https://www.washingtonpost.com/news/business/wp/2015/08/25/comcast-customer-service-rep-goes-viral-after-lengthy-fight-to-cancel-service/

509. Griswold, A. (2014, September 12). Comcast Bills Customer $1,775 for Service It Promised for Free. *Business Insider*. Retrieved from https://www.businessinsider.com/comcast-bills-customer-1775-for-service-it-promised-for-free-2014-9

510. Temkin Group. (2016). *Customer Experience Ratings for the Telecommunications Industry*. Retrieved from https://experiencematters.wordpress.com/2016/08/03/temkin-customer-experience-ratings-for-the-telecommunications-industry/

customers.[511] For instance, many customers have reported being billed for services they were not informed about when signing up, contributing to the perception of deceptive practices.

A particularly troubling case involved a customer who was charged a monthly fee for renting a cable modem, despite owning his own modem and repeatedly notifying Comcast of this fact. The customer spent months attempting to resolve the issue but encountered contradictory and unhelpful responses from customer service.[512] The case, which eventually gained media attention, resulted in Comcast issuing a refund, but it exposed serious issues with the company's transparency and accountability.

The intricacy of Comcast's billing statements is another frequent grievance. Bills often contain numerous line items and charges that are poorly explained, making it challenging for customers to verify their accuracy.[513] This lack of clarity fosters a sense of mistrust and frustration, as customers struggle to understand whether they are being charged correctly.

Legal actions have further highlighted Comcast's questionable billing practices. In 2016, the company settled a lawsuit with the Washington State Attorney General's office for $9.1 million, stemming from allegations that Comcast had charged customers for unrequested services, such as service protection plans.[514] As part of the settlement, Comcast agreed to revise its billing

---

511. Kang, C. (2015, August 25). Comcast Customer Service Rep Goes Viral After Lengthy Fight to Cancel Service. *The Washington Post*. Retrieved from https://www.washingtonpost.com/news/business/wp/2015/08/25/comcast-customer-service-rep-goes-viral-after-lengthy-fight-to-cancel-service/

512. Griswold, A. (2014, September 12). Comcast Bills Customer $1,775 for Service It Promised for Free. *Business Insider*. Retrieved from https://www.businessinsider.com/comcast-bills-customer-1775-for-service-it-promised-for-free-2014-9

513. Kang, C. (2015, August 25). Comcast Customer Service Rep Goes Viral After Lengthy Fight to Cancel Service. *The Washington Post*. Retrieved from https://www.washingtonpost.com/news/business/wp/2015/08/25/comcast-customer-service-rep-goes-viral-after-lengthy-fight-to-cancel-service/

514. WSAG (Washington State Attorney General). (2016). *Attorney General Ferguson Reaches $9.1 Million Settlement with Comcast over Deceptive Practices*. Retrieved from https://www.atg.wa.gov/news/news-releases/ag-ferguson-reaches-91-million-settlement-comcast-over-deceptive-practices

practices and provide restitution to affected customers, though the case reinforced the company's reputation for predatory billing.

Impacts on Customer Relationships and Loyalty

The combination of poor customer service and questionable billing practices has significantly strained Comcast's relationships with its customers. Many feel that the company prioritizes profit over service quality, fostering widespread mistrust and dissatisfaction.[515] This has contributed to Comcast's consistently low customer satisfaction ratings and high churn rates, as frustrated customers actively seek alternatives to its services.

Negative customer experiences have also eroded brand loyalty. Many dissatisfied customers report they would not recommend Comcast to others and would leave if other options were available.[516] In the competitive telecommunications industry, where retaining customers is vital for long-term success, this lack of loyalty poses a serious challenge.

Comcast's poor reputation has broader implications for its business. High-profile cases of inadequate service and predatory billing have not only attracted negative publicity but also intensified regulatory scrutiny and legal challenges.[517] These factors have damaged the company's brand, making it increasingly difficult for Comcast to attract and retain customers.

---

515. ACSI (American Customer Satisfaction Index). (2021). *ACSI Telecommunications Report 2021*. Retrieved from https://www.theacsi.org/news-and-resources/reports/telecommunications-report-2021/

516. Temkin Group. (2016). *Customer Experience Ratings for the Telecommunications Industry*. Retrieved from https://experiencematters.wordpress.com/2016/08/03/temkin-customer-experience-ratings-for-the-telecommunications-industry/

517. Bergmayer, J. (2015). *Overcharged and Underserved: How a Decade of Consolidation Has Reduced Competition and Harmed Consumers in the Cable and Broadband Markets*. Public Knowledge.

Comcast and the Telecommunications Sector's Wider Consequences

Comcast's focus on profit over service quality, combined with its poor customer service and questionable billing practices, has had significant implications not only for the company but also for the broader telecommunications industry. These issues highlight the challenges faced by companies in balancing profitability with customer satisfaction, and they underscore the importance of accountability and transparency in maintaining customer trust.

The Challenges of Balancing Profitability and Customer Satisfaction

One of the key challenges faced by companies like Comcast is finding the right balance between profitability and customer satisfaction. In an industry where competition is fierce and margins are often slim, companies are under constant pressure to maximize revenue and minimize costs.[518] However, as Comcast's experience demonstrates, a focus on short-term profits at the expense of service quality can lead to long-term damage to a company's reputation and customer relationships.

To achieve sustainable success, companies must prioritize customer satisfaction and invest in the resources needed to provide high-quality service. This includes investing in infrastructure, technology, and customer support, as well as ensuring that billing practices are transparent and fair. By focusing on the needs of customers and building strong relationships, companies can create a loyal customer base that is more likely to stay with the company over the long term.[519]

---

518. Griswold, A. (2014, September 12). Comcast Bills Customer $1,775 for Service It Promised for Free. *Business Insider*. Retrieved from https://www.businessinsider.com/comcast-bills-customer-1775-for-service-it-promised-for-free-2014-9

519. ACSI (American Customer Satisfaction Index). (2021). *ACSI Telecommunications Report 2021*. Retrieved from https://www.theacsi.org/news-and-resources/reports/telecommunications-report-2021/

Importance of Accountability and Transparency

The challenges faced by Comcast underscore the critical importance of maintaining accountability and transparency to secure customer trust. Companies need to ensure clarity in their pricing and billing practices, providing customers with detailed and accurate information about the services offered and the associated costs. Additionally, firms must actively respond to complaints, demonstrating accountability by addressing issues promptly and effectively.[520] For Comcast, a persistent lack of transparency and accountability has fueled widespread customer dissatisfaction and mistrust.

Need for Industry-Wide Reform

The challenges faced by Comcast reflect systemic issues prevalent across the telecommunications industry, where the prioritization of profit over service quality has led to widespread customer dissatisfaction. This case highlights the need for industry-wide reform, including stronger regulations and oversight to ensure companies are held accountable for their actions and adopt customer-centric practices.[521]

Regulatory bodies play a critical role in driving these changes, promoting transparency, fairness, and accountability. Enforcing standards around billing, customer service, and competition while equipping consumers with the tools to make informed decisions can foster a more equitable and competitive telecommunications industry.[522]

---

520. WSAG (Washington State Attorney General). (2016). *Attorney General Ferguson Reaches $9.1 Million Settlement with Comcast over Deceptive Practices*. Retrieved from https://www.atg.wa.gov/news/news-releases/ag-ferguson-reaches-91-million-settlement-comcast-over-deceptive-practices

521. Bergmayer, J. (2015). *Overcharged and Underserved: How a Decade of Consolidation Has Reduced Competition and Harmed Consumers in the Cable and Broadband Markets*. Public Knowledge.

522. WSAG (Washington State Attorney General). (2016). *Attorney General Ferguson Reaches $9.1 Million Settlement with Comcast over Deceptive Practices*. Retrieved from https://www.atg.wa.gov/news/news-releases/ag-ferguson-reaches-91-million-settlement-comcast-over-deceptive-practices

Comcast's experience demonstrates the risks of neglecting transparency, ethical behavior, and customer satisfaction. The company's poor service and predatory billing practices have eroded trust, damaged its reputation, and weakened customer loyalty. For Comcast to recover, it must undergo meaningful organizational changes, emphasizing accountability and customer-focused decision-making.

The broader lesson for the telecommunications industry is clear: prioritizing short-term profits at the expense of service quality may lead to temporary gains but risks long-term reputational damage. Companies that prioritize customer needs and invest in high-quality service can achieve sustainable success and maintain a competitive edge in an increasingly discerning market.

Rebuilding Customer Trust and Loyalty: The Way Ahead

In light of the challenges posed by the shift from customer service to customer management, companies must find ways to rebuild customer trust and loyalty. This requires a renewed focus on customer-centric strategies that prioritize personalized service, empathy, and long-term relationship-building.

Embracing a Customer-Centric Approach

To rebuild trust and loyalty, companies must embrace a customer-centric approach that places customers' needs and preferences at the center of decision-making, an approach that reintroduces elements of personalized service, empathy, and care.[523] By moving beyond purely transactional interactions, businesses can better understand and address each customer's unique situation, creating positive experiences that lead to lasting loyalty and stronger relationships.

A customer-centric strategy also involves rethinking the role of technology in shaping customer interactions. While data analytics and automation can

523. Grönroos, C. (2007). *Service Management and Marketing: Customer Management in Service Competition*. Wiley.

certainly enhance service, they should be used in ways that support, rather than replace, genuine human connection.[524] By investing in training that helps customer service representatives use technological tools effectively, without losing the personal touch, companies can ensure that customers feel truly seen, respected, and valued.

Prioritizing Customer Experience

In the customer management model, efficiency and cost-effectiveness often take precedence over customer experience. However, to rebuild trust and loyalty, companies must prioritize customer experience as a key driver of business success. This means focusing on creating positive, memorable interactions at every touchpoint, from initial contact to post-purchase support.[525]

Companies can enhance customer experience by actively seeking and responding to customer feedback, addressing issues promptly and effectively, and going above and beyond to exceed customer expectations. By creating a culture that values and rewards exceptional service, companies can differentiate themselves from competitors and build a loyal customer base that is more likely to stick with the brand over the long term.

Building Long-Term Relationships

Finally, rebuilding customer trust and loyalty requires a renewed focus on building long-term relationships. This means shifting away from short-term, profit-driven strategies and investing in initiatives that foster customer loyalty and engagement.[526] Companies can build long-term relationships by offering loyalty programs, personalized offers, and ongoing support that makes customers feel valued and appreciated.

Building long-term relationships also involves creating a sense of community and connection with customers. Companies can achieve

---

524. Parasuraman, A., Zeithaml, V. A., & Berry, L. L. (1985). A Conceptual Model of Service Quality and Its Implications for Future Research. *Journal of Marketing*, 49(4), 41-50.

525. Zeithaml, V. A., Bitner, M. J., & Gremler, D. D. (2018). *Services Marketing: Integrating Customer Focus Across the Firm*. McGraw-Hill Education.

526. Reichheld, F. F., & Schefter, P. (2000). E-Loyalty: Your Secret Weapon on the Web. *Harvard Business Review*, 78(4), 105-113.

this by engaging with customers through social media, events, and other platforms that allow for meaningful interaction and feedback. By creating a strong sense of community, companies can build brand advocates who are more likely to promote the brand and remain loyal over time.

The shift from customer service to customer management represents a significant change in the way companies interact with their customers. While the customer management model offers short-term gains in efficiency and profitability, it can lead to long-term negative consequences for customer satisfaction, loyalty, and brand reputation.

To address these challenges, companies must embrace a customer-centric approach that prioritizes personalized service, empathy, and long-term relationship-building. By focusing on creating positive customer experiences and building trust and loyalty, companies can differentiate themselves from competitors and achieve sustainable success in an increasingly competitive market.

KEY TAKEAWAYS

The Shift from Personalized Service to Customer Management
Traditional customer service emphasized personalization, empathy, and long-term relationships. However, modern businesses have transitioned toward a customer management model, where efficiency, profitability, and data-driven decision-making take precedence over human interaction.

Data Analytics and Automation Have Transformed Customer Interactions
While data analytics and CRM systems allow businesses to optimize customer interactions and offer targeted recommendations, they also contribute to impersonal, transactional relationships. The rise of automation, such as chatbots and self-service portals, has further reduced human engagement in customer service.

Efficiency and Profitability Often Overshadow Customer Experience
Companies increasingly treat customer interactions as cost centers rather than opportunities to build relationships. The drive for efficiency and cost-cutting has led to standardized, one-size-fits-all approaches that can leave customers feeling like mere numbers rather than valued individuals.

The Shift to Customer Management Has Increased Customer Dissatisfaction
As businesses prioritize automation and segmentation based on customer profitability, many customers feel neglected or undervalued. The loss of personal interaction has led to declining brand loyalty, negative public perception, and an increase in customer frustration.

Rebuilding Customer Trust Requires a Return to Customer-Centric Strategies
To restore trust and loyalty, companies must balance efficiency with personalized service, prioritize customer experience, and invest in long-term relationships. Businesses that integrate empathy, human connection, and responsive service into their strategies can differentiate themselves and foster lasting customer engagement.

Chapter 9

Trust on the Line, Why Cutting Corners Damages Long-Term Success

In the fast-paced world of modern business, the pressure to maximize profits and slash costs has never been greater. Yet, when companies chase short-term gains at the expense of long-term relationships, they risk far more than they realize. Cutting corners might seem like a quick fix, but it often leads to disappointing service and deceptive practices that undermine customer trust. While these tactics may momentarily inflate the bottom line, the real cost is the erosion of loyalty, the very foundation of sustainable success.

Importance of Customer Trust and Loyalty

Customer trust and loyalty are indispensable to the success of any business, as they establish the foundation for a strong, enduring relationship between a company and its customers. Trust, built through consistent, reliable, and transparent interactions, encourages repeat business and drives positive word-of-mouth referrals.[527] These factors directly contribute to a company's ability to sustain long-term revenue growth and maintain a competitive edge in the marketplace.

527. Reichheld, F. F., & Schefter, P. (2000). E-Loyalty: Your Secret Weapon on the Web. *Harvard Business Review*, 78(4), 105-113.

Businesses that focus on fostering trust often find that loyal customers remain committed despite occasional service shortcomings, provided the company demonstrates accountability and resolves issues effectively. Loyalty also serves as a buffer against external challenges, such as economic downturns or market disruptions.

Customers who trust a brand are less likely to switch providers over minor inconveniences or price changes, creating a steady revenue stream even in turbulent times. This stability underscores the immense value of trust; however, it is a fragile resource. Once damaged, rebuilding customer trust often becomes a monumental task, requiring significant time and effort, as seen in numerous high-profile corporate missteps.[528]

Misleading Practices and the Erosion of Trust

One of the most significant ways companies erode customer trust is through misleading practices. These can take many forms, including deceptive advertising, hidden fees, false promises, and unethical sales tactics. While these practices may result in short-term gains, they can have severe long-term consequences for customer relationships.

Deceptive Advertising and False Promises

Deceptive advertising remains a pervasive issue, as companies often exaggerate the benefits of their products or services, make false claims, or obscure critical details in fine print. A company might promote a product by highlighting features or benefits it does not actually possess while downplaying risks or limitations that could affect customer satisfaction.[529] These tactics can create an illusion of value, luring customers into purchases that ultimately fail to meet expectations.

When customers uncover the truth, their trust in the company is significantly undermined, resulting in feelings of betrayal and disillu-

528. Morgan, R. M., & Hunt, S. D. (1994). The Commitment-Trust Theory of Relationship Marketing. *Journal of Marketing*, 58(3), 20-38.

529. Darke, P. R., & Ritchie, R. J. B. (2007). The Defensive Consumer: Advertising Deception, Defensive Processing, and Distrust. *Journal of Marketing Research*, 44(1), 114-127.

sionment.[530] This sense of deception often leads to customer attrition, negative word-of-mouth, and even legal challenges if the practices are particularly egregious.

False promises, such as guaranteeing unattainable results or failing to honor advertised promotions, further exacerbate the erosion of trust between companies and their customers. When customers realize that a company has not fulfilled its commitments, they are unlikely to engage with that business again.[2] Such experiences not only alienate existing customers but also deter potential customers, as dissatisfied individuals often share their negative experiences publicly. Over time, this tarnished reputation can reduce the company's ability to attract new customers, diminishing its competitive position and profitability.

---

530. Darke, P. R., & Ritchie, R. J. B. (2007). The Defensive Consumer: Advertising Deception, Defensive Processing, and Distrust. *Journal of Marketing Research*, 44(1), 114-127.

Volkswagen's Erosion of Customer Trust

Volkswagen, one of the most iconic and respected automotive brands in the world, faced a significant crisis in 2015 when it was revealed that the company had been involved in a massive emissions scandal. The scandal, often referred to as "Dieselgate," involved Volkswagen's use of software to cheat on emissions tests, allowing its diesel vehicles to emit pollutants far beyond legal limits while passing regulatory inspections.

This deliberate deception not only violated environmental regulations but also represented a profound betrayal of the trust that customers and the public had placed in the company. With an emphasis on the breach of environmental pledges, the deterioration of consumer confidence, and the long-term effects on the Volkswagen brand, this case study examines the Volkswagen emissions scandal.

A Betrayal of Environmental Promises

The Volkswagen emissions scandal broke in September 2015 when the United States Environmental Protection Agency (EPA) issued a notice of violation to the company for using "defeat devices" in its diesel engines. These devices were designed to manipulate emissions testing, allowing vehicles to meet regulatory standards in the lab while emitting up to 40 times the legal limit of nitrogen oxides (NOx) during normal driving conditions. The scandal not only revealed serious ethical breaches within Volkswagen but also highlighted the company's betrayal of its environmental promises.

Mechanics of the Scandal

Volkswagen's "defeat devices" were sophisticated software algorithms embedded within the engine control units of their diesel vehicles.[531] These devices could detect when a vehicle was undergoing emissions testing by monitoring various parameters, such as steering wheel movement, speed, and engine operation. During testing, the software would activate the vehicle's full emissions control systems, ensuring that it met the stringent NOx limits set by regulators.

However, once the vehicle returned to normal driving conditions, the software would deactivate these controls, allowing the engine to produce significantly more power and fuel efficiency at the cost of increased NOx emissions.[532] This dual-mode operation enabled Volkswagen to market its diesel vehicles as both environmentally friendly and high-performing, appealing to consumers concerned about reducing their carbon footprint without sacrificing driving pleasure.

The scale of the deception was staggering. It is estimated that around 11 million vehicles worldwide were equipped with these defeat devices, including models from Volkswagen, Audi, and Porsche. The scandal not only involved deliberate deception but also exposed a culture within Volkswagen that prioritized market success over regulatory compliance and ethical considerations.[533]

Violating Environmental Obligations

Volkswagen's marketing strategy for its diesel vehicles heavily centered on their environmental benefits.[534] The company positioned itself as a leader in producing "clean diesel" cars that offered reduced

---

531. Hotten, R. (2015, December 10). Volkswagen: The Scandal Explained. *BBC News*. Retrieved from https://www.bbc.com/news/business-34324772

532. Ewing, J. (2017). *Faster, Higher, Farther: The Inside Story of the Volkswagen Scandal*. W. W. Norton & Company.

533. Hotten, R. (2015, December 10). Volkswagen: The Scandal Explained. *BBC News*. Retrieved from https://www.bbc.com/news/business-34324772

534. *Ibid.*

emissions and fuel efficiency without compromising performance.[535] These claims were central to Volkswagen's branding, particularly in markets like the United States and Europe, where environmental concerns were increasingly influencing consumer choices.

However, the emissions scandal revealed that Volkswagen's environmental promises were based on deception.[536] The company's claims of producing low-emission vehicles were contradicted by the reality of the defeat devices,[537] which allowed cars to emit pollutants at levels far exceeding legal limits.[538] This not only violated environmental regulations but also betrayed the trust of customers who had chosen Volkswagen vehicles based on the company's purported commitment to sustainability.

The scandal was particularly damaging because it involved a company that had cultivated a reputation for engineering excellence and environmental responsibility. Volkswagen's actions undermined its credibility and raised serious questions about the integrity of its leadership and corporate culture. The revelation that the company had knowingly engaged in such widespread deception shattered the trust that consumers, regulators, and the public had placed in Volkswagen.

Global Response and Legal Repercussions

The global response to the Volkswagen emissions scandal was swift and severe. Regulators, governments, and consumer advocacy groups around the world condemned the company's actions, leading to investigations, lawsuits, and significant financial

---

535. Ewing, J. (2017). *Faster, Higher, Farther: The Inside Story of the Volkswagen Scanda*l. W. W. Norton & Company.

536. Morgan, R. M., & Hunt, S. D. (1994). The Commitment-Trust Theory of Relationship Marketing. *Journal of Marketing*, 58(3), 20-38.

537. Reichheld, F. F., & Schefter, P. (2000). E-Loyalty: Your Secret Weapon on the Web. *Harvard Business Review*, 78(4), 105-113.

538. Brand Finance. (2016). *Volkswagen Brand Value Falls in Wake of Emissions Scandal.* Retrieved from https://brandfinance.com/insights/volkswagen-brand-value-falls-in-wake-of-emissions-scandal

penalties.[539] In the United States, the EPA and the California Air Resources Board (CARB) led the charge, with the Department of Justice (DOJ) later filing criminal charges against Volkswagen.

Volkswagen ultimately agreed to a series of settlements and penalties totaling more than $30 billion,[540] including fines, compensation for affected customers, and costs associated with recalling and fixing the affected vehicles. The company also faced criminal charges, with several high-ranking executives being indicted or fined for their roles in the scandal.[541] These legal repercussions were among the largest ever imposed on an automotive company, reflecting the gravity of Volkswagen's deception.

The scandal also led to significant regulatory changes in the automotive industry, with increased scrutiny of emissions testing and a push for more stringent environmental standards. Governments and regulators around the world began re-evaluating their testing procedures to ensure that similar deceptions could not occur in the future.[542] The long-term impact of the scandal on environmental policy and automotive regulation is still being felt today.

Long-Term Impacts on the Volkswagen Brand and Customer Trust

The Volkswagen emissions scandal had profound and lasting effects on the company's brand and customer trust. The deliberate deception, coupled with the scale of the scandal, led to a significant erosion of trust among consumers, regulators, and the public. The long-term impact on Volkswagen's brand and market position continues to be a subject of study and reflection.

---

539. Hotten, R. (2015, December 10). Volkswagen: The Scandal Explained. *BBC News*. Retrieved from https://www.bbc.com/news/business-34324772

540. Ewing, J. (2017). *Faster, Higher, Farther: The Inside Story of the Volkswagen Scandal*. W. W. Norton & Company.

541. Morgan, R. M., & Hunt, S. D. (1994). The Commitment-Trust Theory of Relationship Marketing. *Journal of Marketing*, 58(3), 20-38.

542. Reichheld, F. F., & Schefter, P. (2000). E-Loyalty: Your Secret Weapon on the Web. *Harvard Business Review*, 78(4), 105-113.

Erosion of Customer Trust

One of the most significant consequences of the emissions scandal was the erosion of customer trust in Volkswagen.[543] Trust is a critical component of the relationship between a brand and its customers, and it is particularly important in industries like automotive manufacturing, where safety, reliability, and environmental responsibility are key considerations for consumers.[544]

Many consumers' faith in Volkswagen was destroyed when it was discovered that the company had purposefully misled both regulators and consumers. Customers who had purchased Volkswagen vehicles based on the company's environmental claims felt betrayed, as the vehicles they believed were contributing to a cleaner environment were, in fact, causing significant harm.[545] This sense of betrayal was compounded by the knowledge that Volkswagen had engaged in this deception for years, with millions of vehicles affected.

The loss of trust had immediate and long-term consequences for Volkswagen's customer relationships. In the short term, the company faced a wave of customer dissatisfaction, with many owners of affected vehicles seeking compensation, repairs, or buybacks.[546] The scandal also led to a decline in brand loyalty, as customers who felt betrayed by Volkswagen were less likely to purchase another vehicle from the company in the future.

In the long term, the erosion of trust has made it more difficult for Volkswagen to rebuild its reputation and regain the confidence of consumers. Trust, once broken, is challenging to restore, and Volkswagen has had to invest significant resources in rebranding,

543. Hotten, R. (2015, December 10). Volkswagen: The Scandal Explained. *BBC News*. Retrieved from https://www.bbc.com/news/business-34324772

544. Ewing, J. (2017). *Faster, Higher, Farther: The Inside Story of the Volkswagen Scandal*. W. W. Norton & Company.

545. Morgan, R. M., & Hunt, S. D. (1994). The Commitment-Trust Theory of Relationship Marketing. *Journal of Marketing*, 58(3), 20-38.

546. Reichheld, F. F., & Schefter, P. (2000). E-Loyalty: Your Secret Weapon on the Web. *Harvard Business Review*, 78(4), 105-113.

public relations, and customer outreach to begin the process of rebuilding its image.

Volkswagen's Market Position and Brand Impact

The emissions scandal had a profound impact on Volkswagen's brand and market position.[547] Before the scandal, Volkswagen was one of the most respected and successful automotive brands in the world, known for its engineering excellence, innovation, and commitment to sustainability.[548] The scandal, however, tarnished this reputation, leading to a decline in brand value and a loss of market share.

Volkswagen's brand took a significant hit in the aftermath of the scandal.[549] The company's image as a leader in producing environmentally friendly vehicles was destroyed, and it became synonymous with corporate deception and unethical behavior. The negative publicity surrounding the scandal led to a decline in sales, particularly in markets where environmental concerns were a significant factor in consumer decision-making.[550]

The long-term impact on Volkswagen's market position has been mixed. While the company has managed to recover some of its market share and maintain its position as one of the largest automotive manufacturers in the world, the scandal has left lasting scars on its brand. Volkswagen has had to invest heavily in electric vehicles and other environmentally friendly technologies as part of its efforts to rebuild its reputation and align itself with the growing demand for sustainable transportation.[551]

---

547. Hotten, R. (2015, December 10). Volkswagen: The Scandal Explained. *BBC News*. Retrieved from https://www.bbc.com/news/business-34324772

548. Ewing, J. (2017). *Faster, Higher, Farther: The Inside Story of the Volkswagen Scandal*. W. W. Norton & Company.

549. Morgan, R. M., & Hunt, S. D. (1994). The Commitment-Trust Theory of Relationship Marketing. *Journal of Marketing*, 58(3), 20-38.

550. Reichheld, F. F., & Schefter, P. (2000). E-Loyalty: Your Secret Weapon on the Web. *Harvard Business Review*, 78(4), 105-113.

551. Brand Finance. (2016). *Volkswagen Brand Value Falls in Wake of Emissions Scandal*. Retrieved from https://brandfinance.com/insights/volkswagen-brand-value-falls-in-wake-of-emissions-scandal

Despite these efforts, the shadow of the emissions scandal continues to loom over Volkswagen. The company's brand has been permanently associated with the scandal, and it faces ongoing challenges in convincing consumers, regulators, and the public that it has genuinely reformed its practices and is committed to ethical behavior.[552]

The Wider Effect on the Automobile Sector

The Volkswagen emissions scandal revealed systemic flaws in the regulatory processes for emissions testing, prompting global regulatory bodies to adopt stricter standards and heightened scrutiny. This increased vigilance pushed automakers across the industry to reevaluate their compliance measures and ensure alignment with environmental regulations.[553] The incident underscored the importance of robust oversight, as it became clear that self-regulation alone was insufficient to prevent such misconduct.

In addition to regulatory changes, the scandal acted as a catalyst for the broader adoption of electric vehicles and other low-emission technologies. Governments and regulatory agencies worldwide responded by amplifying support for electric vehicle initiatives, framing them as vital tools for combating climate change and reducing greenhouse gas emissions. In response, Volkswagen announced substantial investments in electric vehicle development, aiming to position itself as a leader in sustainable transportation.[554]

Volkswagen's deceit also highlighted the shortcomings of industry-led sustainability initiatives and self-regulation. It underscored the necessity of stronger oversight mechanisms and accountability

---

552. Victor, D. (2017, April 10). Man Dragged Off Overbooked United Flight. *The New York Times*. Retrieved from https://www.nytimes.com/2017/04/10/business/united-flight-passenger-dragged.html

553. Hotten, R. (2015, December 10). Volkswagen: The Scandal Explained. *BBC News*. Retrieved from https://www.bbc.com/news/business-34324772

554. Ewing, J. (2017). *Faster, Higher, Farther: The Inside Story of the Volkswagen Scandal*. W. W. Norton & Company.

measures to prevent similar breaches in the future, ensuring that environmental promises are met with tangible action.[555]

Difficulties in Rebuilding Trust

Rebuilding trust after a scandal as far-reaching as Volkswagen's emissions deception is a demanding and intricate process. The company has had to undertake significant reforms, including leadership changes, cultural shifts, and systemic operational overhauls. Volkswagen's efforts have centered on fostering transparency and accountability, enhancing oversight of its practices, and improving compliance with environmental regulations.[556] The company has also sought to rebuild its credibility by engaging openly with stakeholders and making substantial investments in electric vehicles and other sustainable technologies, aiming to position itself as a leader in the global transition to a low-carbon economy.

These steps mark progress, but the challenge of regaining consumer trust is far from over. Volkswagen must continuously demonstrate its commitment to ethical practices, environmental stewardship, and genuine reform. This effort is critical not only to restoring the confidence of existing customers but also to reshaping the broader public perception of the brand.[557] The long shadow cast by the emissions scandal underscores the enduring impact of corporate misconduct on brand reputation and market standing.

The Volkswagen scandal is a cautionary tale with implications that resonate far beyond the automotive industry. It emphasizes that trust is the cornerstone of any successful business, and once compromised, it is exceedingly difficult to rebuild. Companies must adopt a forward-thinking approach, prioritizing ethical behavior, transparency, and accountability in every facet of their operations.

---

555. Hotten, R. (2015, December 10). Volkswagen: The Scandal Explained. *BBC News*. Retrieved from https://www.bbc.com/news/business-34324772

556. Ewing, J. (2017). *Faster, Higher, Farther: The Inside Story of the Volkswagen Scandal*. W. W. Norton & Company.

557. Reichheld, F. F., & Schefter, P. (2000). E-Loyalty: Your Secret Weapon on the Web. *Harvard Business Review*, 78(4), 105-113.

Sustained investment in compliance, sustainability, and customer engagement is essential not only for maintaining trust but also for ensuring long-term success in an increasingly values-driven marketplace. The lessons learned from Volkswagen's crisis should serve as a guidepost for industries seeking to navigate the delicate balance between profitability and integrity.

Hidden Fees and Unethical Billing Practices

Hidden fees and unethical billing practices represent a significant threat to customer trust. Customers who discover they have been charged more than expected, or who encounter fees that were not clearly disclosed, often feel misled and resentful. These practices frequently result in disputes, poor reviews, and diminished loyalty.

For instance, a telecommunications company may advertise an attractively low monthly rate but later include numerous undisclosed fees for equipment rental, installation, or other services.[558] When such charges are not transparently presented upfront, customers are likely to perceive these tactics as deceptive. Over time, repeated exposure to these practices fosters dissatisfaction and erodes the loyalty of even the most steadfast customers.[559]

Unethical billing practices exacerbate this erosion of trust, particularly when companies charge for services that were not delivered or continue billing customers after services have been canceled.[560] These behaviors create the perception that profit maximization takes precedence over fairness and customer satisfaction. Such experiences often prompt customers to seek alternatives, file regulatory complaints, or initiate legal action, all of which can damage a company's reputation and financial stability. By prioritizing revenue over ethics, companies risk long-term harm to their brand and bottom line.

---

558. Fournier, S., & Avery, J. (2011). The Uninvited Brand. *Business Horizons*, 54(3), 193-207.
559. Fournier, S., & Avery, J. (2011). The Uninvited Brand. *Business Horizons*, 54(3), 193-207.
560. *Ibid.*

Unethical Sales Tactics

Unethical sales tactics, such as high-pressure sales techniques, upselling unnecessary products or services, or exploiting vulnerable customers, can also erode trust. When customers feel that they have been manipulated or taken advantage of, they are unlikely to return to the company or recommend it to others.

For instance, a financial services company might pressure customers into purchasing expensive insurance products that they do not need or understand. When customers later realize that they have been misled or sold something that does not meet their needs, they are likely to lose trust in the company.[561] This loss of trust can have long-term consequences, as customers who feel betrayed are unlikely to remain loyal or continue doing business with the company.

Poor Service and the Decline of Customer Loyalty

Poor service is another major factor that contributes to the erosion of customer trust and loyalty. When companies cut corners on customer service, it often leads to negative experiences that drive customers away.

Inadequate Customer Support

Inadequate customer support is a common issue that can severely damage customer trust. When customers encounter problems with a product or service, they expect to receive timely and effective assistance.[562] However, if a company has underinvested in customer support, whether by outsourcing services to lower-cost providers, cutting back on staff, or failing to provide adequate training, customers may find it difficult to get the help they need.

Long wait times, unhelpful or rude customer service representatives, and unresolved issues can all contribute to a negative customer experience.

---

561. Morgan, R. M., & Hunt, S. D. (1994). The Commitment-Trust Theory of Relationship Marketing. *Journal of Marketing*, 58(3), 20-38.

562. Zeithaml, V. A., Bitner, M. J., & Gremler, D. D. (2018). Services Marketing: Integrating Customer Focus Across the Firm. McGraw-Hill Education.

When customers feel that their concerns are not being taken seriously, they may lose trust in the company and seek out alternatives.[5] Over time, poor customer support can lead to high churn rates, negative reviews, and a decline in brand reputation.

Service Quality and Reliability

Service quality and reliability are fundamental to maintaining customer trust, yet many companies compromise these elements in the pursuit of cost-cutting measures. Such shortcuts often result in subpar products, frequent outages, or other frustrations for customers. For example, a technology company focused on reducing expenses may release products that are prone to defects or malfunctions due to inadequate quality control.[563] These repeated issues diminish customer confidence in the company's ability to deliver dependable products, undermining trust that is essential for long-term loyalty.

In industries like telecommunications, where reliability is critical, frequent outages or slow response times can exacerbate customer dissatisfaction. Customers who depend on these services for both work and personal needs are likely to grow increasingly frustrated with repeated disruptions.[564] This frustration often prompts them to seek alternatives, turning to competitors with a reputation for better service.[565] The resulting loss of market share and revenue highlights the broader consequences of neglecting service quality and reliability in customer-facing industries.

---

563. Parasuraman, A., Zeithaml, V. A., & Berry, L. L. (1988). SERVQUAL: A Multiple-Item Scale for Measuring Consumer Perceptions of Service Quality. *Journal of Retailing*, 64(1), 12-40.

564. Zeithaml, V. A., Bitner, M. J., & Gremler, D. D. (2018). Services Marketing: Integrating Customer Focus Across the Firm. McGraw-Hill Education.

565. *Ibid.*

United Airlines' Decline in Customer Confidence

In the service industry, customer trust is paramount, particularly in the airline sector, where safety, reliability, and customer care are critical components of a successful business. However, when companies fail to prioritize these elements, they risk losing the trust of their customers, often with significant consequences. United Airlines experienced such a loss of trust in 2017, when a video of a passenger being forcibly dragged off an overbooked flight went viral.

This incident not only sparked widespread outrage but also highlighted broader issues with customer service in the airline industry. This case study examines the infamous passenger dragging incident, its repercussions on United Airlines, and the broader implications for customer service in the airline industry.

The Infamous Passenger Dragging Incident

On April 9, 2017, United Airlines Flight 3411 was scheduled to fly from Chicago O'Hare International Airport to Louisville, Kentucky. The flight was overbooked, a common practice in the airline industry, where airlines sell more tickets than available seats, anticipating that some passengers will not show up. However, on this occasion, all passengers had checked in, and the airline needed to accommodate four United crew members who were required to be in Louisville for another flight.

What Led Up to the Incident

United initially offered passengers incentives, including vouchers and hotel accommodations, to voluntarily give up their seats. When no one accepted the offer, the airline randomly selected four passengers to be removed from the flight. One of those selected was Dr. David Dao, a 69-year-old physician. When Dr. Dao refused to leave the plane, citing his need to see patients the following day, United called security officers, who forcibly removed him from the aircraft.[566] During the altercation, Dr. Dao was dragged down the aisle, his face bloodied after hitting an armrest, and the incident was captured on video by other passengers.

The video quickly went viral, sparking outrage on social media and in the media. The images of a paying customer being violently removed from his seat resonated with people around the world and became a symbol of corporate indifference and mistreatment of customers.[567] The incident raised serious questions about United Airlines' policies, its treatment of passengers, and the broader culture within the airline industry.

United Airlines's Immediate Repercussions

Fallout from United Airlines' incident came swiftly, sparking widespread outrage and severely damaging the airline's reputation. Social media erupted with calls for boycotts, with users expressing anger and disappointment. News outlets worldwide amplified the backlash, covering the story extensively. A video of Dr. Dao being forcibly removed from the plane went viral, drawing sharp criticism and turning the incident into a public relations disaster for United Airlines.[568]

---

566. Victor, D. (2017, April 10). Man Dragged Off Overbooked United Flight. *The New York Times*. Retrieved from https://www.nytimes.com/2017/04/10/business/united-flight-passenger-dragged.html

567. Victor, D. (2017, April 10). Man Dragged Off Overbooked United Flight. *The New York Times*. Retrieved from https://www.nytimes.com/2017/04/10/business/united-flight-passenger-dragged.html

568. *Ibid.*

United's handling of the crisis further worsened the situation. Its initial statement was widely criticized as tone-deaf and lacking empathy. CEO Oscar Munoz described the event as "an upsetting event" and apologized for the need to "re-accommodate" passengers, a phrase that faced backlash for minimizing the severity of the situation.[569]

Increased Difficulties in Airline Customer Support

The incident involving Dr. Dao was not an isolated event but rather a symptom of broader issues with customer service in the airline industry. Airlines have long been criticized for their treatment of passengers, with complaints ranging from overbooking and poor communication to long wait times and inadequate compensation for disrupted travel. The United Airlines incident brought these issues to the forefront and highlighted the need for reform in the industry.

Overbooking and the Treatment of Passengers

The United Airlines incident cast a harsh spotlight on the contentious practice of overbooking, where airlines sell more tickets than seats available, anticipating no-shows. While this method increases revenue and reduces the number of empty seats, it can lead to passengers being involuntarily removed from flights, as exemplified by Dr. Dao's case.[570]

Despite being legal and regulated by the U.S. Department of Transportation, which requires airlines to compensate passengers removed from flights, overbooking remains highly unpopular. Many travelers perceive it as prioritizing profits over their rights.[571] This incident emphasized the urgent need for airlines to address

569. Victor, D., & Stevenson, A. (2017, April 11). United Grapples with PR Crisis Over Videos of Man Dragged Off Plane. *The New York Times*. Retrieved from https://www.nytimes.com/2017/04/11/business/united-flight-passenger-dragged.html

570. Garrow, L. A. (2012). *Airline Operations Research*. CRC Press.

571. *Ibid.*

overbooking with greater transparency and ensure passengers are treated with dignity.

In the airline industry, where cost-cutting and operational efficiency frequently take precedence over customer service, the incident's wider ramifications highlight a structural problem. Passengers frequently find their needs and rights secondary to corporate financial goals, fostering dissatisfaction and a sense of disregard.[572]

Culture of Customer Service in the Airline Industry

The airline industry has long struggled with a culture of poor customer service, leaving many passengers frustrated by inadequate communication, unhelpful staff, and a lack of empathy.[573] These issues are particularly problematic given the inherently stressful nature of air travel, where clear and timely updates about delays, cancellations, and disruptions are essential.

A significant driver of declining service quality is the commoditization of air travel. In an effort to compete on price, airlines have eliminated many previously standard amenities, such as free checked baggage, in-flight meals, and seat selection. This cost-cutting has resulted in a "race to the bottom," where revenue takes precedence over the passenger experience.[574]

Industry consolidation has further compounded the problem. With fewer competitors in the market, airlines hold more power over passengers, who are often left with limited alternatives when faced with poor treatment.[575] This reduced competition fosters

572. Ohlheiser, A. (2017, April 11). United Airlines Faces Growing Backlash Over Doctor's Forcible Removal From Flight. *The Washington Post*. Retrieved from https://www.washingtonpost.com/news/the-switch/wp/2017/04/11/united-faces-growing-backlash-over-doctors-forcible-removal-from-flight/

573. Victor, D., & Stevenson, A. (2017, April 11). United Grapples with PR Crisis Over Videos of Man Dragged Off Plane. *The New York Times*. Retrieved from https://www.nytimes.com/2017/04/11/business/united-flight-passenger-dragged.html

574. Garrow, L. A. (2012). *Airline Operations Research*. CRC Press.

575. Bilotkach, V. (2015). Airline Consolidation and Market Conduct: The Recent Evolution of the US Domestic Airline Industry. *Journal of Air Transport Management*, 47, 23-31.

complacency, as airlines face less pressure to prioritize customer service when there's little threat of losing passengers to a rival.

Cost-Cutting Measures and Their Consequences

Cost-cutting measures in the airline industry have also contributed to the erosion of customer service. In an effort to reduce expenses and increase profitability, airlines have implemented a range of cost-cutting strategies, including reducing staff, outsourcing customer service functions, and cutting back on training for employees. While these measures can improve the airline's bottom line, they often lead to a decline in service quality and a negative impact on the passenger experience.[576]

For example, reducing the number of customer service agents at airports can lead to longer wait times for passengers seeking assistance with check-in, baggage, or rebooking flights. Outsourcing customer service functions to third-party providers, often located in different countries, can result in language barriers, miscommunication, and a lack of understanding of the airline's policies and procedures. Additionally, cutting back on employee training can lead to staff who are ill-prepared to handle difficult situations, such as overbooking or flight disruptions, in a way that is empathetic and customer-focused.[577]

The impact of these cost-cutting measures on customer service was evident in the United Airlines incident. The decision to forcibly remove Dr. Dao from the flight, rather than finding a more humane solution, was likely influenced by a culture of cost-cutting and efficiency that prioritized the airline's operational needs over the well-being of its passengers. This approach ultimately backfired,

---

576. Bilotkach, V. (2015). Airline Consolidation and Market Conduct: The Recent Evolution of the US Domestic Airline Industry. *Journal of Air Transport Management*, 47, 23-31.

577. Garrow, L. A. (2012). *Airline Operations Research*. CRC Press.

as the negative publicity and financial repercussions of the incident far outweighed any short-term savings.[578]

The Need for Regulatory and Industry-Wide Reforms

The United Airlines incident highlighted the need for regulatory and industry-wide reforms to protect passengers' rights and improve customer service in the airline industry. In the wake of the incident, there were calls for changes to the rules governing overbooking, as well as for increased transparency and accountability from airlines.

One of the key areas for reform is the practice of overbooking. While overbooking is a legal and common practice, there is a need for clearer guidelines on how airlines should handle situations where there are more passengers than available seats. This includes ensuring that passengers are fully informed of their rights and options when they are asked to give up their seats and that airlines offer adequate compensation for their inconvenience.[579]

There is also a need for greater transparency in the airline industry's customer service practices. Airlines should be required to provide clear and accurate information to passengers about their rights, as well as about any fees or charges associated with changes to their travel plans.[580] Additionally, airlines should be held accountable for their treatment of passengers, with stronger penalties for instances of mistreatment or poor service.

Finally, there is a need for a cultural shift within the airline industry, where customer service is prioritized and where passengers are treated with the respect and dignity they deserve. This requires a commitment from airlines to invest in their employees, provide

---

578. Ohlheiser, A. (2017, April 11). United Airlines Faces Growing Backlash Over Doctor's Forcible Removal From Flight. *The Washington Post*. Retrieved from https://www.washingtonpost.com/news/the-switch/wp/2017/04/11/united-faces-growing-backlash-over-doctors-forcible-removal-from-flight/

579. Garrow, L. A. (2012). *Airline Operations Research*. CRC Press.

580. Bilotkach, V. (2015). Airline Consolidation and Market Conduct: The Recent Evolution of the US Domestic Airline Industry. *Journal of Air Transport Management*, 47, 23-31.

adequate training, and foster a customer-centric culture that values the passenger experience over short-term financial gains.[581]

Long-Term Impacts on United Airlines and the Airline Industry

The United Airlines passenger removal incident had far-reaching consequences for the airline and the broader industry, emphasizing the urgent need for reform in passenger treatment and airline operations. It became a turning point, prompting both airlines and regulators to reconsider policies that prioritize efficiency and profit over passenger dignity.

The shocking images of Dr. Dao's forcible removal became a global symbol of corporate negligence and passenger mistreatment. The widespread outrage eroded customer trust, leading to a measurable decline in satisfaction and loyalty.[582] The incident cemented United's association with disregard for passenger welfare, tarnishing its brand image.

In response, United Airlines took steps to mitigate the fallout and address public criticism. The company introduced policy changes, such as increasing compensation for passengers denied boarding, reducing reliance on overbooking, and enhancing employee training to better manage difficult situations.[583] These efforts were part of a broader strategy to improve customer service and rebuild its tarnished reputation.

Despite these initiatives, the long-term stain on United's reputation has proven difficult to remove. The incident remains a cautionary example of the risks inherent in neglecting customer experience and trust. For the industry as a whole, the episode underscores

---

581. Victor, D., & Stevenson, A. (2017, April 11). United Grapples with PR Crisis Over Videos of Man Dragged Off Plane. *The New York Times*. Retrieved from https://www.nytimes.com/2017/04/11/business/united-flight-passenger-dragged.html

582. *Ibid.*

583. Ohlheiser, A. (2017, April 11). United Airlines Faces Growing Backlash Over Doctor's Forcible Removal From Flight. *The Washington Post*. Retrieved from https://www.washingtonpost.com/news/the-switch/wp/2017/04/11/united-faces-growing-backlash-over-doctors-forcible-removal-from-flight/

the importance of rethinking operational practices to ensure passengers feel respected and valued.[584]

Lessons for the Airline Industry

The United Airlines passenger dragging incident had far-reaching consequences, not only for the airline itself but also for the entire industry. It ignited a nationwide conversation about passenger treatment and prompted increased scrutiny of airline policies and practices by regulators, lawmakers, and the public.[585] The public backlash underscored the urgency of addressing systemic issues in the industry and catalyzed changes aimed at improving the passenger experience.

In response to the incident, airlines began revisiting and revising their policies. Measures such as reducing overbooking, increasing compensation for bumped passengers, and enhancing customer service training for employees became more prevalent across the industry. Legislative proposals also emerged, advocating for stronger passenger rights and greater accountability from airlines. While these steps mark progress, the incident served as a stark reminder that reactive changes are not enough; a proactive shift toward prioritizing passenger experience and trust is essential.[586]

This incident underscored the necessity for the airline industry to prioritize transparency, fairness, and respect in its dealings with passengers. For long-term success, airlines must focus on building trust by creating policies that are customer-centric and ensuring consistent, positive interactions. This includes investing in employee training, revisiting practices like overbooking, and fostering a corporate culture that values customer relationships.[587]

---

584. Victor, D., & Stevenson, A. (2017, April 11). United Grapples with PR Crisis Over Videos of Man Dragged Off Plane. *The New York Times*. Retrieved from https://www.nytimes.com/2017/04/11/business/united-flight-passenger-dragged.html

585. Garrow, L. A. (2012). *Airline Operations Research*. CRC Press.

586. Bilotkach, V. (2015). Airline Consolidation and Market Conduct: The Recent Evolution of the US Domestic Airline Industry. *Journal of Air Transport Management*, 47, 23-31.

587. Bilotkach, V. (2015). Airline Consolidation and Market Conduct: The Recent Evolution of the US Domestic Airline Industry. *Journal of Air Transport Management*, 47, 23-31.

The lessons from the United Airlines incident extend beyond the airline sector, offering a cautionary tale for businesses across industries. Prioritizing short-term gains over customer trust can have disastrous consequences for reputation, market position, and long-term profitability. Transparency, accountability, and ethical practices are essential to maintaining customer loyalty and confidence. Companies that fail to adapt risk facing similar public backlash, reputational harm, and financial losses.

Ultimately, the United Airlines passenger dragging incident serves as a pivotal moment in the ongoing evolution of the airline industry. It demonstrated that customer trust and dignity are non-negotiable, reinforcing the critical need for reform, proactive engagement, and a renewed commitment to providing respectful and reliable service. By embedding these principles into their operations, airlines and businesses alike can build stronger relationships with their customers and achieve sustainable success in an increasingly competitive market.

The Impact of Cost-Cutting on Customer Experience

Cost-cutting measures that negatively impact the customer experience can have long-lasting effects on trust and loyalty. For example, a company that reduces its workforce to save money may find that its remaining employees are overworked and unable to provide the level of service that customers expect.[588] Similarly, companies that cut corners on product development, quality control, or after-sales support may deliver products that fail to meet customer expectations.

When customers feel that a company is more focused on reducing costs than on providing quality products or services, they may become disillusioned and lose trust in the brand.[589] This erosion of trust can lead to a decline in customer loyalty, as dissatisfied customers seek out competitors who prioritize their needs and offer better value.

---

588. Fornell, C., & Wernerfelt, B. (1987). Defensive Marketing Strategy by Customer Complaint Management: A Theoretical Analysis. *Journal of Marketing Research*, 24(4), 337-346.

589. Zeithaml, V. A., Bitner, M. J., & Gremler, D. D. (2018). Services Marketing: Integrating Customer Focus Across the Firm. McGraw-Hill Education.

The Long-Term Consequences of Eroding Customer Trust

The erosion of customer trust due to misleading practices and poor service can have significant long-term consequences for businesses. These consequences include a decline in customer loyalty, negative word-of-mouth, legal and regulatory challenges, and damage to the company's reputation and brand.

Decline in Customer Loyalty and Repeat Business

When customer trust is eroded, loyalty and repeat business often decline. Customers who feel betrayed or dissatisfied are unlikely to continue doing business with a company, and they may seek out alternatives that offer better service or more transparent practices.[590] This decline in loyalty can have a direct impact on a company's revenue, as it becomes more difficult and costly to retain existing customers and attract new ones.

The loss of repeat business is particularly damaging in industries where customer lifetime value is high, such as financial services, telecommunications, and technology.[591] Companies that rely on long-term customer relationships to drive revenue may find themselves struggling to maintain growth if they fail to address the underlying issues that are eroding trust and loyalty.

Negative Word-of-Mouth and Reputation Damage

Negative word-of-mouth is another significant consequence of eroding customer trust. Dissatisfied customers are more likely to share their negative experiences with others, both in person and online.[592] In today's digital age, negative reviews and social media posts can quickly spread, amplifying the impact of poor service or misleading practices and damaging a company's reputation.

---

590. Reichheld, F. F., & Schefter, P. (2000). E-Loyalty: Your Secret Weapon on the Web. *Harvard Business Review*, 78(4), 105-113.

591. Fornell, C., & Wernerfelt, B. (1987). Defensive Marketing Strategy by Customer Complaint Management: A Theoretical Analysis. *Journal of Marketing Research*, 24(4), 337-346.

592. Fournier, S., & Avery, J. (2011). The Uninvited Brand. *Business Horizons*, 54(3), 193-207.

Reputation damage can have far-reaching effects on a company's ability to attract and retain customers. A tarnished reputation can lead to a decline in brand equity, reduced market share, and increased customer acquisition costs. Companies with a poor reputation may also find it more difficult to compete for talent, as prospective employees may be wary of working for a company with a history of unethical practices or poor customer service.[593]

Legal and Regulatory Challenges

Misleading practices and unethical behavior can also lead to legal and regulatory challenges. Companies that engage in deceptive advertising, hidden fees, or other unethical practices may face lawsuits from customers, regulatory fines, and other penalties.[594] These legal challenges can be costly and time-consuming, and they can further damage a company's reputation and financial standing.

There are also legal challenges; companies may face increased scrutiny from regulators, particularly in industries where consumer protection is a priority. Regulatory bodies may impose stricter oversight, require changes to business practices, or introduce new regulations to protect consumers from misleading practices.[595] These changes can increase operational costs and create additional challenges for companies that have already damaged their reputation and eroded customer trust.

Difficulty of Rebuilding Trust

Rebuilding customer trust, once eroded, is an uphill battle that requires sustained effort and resources. Trust, painstakingly built over time through consistent and positive interactions, is fragile and difficult to restore once broken. Companies that have lost customer confidence due to misleading practices or subpar service must demonstrate a clear commitment to change by improving service quality, addressing grievances effectively,

---

593. Fornell, C., & Wernerfelt, B. (1987). Defensive Marketing Strategy by Customer Complaint Management: A Theoretical Analysis. *Journal of Marketing Research*, 24(4), 337-346.

594. *Ibid.*

595. Morgan, R. M., & Hunt, S. D. (1994). The Commitment-Trust Theory of Relationship Marketing. *Journal of Marketing*, 58(3), 20-38.

and upholding ethical standards. Even with these efforts, some customers may never return, leaving a lasting scar on the company's reputation.[596]

The consequences of prioritizing short-term profits over long-term customer relationships are profound. Misleading practices, poor service, and a disregard for transparency can lead to customer churn, negative word-of-mouth, regulatory scrutiny, and reputational damage that takes years to repair.[597] The costs of these actions often outweigh the temporary gains, leaving companies at a competitive disadvantage in the long run.

To thrive in today's market, businesses must prioritize trust and loyalty, placing customers at the center of their operations. This means committing to quality, transparency, and ethical conduct at every level of the organization. By doing so, companies not only safeguard their reputation but also create the foundation for lasting growth, competitive strength, and meaningful customer relationships.

---

596. Morgan, R. M., & Hunt, S. D. (1994). The Commitment-Trust Theory of Relationship Marketing. *Journal of Marketing*, 58(3), 20-38.

597. Reichheld, F. F., & Schefter, P. (2000). E-Loyalty: Your Secret Weapon on the Web. *Harvard Business Review*, 78(4), 105-113.

KEY TAKEAWAYS

- **Trust is the Cornerstone of Long-Term Business Success**
  Customer trust and loyalty are fundamental to sustaining long-term revenue and maintaining a competitive advantage. Once trust is broken, rebuilding it is extremely difficult and costly. Companies that prioritize transparency and ethical conduct foster stronger relationships with their customers, which helps them weather economic downturns and market disruptions.

- **Misleading Practices Lead to Irreparable Reputation Damage**
  Deceptive advertising, hidden fees, false promises, and unethical sales tactics may generate short-term profits but can severely damage a company's reputation. Customers who feel misled are likely to leave, share their negative experiences, and deter potential customers, ultimately leading to a decline in brand credibility and profitability. The Volkswagen emissions scandal serves as a cautionary tale of how corporate deception can result in financial and legal consequences.

- **Poor Customer Service Accelerates the Loss of Trust and Loyalty**
  Cutting costs in customer service, such as reducing support staff, outsourcing, or failing to properly train employees, leads to frustration, negative word-of-mouth, and customer churn. The United Airlines passenger removal incident demonstrated how inadequate customer support and disregard for passenger rights can escalate into a full-blown crisis that severely damages public perception.

- **Cost-Cutting Measures That Undermine Quality Can Backfire**
  Businesses that prioritize cost reductions over product quality, service reliability, and customer experience often face long-term consequences. Short-term savings achieved by cutting corners can result in lost customer confidence, decreased market share, and increased regulatory scrutiny. Sustainable success requires balancing operational efficiency with a commitment to quality and customer satisfaction.

Rebuilding Customer Trust Requires Proactive and Ethical Reforms Once trust is eroded, companies must invest significant time and resources to restore credibility. This includes implementing transparent policies, improving service standards, addressing past grievances, and demonstrating a clear commitment to ethical business practices. While some customers may never return, a proactive approach can help mitigate reputational damage and rebuild long-term customer relationships.

Chapter 10

The Shareholder Value Paradigm

The concept of shareholder value, which posits that a company's primary responsibility is to maximize returns for its shareholders, has dominated corporate governance and business strategy for the past several decades. This paradigm, popularized in the 1980s, has profoundly shaped the priorities and operations of companies worldwide. While it has led to substantial wealth creation for shareholders, the obsession with maximizing shareholder returns has often come at the expense of other key stakeholders, particularly employees and customers.

How the Shareholder Value Paradigm Began and How It Spread

The shareholder value paradigm took shape in the 1970s and 1980s, fueled by shifts in corporate governance, economic theory, and the expanding influence of financial markets. Milton Friedman, a prominent economist, argued in a 1970 *New York Times* article that the primary social responsibility of business is to increase its profits. He maintained that businesses exist to serve their shareholders and are obligated to maximize returns within legal boundaries, an idea that soon became the foundation of the shareholder value paradigm.[598] This perspective

598. Friedman, M. (1970, September 13). The Social Responsibility of Business Is to Increase Its Profits. *The New York Times Magazine*. Retrieved from https://www.nytimes.com/1970/09/13/archives/a-friedman-doctrine-the-social-responsibility-of-business-is-to.html

quickly rose to prominence in corporate governance and reshaped how businesses prioritized their objectives.

By the 1980s, this paradigm gained momentum as corporate raiders and activist investors used leveraged buyouts and hostile takeovers to compel companies to focus on short-term profits and shareholder returns.[599] These investors contended that many businesses were underperforming and that prioritizing shareholder value could unlock higher financial gains. Executive compensation increasingly tied CEO pay to stock performance during this period, further incentivizing corporate leaders to prioritize immediate profits over long-term stability, a shift that had profound implications for corporate strategy.

Institutional investors, such as pension funds and mutual funds, also played a pivotal role in solidifying the shareholder value model. Collectively holding substantial stakes in public companies, they advocated for strategies that maximized their returns.[600] This often sidelined the interests of other stakeholders and shifted businesses' focus toward financial metrics like earnings per share and return on equity, while broader measures of success, such as employee well-being, customer satisfaction, and social impact, were deprioritized.

Impact on Corporate Behavior

The shareholder value paradigm has had profound effects on corporate behavior, influencing everything from strategic decision-making to day-to-day operations. While it has driven companies to become more efficient and profitable, it has also led to practices that prioritize short-term gains over long-term sustainability and that de-prioritize the needs of employees and customers.

Cost-Cutting and Workforce Reductions

One of the most significant impacts of the shareholder value paradigm has been the emphasis on cost-cutting and workforce reductions as

599. Lazonick, W., & O'Sullivan, M. (2000). Maximizing Shareholder Value: A New Ideology for Corporate Governance. *Economy and Society*, 29(1), 13-35.

600. Useem, M. (1996). *Investor Capitalism: How Money Managers Are Changing the Face of Corporate America*. Basic Books.

a means of boosting profitability. In the pursuit of higher returns for shareholders, many companies have sought to reduce labor costs by outsourcing jobs, automating processes, and cutting employee benefits.[601] These practices have often resulted in job insecurity, wage stagnation, and reduced employee morale, particularly in industries that have been heavily affected by globalization and technological change.

For example, during the 1990s and 2000s, many large corporations in the United States and Europe engaged in widespread downsizing and restructuring, often laying off thousands of workers in an effort to improve their financial performance.[602] These layoffs were frequently justified as necessary to increase efficiency and competitiveness, but they also had the effect of boosting short-term profits and stock prices, which benefited shareholders and executives but came at a significant cost to employees.

The focus on cost-cutting has also led to a decline in investment in employee development and training. As companies have sought to maximize returns, they have often reduced spending on programs that would enhance employee skills, foster innovation, and improve long-term productivity. This has contributed to a widening skills gap in many industries and has left workers less prepared to adapt to changes in the economy.[603]

---

601. Lazonick, W. (2014). Profits Without Prosperity: Stock Buybacks Manipulate the Market and Leave Most Americans Worse Off. *Harvard Business Review*, 92(9), 46-55.

602. Cappelli, P. (1999). *The New Deal at Work: Managing the Market-Driven Workforce*. Harvard Business Review Press.

603. Barton, D., Manyika, J., & Williamson, S. (2017). Finally, Evidence That Managing for the Long Term Pays Off. *Harvard Business Review*. Retrieved from https://hbr.org/2017/02/finally-proof-that-managing-for-the-long-term-pays-off

Profit-Driven Decisions Behind the Boeing 737 Max Crisis

Boeing, long celebrated for its engineering prowess and role as a leading aerospace manufacturer, found its reputation profoundly shaken by the 737 Max disaster. This crisis, involving the fatal crashes of Lion Air Flight 610 in October 2018 and Ethiopian Airlines Flight 302 in March 2019, claimed 346 lives and revealed troubling lapses in safety prioritization. At the heart of the disaster was a malfunction in the Maneuvering Characteristics Augmentation System (MCAS), a software feature intended to prevent stalls by automatically adjusting the plane's nose downward.

Investigations uncovered that Boeing's implementation of MCAS, coupled with its lack of transparency about the system's risks, stemmed from a relentless drive to maintain market dominance and satisfy shareholder demands. The decision to rush the 737 Max into production, minimize pilot retraining costs, and bypass rigorous oversight marked a stark example of profits taking precedence over passenger safety. The resulting human and reputational toll underscored the dangers of sacrificing long-term reliability for short-term gains.

Development of the 737 Max and the Role of MCAS

The 737 Max was developed as a response to increasing competition from Airbus, particularly the Airbus A320neo, which offered airlines improved fuel efficiency and lower operating costs. To compete, Boeing needed to produce a new version of its popular 737 model that could offer similar advantages without requiring airlines to undergo costly pilot retraining. The result was the 737 Max, which featured larger, more fuel-efficient engines and a range of other modifications.[604] However, the larger engines affected the aircraft's aerodynamics, particularly the tendency for the nose to pitch up during certain flight conditions, increasing the risk of a stall.

To address this issue, Boeing developed the MCAS software, which was designed to automatically adjust the plane's nose downward if it detected a potential stall. However, to avoid triggering a more expensive and time-consuming regulatory process, Boeing did not initially disclose the existence of MCAS to airlines or pilots, nor did it include detailed training on the system. Instead, the company downplayed the significance of MCAS, presenting it as a minor adjustment that did not require additional pilot training.[605]

The decision to minimize the importance of MCAS and to limit training on the system was driven by a desire to reduce costs and speed up the certification process for the 737 Max.[606] Boeing was under intense pressure to deliver the new aircraft quickly and to compete with Airbus, and the company's leadership prioritized these financial and competitive concerns over the potential safety risks posed by the new software.

Fatal Crashes and Their Devastating Consequences

The flaws in MCAS became tragically apparent with the crash of Lion Air Flight 610 in October 2018. The aircraft experienced repeated nose-down commands from the MCAS system, which the pilots were unable to counteract, leading to the plane crashing

604. Gelles, D. (2019, October 28). *The Roots of Boeing's 737 Max Crisis: A Regulator Relaxes Its Oversight.* The New York Times. Retrieved from https://www.nytimes.com/2019/10/27/business/boeing-737-max-faa.html

605. Kitroeff, N., & Gelles, D. (2019, June 1). *The Inside Story of MCAS: How Boeing's 737 Max System Got a Pass.* The New York Times. Retrieved from https://www.nytimes.com/2019/06/01/business/boeing-737-max-crash.html

606. Gelles, D. (2019, October 28). *The Roots of Boeing's 737 Max Crisis: A Regulator Relaxes Its Oversight.* The New York Times. Retrieved from https://www.nytimes.com/2019/10/27/business/boeing-737-max-faa.html

into the Java Sea shortly after takeoff.[607] Despite the crash, Boeing did not immediately ground the 737 Max or fully disclose the risks associated with MCAS. Instead, the company issued a bulletin reminding pilots of existing procedures for handling an erroneous activation of the system but did not acknowledge the system's inherent flaws.

Five months later, Ethiopian Airlines Flight 302 suffered a similar fate, with the MCAS system once again playing a central role in the crash. In the wake of the second crash, Boeing and aviation authorities worldwide faced intense scrutiny.[608] The 737 Max was eventually grounded globally, and investigations revealed a troubling pattern of cost-cutting, inadequate oversight, and a culture within Boeing that prioritized meeting production deadlines and financial targets over ensuring the safety of its aircraft.

Profit Over Safety in Shareholder Value Dilemma

The 737 Max disaster is a stark example of the dangers of the shareholder value paradigm, where the relentless pursuit of profit and shareholder returns can lead to the erosion of safety standards and ethical considerations. In the case of Boeing, the company's focus on maintaining its competitive edge and maximizing returns for shareholders played a significant role in the decisions that ultimately led to the 737 Max crashes.

Cost-Cutting and Production Pressures

One of the key factors that contributed to the 737 Max disaster was the cost-cutting measures implemented by Boeing in the years leading up to the aircraft's development. Under the leadership of CEO Dennis Muilenburg, Boeing increasingly focused on reducing

---

607. Kitroeff, N., & Gelles, D. (2019, June 1). *The Inside Story of MCAS: How Boeing's 737 Max System Got a Pass*. The New York Times. Retrieved from https://www.nytimes.com/2019/06/01/business/boeing-737-max-crash.html

608. Gelles, D. (2019, October 28). *The Roots of Boeing's 737 Max Crisis: A Regulator Relaxes Its Oversight*. The New York Times. Retrieved from https://www.nytimes.com/2019/10/27/business/boeing-737-max-faa.html

costs, improving efficiency, and maximizing profitability.[609] This shift was driven in part by pressure from shareholders and the need to maintain Boeing's stock price, which was a key metric of success under the shareholder value paradigm.

To achieve these goals, Boeing made a series of decisions prioritizing cost savings over safety. For example, the company outsourced significant portions of the 737 Max's development to lower-cost suppliers, which raised concerns about the quality and reliability of the components used in the aircraft. Boeing also pushed for a speedy certification process with little Federal Aviation Administration (FAA) oversight in an effort to reduce the regulatory obstacles related to the 737 Max. This was done by downplaying the importance of modifications to the aircraft, such as the installation of MCAS.[610]

The pressure to deliver the 737 Max quickly and to keep costs low also led to a culture of silence within Boeing, where employees were discouraged from raising safety concerns or questioning the company's decisions. Internal emails and documents released during investigations revealed that some engineers and employees had raised concerns about the safety of MCAS and other aspects of the 737 Max's design but were either ignored or pressured to remain silent.[611] This culture of prioritizing financial goals over safety contributed to the failure to identify and address the flaws in the aircraft before it was released to the market.

Executive Pay and Shareholder Demands

Executive compensation at Boeing was closely tied to the company's financial performance, with a significant portion of CEO and executive pay linked to stock price and shareholder

609. Pasztor, A. (2019, December 23). *Boeing's Downfall: How the 737 Max Grounding Flipped the Company's Leadership.* The Wall Street Journal. Retrieved from https://www.wsj.com/articles/boeing-737-max-crash-faa-dennis-muilenburg-11576978409

610. Lazonick, W. (2014). *Profits Without Prosperity: Stock Buybacks Manipulate the Market and Leave Most Americans Worse Off.* Harvard Business Review, 92(9), 46-55.

611. Gelles, D. (2019, October 28). *The Roots of Boeing's 737 Max Crisis: A Regulator Relaxes Its Oversight.* The New York Times. Retrieved from https://www.nytimes.com/2019/10/27/business/boeing-737-max-faa.html

returns. This created strong incentives for Boeing's leadership to focus on short-term financial gains, often at the expense of long-term safety and sustainability. The emphasis on boosting stock prices through cost-cutting, share buybacks, and other financial maneuvers reinforced the shareholder value paradigm and contributed to the decisions that ultimately led to the 737 Max disaster.[612]

In the years leading up to the crisis, Boeing engaged in aggressive share buybacks, spending billions of dollars to repurchase its own stock. While these buybacks helped to inflate the company's stock price and deliver returns to shareholders, they also diverted resources away from critical investments in research and development, employee training, and safety measures.[613] The focus on maximizing shareholder value through financial engineering left Boeing ill-prepared to address the challenges and risks associated with the 737 Max.

The shareholder value paradigm also influenced Boeing's interactions with regulators and customers. The company's leadership was determined to maintain its market position and to meet the expectations of shareholders, even if it meant cutting corners or compromising on safety. This approach was evident in Boeing's efforts to downplay the significance of MCAS and to minimize the training requirements for pilots, which were driven by a desire to reduce costs and expedite the aircraft's approval process.[614]

Crisis Fallout and Erosion of Trust

The fallout from the 737 Max disaster has been profound, both for Boeing and for the broader aerospace industry. The crisis has led to significant financial, legal, and reputational consequences for

612. Lazonick, W. (2014). *Profits Without Prosperity: Stock Buybacks Manipulate the Market and Leave Most Americans Worse Off.* Harvard Business Review, 92(9), 46-55.

613. *Ibid.*

614. Gelles, D. (2019, October 28). *The Roots of Boeing's 737 Max Crisis: A Regulator Relaxes Its Oversight.* The New York Times. Retrieved from https://www.nytimes.com/2019/10/27/business/boeing-737-max-faa.html

Boeing, as well as a loss of trust among regulators, customers, and the public.

Financial and Legal Consequences

The grounding of the 737 Max had a significant financial impact on Boeing, resulting in billions of dollars in lost revenue, compensation payments to airlines, and legal settlements. The company faced numerous lawsuits from the families of crash victims, as well as investigations by regulatory authorities in the United States and around the world.[615] Boeing's stock price plummeted in the wake of the crisis, and the company's reputation as a leader in aviation was severely damaged.

As well as the financial costs, Boeing faced intense scrutiny from regulators, lawmakers, and the media. The FAA's certification process for the 737 Max came under fire, with critics arguing that the agency had been too lenient in its oversight of Boeing and had allowed the company to effectively self-regulate.[616] The crisis also led to calls for reform in the aviation industry, with demands for greater transparency, accountability, and safety standards.

Boeing's leadership faced significant consequences as well. CEO Dennis Muilenburg was forced to resign in December 2019, and several other executives were also removed or reassigned.[617] The company's board of directors came under pressure to improve governance and oversight, and Boeing was forced to undertake a major restructuring of its operations and corporate culture to address the failures that led to the crisis.

---

615. Lazonick, W. (2014). *Profits Without Prosperity: Stock Buybacks Manipulate the Market and Leave Most Americans Worse Off.* Harvard Business Review, 92(9), 46-55.

616. Gelles, D. (2019, October 28). *The Roots of Boeing's 737 Max Crisis: A Regulator Relaxes Its Oversight.* The New York Times. Retrieved from https://www.nytimes.com/2019/10/27/business/boeing-737-max-faa.html

617. Lazonick, W. (2014). *Profits Without Prosperity: Stock Buybacks Manipulate the Market and Leave Most Americans Worse Off.* Harvard Business Review, 92(9), 46-55.

Eroding Trust and Damaged Reputation

The 737 Max disaster has had a lasting impact on Boeing's reputation and the trust that customers, regulators, and the public place in the company. The crisis revealed deep flaws in Boeing's safety culture and decision-making processes, and it exposed the extent to which the company had prioritized profit over safety.[618] As a result, many customers and stakeholders have lost confidence in Boeing's ability to deliver safe and reliable products.

The loss of trust has been particularly damaging for Boeing because of the critical role that trust plays in the aerospace industry. Airlines, passengers, and regulators must have confidence in the safety and reliability of aircraft, and any doubts about a manufacturer's commitment to safety can have serious consequences. The 737 Max disaster has led to a decline in orders for Boeing's aircraft, with some airlines canceling or delaying their purchases, and has raised questions about the company's long-term viability.[619]

The crisis has also had broader implications for the aerospace industry as a whole. The grounding of the 737 Max disrupted global air travel and created significant challenges for airlines that relied on the aircraft. The crisis has also led to increased scrutiny of other aircraft manufacturers and has prompted calls for stricter regulation and oversight of the industry. The 737 Max disaster has served as a cautionary tale for the entire aerospace sector, highlighting the dangers of prioritizing profit over safety and the importance of maintaining a strong safety culture.[620]

---

618. Gelles, D. (2019, October 28). *The Roots of Boeing's 737 Max Crisis: A Regulator Relaxes Its Oversight.* The New York Times. Retrieved from https://www.nytimes.com/2019/10/27/business/boeing-737-max-faa.html

619. Gelles, D. (2019, October 28). *The Roots of Boeing's 737 Max Crisis: A Regulator Relaxes Its Oversight.* The New York Times. Retrieved from https://www.nytimes.com/2019/10/27/business/boeing-737-max-faa.html

620. Lazonick, W. (2014). *Profits Without Prosperity: Stock Buybacks Manipulate the Market and Leave Most Americans Worse Off.* Harvard Business Review, 92(9), 46-55.

Efforts to Rebuild Trust and Reform the Company

In the wake of the crisis, Boeing has made significant efforts to rebuild trust and reform its operations. The company has implemented a range of changes to its corporate governance, safety procedures, and culture in an effort to address the failures that led to the 737 Max disaster.[621] These changes include restructuring the safety and engineering teams, improving oversight and accountability, and enhancing transparency with regulators and customers.

Boeing has also made a concerted effort to communicate its commitment to safety and to demonstrate that it has learned from the crisis. The company has publicly acknowledged its mistakes and has taken steps to address the issues with the 737 Max, including redesigning the MCAS system and providing additional training for pilots.[622] Boeing has also worked closely with regulators to ensure that the 737 Max meets the highest safety standards before it is allowed to return to service.

Rebuilding trust after the 737 Max disaster is an uphill battle. Boeing's reputation, once synonymous with innovation and safety, has been irreparably damaged. The company's name is now linked to the preventable loss of 346 lives, a tragedy born from a culture that prioritized profit over people. This isn't a crisis that can be resolved with policy changes or carefully crafted statements; it requires a complete cultural overhaul and sustained effort to prove that safety and ethics are truly at the core of its operations.

The 737 Max disaster is a stark lesson in the dangers of putting shareholder value above all else. Cost-cutting measures and rushed decisions aimed at boosting short-term profits led to a crisis that tarnished Boeing's legacy and sent shockwaves through the aerospace industry. The fallout wasn't just financial, it exposed

---

621. *Ibid.*

622. Gelles, D. (2019, October 28). *The Roots of Boeing's 737 Max Crisis: A Regulator Relaxes Its Oversight.* The New York Times. Retrieved from https://www.nytimes.com/2019/10/27/business/boeing-737-max-faa.html

fundamental flaws in the company's priorities, governance, and commitment to its customers.

This case should serve as a wake-up call not only for Boeing but for all industries that rely on public trust. Pursuing short-term gains at the expense of safety, ethics, and accountability is a recipe for disaster. Companies must recognize that trust, once lost, is nearly impossible to regain. The path forward demands a balance between financial performance and a genuine commitment to the people and communities they serve. If Boeing, or any company, hopes to recover, it must demonstrate that lessons have been learned and that human lives will never again be overshadowed by the pursuit of profit.

Short-Termism and the Neglect of Long-Term Strategy

The shareholder value paradigm has also fostered a culture of short-termism, where companies prioritize immediate financial results over long-term strategic planning. This focus on short-term gains has led many companies to engage in practices that may boost earnings in the near term but undermine long-term sustainability and growth.

One of the most common manifestations of short-termism is the practice of share buybacks, where companies use their profits to repurchase their own shares rather than reinvest in their business. Share buybacks can temporarily boost stock prices and improve financial metrics, but they do little to enhance the company's long-term value or competitiveness. In fact, excessive buybacks can drain resources that could otherwise be used for research and development, capital investment, or employee compensation.[623]

Some businesses have also taken shortcuts that jeopardize ethical standards, customer service, and product quality as a result of their focus on immediate financial gain. For example, the Volkswagen emissions scandal, in which the company used illegal software to cheat on emissions tests, was driven by a desire to protect market share and profitability in

623. Lazonick, W. (2014). Profits Without Prosperity: Stock Buybacks Manipulate the Market and Leave Most Americans Worse Off. *Harvard Business Review*, 92(9), 46-55.

the short term, even at the expense of environmental regulations and customer trust.

Similarly, Wells Fargo's fraudulent account scandal, where employees opened millions of unauthorized accounts to meet aggressive sales targets, was rooted in a corporate culture that prioritized short-term financial performance over ethical behavior and customer satisfaction.[624]

The Marginalization of Customers

In order to maximize shareholder returns, the shareholder value paradigm has progressively neglected the interests of customers. Companies focused on profitability often implement practices that prioritize short-term gains over customer satisfaction and loyalty. This is particularly evident in industries with limited competition, where firms rely on market dominance to sustain profits, even as customer dissatisfaction grows.

A prominent example is the telecommunications industry, which has faced widespread criticism for deceptive billing, subpar customer service, and aggressive sales tactics aimed at boosting revenue. Such strategies frequently alienate customers rather than foster loyalty. Similarly, in the airline industry, cost-cutting measures have degraded service quality, leaving passengers to contend with overcrowded flights, hidden fees, and a lack of transparency. The infamous 2017 United Airlines incident, where a passenger was forcibly removed from an overbooked flight, underscored how corporate priorities can eclipse customer needs.[625]

By focusing on short-term revenue generation rather than cultivating lasting customer relationships, many companies have experienced an erosion of trust and loyalty.[626] Customers increasingly perceive businesses as prioritizing profits over their needs, undermining the goodwill and long-term relationships essential to sustained success.

---

624. Corkery, M., & Cowley, S. (2016, October 12). Wells Fargo Struggling in Aftermath of Fraud Scandal. *The New York Times*. Retrieved from https://www.nytimes.com/2016/10/13/business/dealbook/wells-fargo-scandal.html

625. Victor, D., & Stevenson, A. (2017, April 11). United Grapples with PR Crisis Over Videos of Man Dragged Off Plane. *The New York Times*. Retrieved from https://www.nytimes.com/2017/04/11/business/united-flight-passenger-dragged.html

626. Fournier, S., & Avery, J. (2011). The Uninvited Brand. *Business Horizons*, 54(3), 193-207.

Societal Impact of Shareholder-Centric Practices

The shareholder value paradigm has not only affected corporate behavior but has also had broader consequences for society. By de-prioritizing employees and customers, companies have contributed to growing economic inequality, a decline in social cohesion, and a loss of trust in business and government institutions.

Economic Inequality and Job Insecurity

One of the most significant societal impacts of the shareholder value paradigm has been the increase in economic inequality. As companies have focused on maximizing shareholder returns, they have often done so at the expense of workers, leading to wage stagnation, job insecurity, and a decline in labor's share of national income.

In many industries, the emphasis on cost-cutting and outsourcing has resulted in the loss of well-paying jobs, particularly in manufacturing and other blue-collar sectors. At the same time, the rise of the gig economy and the use of temporary or contract labor have further eroded job security and benefits for many workers. While these practices have helped companies reduce labor costs and increase profits, they have also contributed to a widening gap between the rich and poor, as the benefits of economic growth have increasingly accrued to shareholders and executives rather than to the broader workforce.[627]

The focus on shareholder value has also contributed to the decline of unions and collective bargaining, as companies have sought to weaken labor's bargaining power in order to reduce costs and increase flexibility. This has further exacerbated economic inequality, as workers have less leverage to negotiate for higher wages, better benefits, or improved working conditions.[628]

---

627. Autor, D. H. (2014). Skills, Education, and the Rise of Earnings Inequality Among the "Other 99 Percent". *Science*, 344(6186), 843-851.

628. Western, B., & Rosenfeld, J. (2011). Unions, Norms, and the Rise in American Wage Inequality. *American Sociological Review*, 76(4), 513-537.

Purdue Pharma's Betrayal of Public Trust

Purdue Pharma, a pharmaceutical company owned by the Sackler family, has been at the center of one of the most devastating public health crises in modern history, the opioid epidemic. The company's aggressive marketing of OxyContin, a powerful prescription painkiller, played a significant role in fueling the widespread abuse of opioids in the United States. Purdue Pharma's actions not only led to a dramatic increase in addiction and overdose deaths but also severely eroded public trust in the pharmaceutical industry and the healthcare system.

Purdue Pharma's Role in the Opioid Epidemic

The opioid crisis in the United States has its roots in the 1990s, when pharmaceutical companies began promoting prescription opioids for pain management. Among these companies, Purdue Pharma was particularly influential due to its development and marketing of OxyContin, a time-release formulation of oxycodone. OxyContin was introduced to the market in 1996, and its success was driven by Purdue's aggressive marketing strategies, which included misleading claims about the drug's safety and efficacy.

OxyContin's Development and Aggressive Marketing

OxyContin was developed as a long-acting opioid painkiller designed to provide extended relief for patients suffering from chronic pain. Purdue Pharma marketed the drug as a revolutionary solution for pain management, claiming that its time-release formulation made it less likely to be abused compared to other opioids. The company emphasized that OxyContin had a low risk of addiction, which was a key selling point for doctors who were increasingly concerned about the potential for opioid abuse.[629]

To promote OxyContin, Purdue Pharma launched an aggressive marketing campaign that targeted physicians, particularly those in primary care, who were not typically experienced in managing patients with chronic pain.[630] The company's sales representatives were trained to downplay the risks of addiction and to promote OxyContin as a safe and effective treatment for a wide range of pain conditions, including moderate pain that might not have previously warranted opioid treatment.

Purdue also invested heavily in educational programs, sponsored medical conferences, and provided free samples of OxyContin to doctors. The company's marketing efforts were highly successful, leading to a significant increase in the prescribing of OxyContin and other opioids. By 2001, OxyContin had become the most prescribed brand-name narcotic in the United States, generating billions of dollars in revenue for Purdue Pharma.[631]

Misleading Claims Fueling Opioid Abuse

Despite Purdue Pharma's claims that OxyContin had a low risk of addiction, evidence began to emerge that the drug was being widely abused. Patients who were prescribed OxyContin for legitimate medical reasons often became addicted, and the drug soon became popular among those seeking to misuse it. One of the factors that contributed to OxyContin's abuse was its time-release formulation, which could be easily circumvented by

---

629. Van Zee, A. (2009). *The Promotion and Marketing of OxyContin: Commercial Triumph, Public Health Tragedy.* American Journal of Public Health, 99(2), 221-227.

630. Meier, B. (2003). *Pain Killer: An Empire of Deceit and the Origin of America's Opioid Epidemic.* Rodale Books.

631. Van Zee, A. (2009). *The Promotion and Marketing of OxyContin: Commercial Triumph, Public Health Tragedy.* American Journal of Public Health, 99(2), 221-227.

crushing the pills to release the full dose of oxycodone at once.[632] This made the drug highly desirable for recreational use and led to a surge in opioid-related overdoses and deaths.

Purdue Pharma was aware of the growing problems with OxyContin abuse but continued to market the drug aggressively. Internal documents later revealed that the company had received reports of widespread abuse as early as the late 1990s but did little to address the issue. Instead, Purdue downplayed the risks and continued to promote OxyContin as a safe and effective treatment for pain.[633]

Devastating outcomes resulted from Purdue Pharma's false statements regarding the safety of OxyContin and its inaction in the face of mounting abuse evidence. By the early 2000s, opioid addiction had reached epidemic levels in the United States, with millions of people addicted to prescription opioids.[634] The widespread availability of OxyContin and other opioids contributed to a dramatic increase in overdose deaths, which have continued to rise in the years since.

Public Health Consequences of the Opioid Crisis

The opioid crisis has had a devastating impact on public health in the United States. Since the late 1990s, more than 500,000 people have died from opioid overdoses, with prescription opioids like OxyContin playing a significant role in the epidemic. The rise in opioid addiction has also led to increases in related health problems, including hepatitis C, HIV, and neonatal abstinence

---

632. Meier, B. (2003). *Pain Killer: An Empire of Deceit and the Origin of America's Opioid Epidemic.* Rodale Books.

633. Van Zee, A. (2009). *The Promotion and Marketing of OxyContin: Commercial Triumph, Public Health Tragedy.* American Journal of Public Health, 99(2), 221-227.

634. Kolodny, A., Courtwright, D. T., Hwang, C. S., Kreiner, P., Eadie, J. L., Clark, T. W., & Alexander, G. C. (2015). *The Prescription Opioid and Heroin Crisis: A Public Health Approach to an Epidemic of Addiction.* Annual Review of Public Health, 36, 559-574.

syndrome (NAS) in infants born to mothers who used opioids during pregnancy.[635]

With hospitals and emergency rooms overcrowded with patients experiencing opioid-related complications, the opioid crisis has also put a strain on the healthcare system. The cost of treating opioid addiction and its associated health problems has been estimated in billions of dollars, placing a significant burden on public health resources.[636]

In addition to the health effects, the opioid crisis has had significant social and financial repercussions. Communities across the United States have been devastated by the epidemic, with many areas experiencing increased crime, unemployment, and family breakdowns as a result of widespread addiction.[637] The opioid crisis has also contributed to a decline in life expectancy in the United States, reversing decades of progress in public health.

The Role of Purdue Pharma in the Crisis

Purdue Pharma's role in the opioid crisis has been the subject of intense scrutiny and legal action. The company's aggressive marketing of OxyContin, coupled with its misleading claims about the drug's safety, has been widely blamed for fueling the epidemic. Purdue's actions have been described as a textbook example of corporate irresponsibility, with the company prioritizing profits over public health.[638]

---

635. Scholl, L., Seth, P., Kariisa, M., Wilson, N., & Baldwin, G. (2019). *Drug and Opioid-Involved Overdose Deaths, United States, 2013, 2017.* Morbidity and Mortality Weekly Report, 67(51-52), 1419-1427.

636. Florence, C. S., Zhou, C., Luo, F., & Xu, L. (2016). *The Economic Burden of Prescription Opioid Overdose, Abuse, and Dependence in the United States, 2013.* Medical Care, 54(10), 901-906.

637. Case, A., & Deaton, A. (2017). *Mortality and Morbidity in the 21st Century.* Brookings Papers on Economic Activity, 2017(1), 397-476.

638. Van Zee, A. (2009). *The Promotion and Marketing of OxyContin: Commercial Triumph, Public Health Tragedy.* American Journal of Public Health, 99(2), 221-227.

Accountability and Legal Repercussions for Purdue Pharma

In 2007, Purdue Pharma and three of its top executives pleaded guilty to federal charges of misbranding OxyContin and agreed to pay over $600 million in fines.[639] The company admitted that it had misled doctors and patients about the risks of addiction associated with OxyContin and had downplayed the potential for abuse. Despite this settlement, Purdue continued to face legal challenges, with thousands of lawsuits filed by states, municipalities, and individuals seeking to hold the company accountable for its role in the opioid crisis.

The legal battles culminated in a landmark settlement in 2020, in which Purdue Pharma agreed to plead guilty to three federal criminal charges, including conspiracy to defraud the United States and violating anti-kickback laws. As part of the settlement, Purdue agreed to pay $8.3 billion in fines, forfeitures, and civil liabilities, and the Sackler family agreed to pay $225 million in civil penalties.[640] The settlement also required Purdue to dissolve and reorganize as a public benefit company, with its future profits used to address the opioid crisis.

Despite the settlement, many critics argue that the penalties imposed on Purdue Pharma and the Sackler family were insufficient given the scale of the harm caused by the opioid crisis. The Sacklers, who amassed billions of dollars in profits from the sale of OxyContin, have faced widespread criticism for their role in the epidemic, with many calling for more severe legal and financial consequences.[641]

---

639. Meier, B. (2003). *Pain Killer: An Empire of Deceit and the Origin of America's Opioid Epidemic.* Rodale Books.

640. Lovelace, B. (2020, October 21). Purdue Pharma to Plead Guilty to Three Criminal Charges Over OxyContin Sales. CNBC. Retrieved from https://www.cnbc.com/2020/10/21/purdue-pharma-to-plead-guilty-to-three-criminal-charges-over-oxycontin-sales.html

641. Lovelace, B. (2020, October 21). Purdue Pharma to Plead Guilty to Three Criminal Charges Over OxyContin Sales. CNBC. Retrieved from https://www.cnbc.com/2020/10/21/purdue-pharma-to-plead-guilty-to-three-criminal-charges-over-oxycontin-sales.html

Public Trust Eroded and Purdue Pharma's Controversial Legacy

Public confidence in the pharmaceutical sector and the healthcare system has been significantly impacted by the opioid crisis and Purdue Pharma's role in escalating the epidemic. The company's actions have been widely condemned as a betrayal of the trust that patients and healthcare providers place in pharmaceutical companies, and the legacy of Purdue Pharma is one of corporate greed and disregard for public health.

Collapse of Trust in the Pharmaceutical Industry

Purdue Pharma's aggressive marketing of OxyContin, coupled with its misleading claims about the drug's safety, has contributed to a perception that pharmaceutical companies prioritize profits over patient well-being. This perception has been reinforced by the actions of other pharmaceutical companies that have engaged in similar practices, including the promotion of other opioids and the aggressive marketing of prescription drugs more broadly.[642]

The loss of trust in the pharmaceutical industry has had serious implications for public health. Patients and healthcare providers are now more skeptical of new medications and more wary of the claims made by pharmaceutical companies. This skepticism can lead to delays in the adoption of new treatments and a reluctance to prescribe medications that may be beneficial but are perceived as risky.[643] The erosion of trust has also fueled a broader backlash against the pharmaceutical industry, with calls for greater regulation, transparency, and accountability.

Agencies like the U.S. Food and Drug Administration (FDA) have faced significant criticism for permitting the aggressive marketing of OxyContin and other opioids, even as mounting evidence revealed their high potential for abuse. The crisis has led to calls

---

642. Kolodny, A., Courtwright, D. T., Hwang, C. S., Kreiner, P., Eadie, J. L., Clark, T. W., & Alexander, G. C. (2015). *The Prescription Opioid and Heroin Crisis: A Public Health Approach to an Epidemic of Addiction.* Annual Review of Public Health, 36, 559-574.

643. Meier, B. (2003). *Pain Killer: An Empire of Deceit and the Origin of America's Opioid Epidemic.* Rodale Books.

for reforms to the regulatory process, including more rigorous testing of new drugs, stricter limits on marketing practices, and greater transparency in the approval process.[644]

Purdue Pharma's Enduring Stain on Public Health

Purdue Pharma's legacy is inextricably linked to the opioid crisis, and the company is widely viewed as one of the primary culprits in the epidemic.[645] The aggressive marketing of OxyContin and the company's misleading claims about the drug's safety have left a lasting stain on Purdue's reputation, and the company is now synonymous with corporate greed and irresponsibility.

The Sackler family, which owned Purdue Pharma, has also seen its reputation tarnished by the opioid crisis. The Sacklers were once known for their philanthropy and contributions to the arts and education, but their role in the opioid crisis has overshadowed these efforts. Many institutions that once accepted donations from the Sacklers have distanced themselves from the family, and there have been calls for the removal of the Sackler name from museums, universities, and other public institutions.[646]

Purdue Pharma's actions have sparked a broader debate about the ethics of drug marketing and the extent to which companies should be held accountable for the public health consequences of their products. The crisis has led to calls for stronger corporate governance, greater accountability for pharmaceutical executives, and more robust regulation of the industry.[647]

---

644. Van Zee, A. (2009). *The Promotion and Marketing of OxyContin: Commercial Triumph, Public Health Tragedy.* American Journal of Public Health, 99(2), 221-227.

645. Lovelace, B. (2020, October 21). Purdue Pharma to Plead Guilty to Three Criminal Charges Over OxyContin Sales. CNBC. Retrieved from https://www.cnbc.com/2020/10/21/purdue-pharma-to-plead-guilty-to-three-criminal-charges-over-oxycontin-sales.html

646. Lovelace, B. (2020, October 21). Purdue Pharma to Plead Guilty to Three Criminal Charges Over OxyContin Sales. CNBC. Retrieved from https://www.cnbc.com/2020/10/21/purdue-pharma-to-plead-guilty-to-three-criminal-charges-over-oxycontin-sales.html

647. Meier, B. (2003). *Pain Killer: An Empire of Deceit and the Origin of America's Opioid Epidemic.* Rodale Books.

Lessons from the Opioid Crisis

OxyContin's aggressive marketing and the company's disregard for mounting abuse evidence highlight the dangers of a profit-driven approach to healthcare. The crisis has underscored the need for stronger regulation of the pharmaceutical industry, greater transparency in drug marketing, and a more balanced approach to pain management that takes into account the risks of addiction.[648]

Other industries have also learned a valuable lesson from the opioid crisis, which highlights the possible negative effects of corporate greed and the breakdown of public confidence. The legacy of Purdue Pharma is a reminder that companies have a responsibility to prioritize the well-being of their customers and the broader community and that the pursuit of profit at the expense of public health can have devastating consequences.[649]

Purdue Pharma's role in the opioid crisis stands as a stark example of corporate greed prioritizing profit over public health, with devastating consequences. The company's aggressive and misleading marketing of OxyContin fueled an epidemic of addiction and overdose, leaving millions affected and irrevocably damaging trust in the pharmaceutical industry.

This crisis has cemented Purdue's legacy as a symbol of irresponsibility, underscoring the urgent need for stronger regulation, transparency, and accountability within the healthcare sector. The opioid epidemic serves as a powerful warning of the catastrophic outcomes that arise when profit is placed above people, emphasizing the critical importance of ethical corporate behavior and unwavering commitment to public well-being.

---

648. Kolodny, A., Courtwright, D. T., Hwang, C. S., Kreiner, P., Eadie, J. L., Clark, T. W., & Alexander, G. C. (2015). *The Prescription Opioid and Heroin Crisis: A Public Health Approach to an Epidemic of Addiction.* Annual Review of Public Health, 36, 559-574.

649. Van Zee, A. (2009). *The Promotion and Marketing of OxyContin: Commercial Triumph, Public Health Tragedy.* American Journal of Public Health, 99(2), 221-227.

Social Trust Is Being Lost

A further factor in the decline of public confidence in government and corporate institutions is the shareholder value paradigm. As companies have prioritized shareholder returns over other stakeholders, they have often engaged in practices that are perceived as exploitative or unethical, leading to a decline in public confidence in the business sector.

Scandals such as those at Enron, Wells Fargo, and Volkswagen have highlighted the extent to which corporate leaders are willing to engage in deceptive or illegal practices to boost short-term profits. These scandals have not only damaged the reputations of the companies involved but have also contributed to a broader sense of distrust in the business community. Many people now view corporations as self-serving entities that prioritize profits over the public good, leading to increased skepticism and calls for greater regulation and oversight.[650]

The erosion of social trust has also extended to government institutions, particularly as policymakers have been seen as prioritizing the interests of corporations and wealthy individuals over those of ordinary citizens.[651] The influence of corporate lobbying and campaign contributions on public policy has led to a perception that the political system is rigged in favor of the wealthy and powerful, further eroding trust in government and contributing to political polarization and social unrest.

---

650. Ewing, J. (2017). *Faster, Higher, Farther: The Inside Story of the Volkswagen Scandal*. W. W. Norton & Company.

651. Gilens, M., & Page, B. I. (2014). Testing Theories of American Politics: Elites, Interest Groups, and Average Citizens. *Perspectives on Politics*, 12(3), 564-581.

How Facebook Lost Users' Trust

Facebook, once heralded as a revolutionary platform connecting billions of people worldwide, has faced significant scrutiny over the years due to its handling of user data. The platform, which thrives on user engagement, has been criticized for its data privacy practices and the exploitation of user information. These issues have not only eroded trust among its vast user base but have also raised broader concerns about privacy, security, and the influence of technology companies in society.

Facebook's Data Collection Practices

Facebook's platform is free to use, but this accessibility comes at a cost: users' personal data. Facebook collects vast amounts of data from its users, including personal details, browsing habits, location data, and social interactions. This data is then used to build detailed profiles of users, which can be leveraged for targeted advertising, one of the company's primary revenue streams.[652]

The platform's data collection practices extend beyond what users explicitly share. Facebook tracks users across the web, collecting data even when they are not actively using the platform. This is done through various means, such as the Facebook Pixel, a piece of code embedded in websites that allows Facebook to track user activity across the internet, and the "Like" and "Share" buttons found on countless websites, which also collect data on user behavior.[653]

---

652. Andrejevic, M. (2014). *Infoglut: How Too Much Information Is Changing the Way We Think and Know*. Routledge.

653. Isaak, J., & Hanna, M. J. (2018). User Data Privacy: Facebook, Cambridge Analytica, and Privacy Protection. *Computer*, 51(8), 56-59.

Through its vast network of third-party partners and applications, Facebook has also been known to gather information from non-users. This pervasive data collection has raised significant concerns about user privacy, particularly as many users are unaware of the extent to which their data is being collected and used.[654]

Facebook's Role in the Cambridge Analytica Scandal

One of the most significant data privacy scandals involving Facebook was the Cambridge Analytica scandal, which came to light in 2018. Cambridge Analytica, a political consulting firm, was found to have harvested the personal data of millions of Facebook users without their consent. This data was used to create psychographic profiles of voters, which were then used to target political advertising during the 2016 U.S. presidential election and the Brexit referendum.[655]

The scandal exposed how Facebook's lax data privacy practices allowed third parties to exploit user information for political purposes. The data was collected through a third-party app called "This Is Your Digital Life," which was disguised as a personality quiz. While only a few hundred thousand users directly interacted with the app, the app was able to access the data of millions of users through their friends' networks, thanks to Facebook's then-lenient data-sharing policies.[656]

The Cambridge Analytica scandal was a turning point for Facebook, as it brought global attention to the platform's data privacy issues.[657]

---

654. Cadwalladr, C., & Graham-Harrison, E. (2018, March 17). Revealed: 50 Million Facebook Profiles Harvested for Cambridge Analytica in Major Data Breach. *The Guardian*. Retrieved from https://www.theguardian.com/news/2018/mar/17/cambridge-analytica-facebook-influence-us-election

655. Isaak, J., & Hanna, M. J. (2018). User Data Privacy: Facebook, Cambridge Analytica, and Privacy Protection. *Computer*, 51(8), 56-59.

656. Cadwalladr, C., & Graham-Harrison, E. (2018, March 17). Revealed: 50 Million Facebook Profiles Harvested for Cambridge Analytica in Major Data Breach. *The Guardian*. Retrieved from https://www.theguardian.com/news/2018/mar/17/cambridge-analytica-facebook-influence-us-election

657. *Ibid.*

The scandal led to widespread outrage, multiple investigations, and calls for greater regulation of social media platforms. It also marked a significant breach of trust between Facebook and its users, many of whom were unaware that their data could be used in such a manner.

Other Data Privacy Controversies

As well as the Cambridge Analytica scandal, Facebook has been involved in numerous other data privacy controversies. For example, in 2018, it was revealed that Facebook had given access to user data to over 150 companies, including tech giants like Amazon, Apple, Microsoft, and Netflix. These companies were able to access users' private messages, contact information, and other personal data without explicit user consent.[658]

Facebook has also faced criticism for its handling of passwords. In 2019, it was reported that Facebook had stored hundreds of millions of user passwords in plain text, making them easily accessible to thousands of Facebook employees.[659] This security lapse further undermined user trust and raised serious concerns about the company's ability to protect sensitive user information.

These controversies highlight a pattern of behavior in which Facebook prioritizes data collection and monetization over user privacy and security. The company's repeated failures to safeguard user data have contributed to a growing sense of distrust among users, regulators, and the public.[660]

---

658. Dance, G. J. X., LaForgia, M., & Confessore, N. (2018, December 18). As Facebook Raised a Privacy Wall, It Carved an Opening for Tech Giants. *The New York Times*. Retrieved from https://www.nytimes.com/2018/12/18/technology/facebook-privacy.html

659. Krebs, B. (2019, March 21). Facebook Stored Hundreds of Millions of User Passwords in Plain Text for Years. *Krebs on Security*. Retrieved from https://krebsonsecurity.com/2019/03/facebook-stored-hundreds-of-millions-of-user-passwords-in-plain-text-for-years/

660. Isaak, J., & Hanna, M. J. (2018). User Data Privacy: Facebook, Cambridge Analytica, and Privacy Protection. *Computer*, 51(8), 56-59.

The Impact on User Trust

The erosion of trust in Facebook has been significant. Following the Cambridge Analytica scandal, surveys revealed that a large percentage of Facebook users had lost trust in the platform. A 2018 survey by the Ponemon Institute found that only 27% of users believed Facebook was committed to protecting their privacy, a sharp decline from 79% the previous year.[661]

This decline in trust has had tangible effects on user behavior. Many users have become more cautious about what they share on Facebook, with some opting to delete their accounts altogether. The #DeleteFacebook movement, which gained traction after the Cambridge Analytica scandal, is one example of the growing backlash against the platform.[662] While the movement did not lead to a mass exodus from Facebook, it did highlight the growing concerns about the platform's data practices.

Facebook's operations have also been impacted by the erosion of trust. In the wake of the Cambridge Analytica scandal, Facebook's stock price took a significant hit, and the company faced increased scrutiny from regulators and lawmakers around the world.[663] The scandal also led to a loss of advertising revenue as companies became more cautious about associating their brands with a platform embroiled in controversy.

Implications of Facebook's Failures for Social Media and Tech Giants

Facebook's declining reputation has had wider effects on the technology and social media sectors. Facebook's controversies have sparked a wider debate about data privacy, the ethical use of technology, and the responsibility of tech companies to protect user information.

---

661. Ponemon Institute. (2018). *Consumer Sentiment Study on Data Privacy.* Retrieved from https://www.ponemon.org/library/consumer-sentiment-study-on-data-privacy

662. Vogels, E. A. (2018, April 2). *How Americans Feel About Social Media and Privacy.* Pew Research Center. Retrieved from https://www.pewresearch.org/fact-tank/2018/04/02/how-americans-feel-about-social-media-and-privacy/

663. *Ibid.*

One of the key issues raised by Facebook's data privacy scandals is the lack of transparency in how social media platforms collect and use data. Many users are unaware of the extent to which their data is being collected, shared, and monetized by these platforms. This lack of transparency has led to calls for greater regulation of the tech industry, with policymakers advocating for stricter data privacy laws and greater accountability for tech companies.[664]

The Facebook scandals have also highlighted the need for users to have more control over their data. Many critics argue that social media platforms should provide users with clearer options for managing their privacy settings and should be more transparent about how their data is being used.[665] This has led to increased interest in alternative social media platforms that prioritize privacy and security, such as encrypted messaging apps like Signal and privacy-focused social networks like Mastodon.

Finally, the erosion of trust in Facebook has underscored the broader societal implications of data privacy issues. The misuse of personal data can have far-reaching consequences, from influencing political outcomes to enabling discrimination and surveillance. The Facebook controversies have prompted a global conversation about the ethical use of technology and the need for stronger protections for users' digital rights.[666]

Societal Impact of Facebook's Privacy Failures

The data privacy issues associated with Facebook have not only eroded user trust but have also had broader implications for society as a whole. These issues have raised important questions about the role of technology companies in modern society, the protection of personal data, and the impact of social media on democracy and public discourse.

---

664. Andrejevic, M. (2014). *Infoglut: How Too Much Information Is Changing the Way We Think and Know*. Routledge.

665. Isaak, J., & Hanna, M. J. (2018). User Data Privacy: Facebook, Cambridge Analytica, and Privacy Protection. *Computer*, 51(8), 56-59.

666. *Ibid.*

Undermining Democracy and Public Discourse

One of the most significant implications of Facebook's data privacy issues is their impact on democracy and public discourse. The Cambridge Analytica scandal, in particular, highlighted how personal data can be used to manipulate political outcomes. By harvesting data from millions of Facebook users, Cambridge Analytica was able to create detailed profiles of voters and target them with personalized political ads.[667] This type of microtargeting can be used to influence voter behavior, spread misinformation, and undermine democratic processes.

The use of Facebook for political manipulation has raised serious concerns about the role of social media in modern elections. Critics argue that the platform's data-driven advertising model allows for the spread of misinformation and divisive content, which can distort public discourse and polarize societies. The spread of fake news and conspiracy theories on Facebook has been linked to political violence, social unrest, and the erosion of trust in democratic institutions.[668]

In response to these concerns, Facebook has implemented measures to improve transparency in political advertising and to combat the spread of misinformation. However, many critics argue that these efforts have been insufficient and that more needs to be done to address the broader societal impacts of social media on democracy.[669]

Demanding Robust Data Privacy Protections

The Facebook data privacy controversies have also highlighted the need for stronger protections for personal data. In the wake of the Cambridge Analytica scandal, there has been growing

---

667. Cadwalladr, C., & Graham-Harrison, E. (2018, March 17). Revealed: 50 Million Facebook Profiles Harvested for Cambridge Analytica in Major Data Breach. *The Guardian*. Retrieved from https://www.theguardian.com/news/2018/mar/17/cambridge-analytica-facebook-influence-us-election

668. Isaak, J., & Hanna, M. J. (2018). User Data Privacy: Facebook, Cambridge Analytica, and Privacy Protection. *Computer*, 51(8), 56-59.

669. *Ibid.*

recognition of the need for comprehensive data privacy legislation that sets clear standards for how companies collect, store, and use personal data.

In 2018, the European Union implemented the General Data Protection Regulation (GDPR), which is one of the most comprehensive data privacy laws in the world. GDPR grants individuals greater control over their personal data and imposes strict requirements on companies to protect user information. The implementation of GDPR has set a new standard for data privacy and has prompted other countries to consider similar legislation.[670]

There have been requests for a federal data privacy law in the US that would offer comparable safeguards to the GDPR. While some states, such as California, have enacted their own data privacy laws, there is currently no comprehensive federal legislation. The Facebook controversies have added urgency to the debate over data privacy in the U.S., with policymakers, privacy advocates, and tech companies all calling for clearer rules and stronger protections for users.[671]

The Ethical Responsibilities of Technology Companies

The erosion of trust in Facebook has also raised important questions about the ethical responsibilities of technology companies. As platforms like Facebook become increasingly central to our lives, there is growing concern about the power and influence these companies wield. The Facebook data privacy controversies have highlighted the need for tech companies to prioritize user privacy, transparency, and ethical behavior in their operations.

Many critics argue that tech companies have a responsibility to protect their users from harm, whether it be through data breaches, misinformation, or exploitation of personal data. This includes

---

670. European Commission. (2018). Data Protection in the EU. Retrieved from https://ec.europa.eu/info/law/law-topic/data-protection/data-protection-eu_en

671. Solove, D. J. (2020). *The Future of Privacy Law: The Need for Comprehensive Legislation in the U.S.* Yale Law Journal.

being transparent about how data is collected and used, providing users with meaningful control over their information, and taking steps to prevent the misuse of data by third parties.[672]

Facebook's controversies over data privacy and the exploitation of user information have profoundly shaken trust in the platform and raised critical questions about the ethical responsibilities of technology companies. As platforms like Facebook become integral to daily life, the influence and power these companies wield must come with a commitment to user privacy, transparency, and ethical behavior.

Critics argue that tech companies must take active responsibility for protecting their users from harm, including safeguarding against data breaches, misinformation, and exploitation of personal data. This responsibility demands clear communication about data collection practices, providing users with meaningful control over their information, and ensuring robust measures to prevent misuse by third parties.

Moreover, Facebook's repeated missteps highlight the insufficiency of self-regulation in the tech industry. Stronger oversight and enforcement of data privacy laws are essential to holding companies accountable for breaches and violations. Users must have clear avenues for recourse in cases of harm, ensuring that companies prioritize their ethical obligations alongside financial objectives.

The Facebook case underscores the urgent need for comprehensive data privacy protections, increased transparency, and accountability across the tech industry. As society becomes increasingly dependent on digital platforms, these companies must prioritize user trust and security, adhere to strict ethical standards, and proactively prevent data exploitation. The erosion of trust in Facebook serves as a potent reminder that safeguarding user information is not just a regulatory necessity but a moral imperative for a more ethical digital future.

---

672. Andrejevic, M. (2014). *Infoglut: How Too Much Information Is Changing the Way We Think and Know*. Routledge.

Loss of Long-Term Value Creation

Finally, the shareholder value paradigm has led to a loss of long-term value creation, as companies have focused on short-term financial performance at the expense of long-term sustainability and innovation. By prioritizing shareholder returns, companies have often neglected investments in research and development, employee training, and other areas that are critical to long-term growth and competitiveness.

This focus on short-termism has contributed to a decline in innovation in many industries, as companies have been more concerned with meeting quarterly earnings targets than with developing new products or services that could drive future growth. It has also led to a decline in corporate responsibility, as companies have been less willing to invest in environmental sustainability, social programs, or other initiatives that do not provide immediate financial returns.[673]

Because it makes it more difficult for businesses to compete internationally, adjust to shifting market conditions, and support economic growth, the loss of long-term value creation has a big impact on the overall economy.[674] It also has implications for society, as the focus on short-term profits can lead to environmental degradation, social inequality, and other negative outcomes that affect the well-being of communities and future generations.

Moving Beyond the Shareholder Value Paradigm

Given the negative consequences of the shareholder value paradigm, there is growing recognition of the need for a more balanced approach to corporate governance that takes into account the interests of all stakeholders, including employees, customers, communities, and the environment.

---

673. Lazonick, W. (2014). Profits Without Prosperity: Stock Buybacks Manipulate the Market and Leave Most Americans Worse Off. *Harvard Business Review*, 92(9), 46-55.

674. Bilotkach, V. (2015). Airline Consolidation and Market Conduct: The Recent Evolution of the US Domestic Airline Industry. *Journal of Air Transport Management*, 47, 23-31.

Embracing Stakeholder-Centric Models

One alternative to the shareholder value paradigm is the concept of stakeholder capitalism, which holds that companies have a responsibility to all of their stakeholders, not just their shareholders. Under this model, companies are encouraged to consider the long-term impact of their decisions on employees, customers, suppliers, communities, and the environment, rather than focusing solely on maximizing short-term profits.

The idea of stakeholder capitalism has gained traction in recent years, particularly in the wake of the 2008 financial crisis and the growing concerns about economic inequality and environmental sustainability. Some companies, such as Patagonia and Unilever, have embraced this approach, prioritizing social and environmental responsibility alongside financial performance. Additionally, organizations such as the Business Roundtable, a group of CEOs from major U.S. corporations, have publicly endorsed the idea that companies should serve the interests of all stakeholders, not just shareholders.[675]

Regulation and Policy as Drivers of Corporate Responsibility

Regulation and public policy also have a critical role to play in moving beyond the shareholder value paradigm. Policymakers can encourage more balanced corporate governance by enacting regulations that promote transparency, accountability, and social responsibility. For example, governments can require companies to disclose information about their environmental and social impact, strengthen labor protections, and enforce antitrust laws to ensure that markets remain competitive.

Public policy can also incentivize long-term investment by providing tax incentives or other benefits to companies that invest in research and development, employee training, and sustainable practices. By creating a regulatory environment that supports long-term value creation, governments

675. Bilotkach, V. (2015). Airline Consolidation and Market Conduct: The Recent Evolution of the US Domestic Airline Industry. *Journal of Air Transport Management*, 47, 23-31.

can help shift the focus away from short-term profits and towards a more holistic approach to business that benefits all stakeholders.[676]

Corporate Leadership's Role in Shaping Ethical Business Practices

Shifting away from the shareholder value paradigm requires bold leadership and a commitment to redefining corporate success. Corporate leaders must challenge entrenched norms and champion a broader vision that prioritizes long-term thinking, ethical behavior, and the well-being of all stakeholders. This shift involves fostering a culture of accountability and transparency where financial success aligns with the interests of employees, customers, and communities.

Leadership also plays a pivotal role in advocating for and implementing policies that support stakeholder capitalism. By setting an example, leaders can demonstrate that businesses can thrive financially while embracing social responsibility and sustainability.[677] Companies that champion inclusive governance and equitable practices pave the way for others, helping to create a business environment where ethical decision-making becomes the standard.

The shareholder value paradigm has driven wealth creation for decades, but often at the expense of equity, trust, and long-term sustainability. Economic inequality, social disillusionment, and a loss of innovation have been significant costs of this narrow focus. A more balanced approach, rooted in stakeholder capitalism and guided by visionary leadership, can address these challenges while fostering prosperity for all.

By adopting stakeholder-focused strategies, supporting progressive public policies, and embracing inclusive corporate leadership, companies have the opportunity to redefine their impact on society. In doing so, they can contribute to a more sustainable, equitable future, one that balances profitability with the broader needs of the people and communities they serve.

---

676. Gilens, M., & Page, B. I. (2014). Testing Theories of American Politics: Elites, Interest Groups, and Average Citizens. *Perspectives on Politics*, 12(3), 564-581.

677. Lazonick, W., & O'Sullivan, M. (2000). Maximizing Shareholder Value: A New Ideology for Corporate Governance. *Economy and Society*, 29(1), 13-35.

KEY TAKEAWAYS

The Rise of Shareholder Value Culture
The shareholder value paradigm, popularized in the 1980s, reshaped corporate governance by prioritizing short-term financial returns over long-term stability, employee well-being, and ethical responsibility.

Short-Term Profits at the Expense of Safety and Ethics
High-profile corporate scandals, including the Boeing 737 Max crisis, Purdue Pharma's role in the opioid epidemic, and Facebook's data privacy failures, illustrate the dangers of prioritizing profits over public safety, trust, and well-being.

Erosion of Workforce Stability and Customer Trust
Cost-cutting measures driven by shareholder value, such as mass layoffs, wage suppression, and reduced investment in customer service, have contributed to job insecurity, economic inequality, and declining trust in corporations.

Public Backlash and Calls for Regulation
The consequences of profit-driven decision-making have sparked growing public demand for stronger corporate accountability, with increased regulation and legal repercussions for companies that exploit workers, consumers, or the environment.

The Shift Toward Stakeholder Capitalism
There is a growing push for stakeholder capitalism, which advocates for a more balanced approach where businesses consider the interests of employees, customers, communities, and the environment, not just shareholders, in their decision-making.

Chapter 11

Business Beyond the Bottom Line

Corporate practices, especially those driven by profit maximization and the shareholder value paradigm, have far-reaching effects that extend beyond the confines of the companies themselves. These practices can significantly impact society at large, contributing to various social, economic, and public health issues. From exacerbating economic inequality to influencing public health outcomes, the ripple effect of corporate decisions often manifests in ways that profoundly shape the lives of individuals and communities.

Economic Inequality and Corporate Practices

Economic inequality has been a growing concern in many parts of the world, particularly in the United States. Corporate practices, especially those focused on maximizing shareholder value, have played a significant role in exacerbating this inequality. The pursuit of profit often leads to decisions that prioritize the interests of shareholders and executives over those of employees and other stakeholders, contributing to a widening gap between the wealthy and the rest of society.

Wage Stagnation and the Decline of Labor's Share of Income

One of the most direct ways in which corporate practices contribute to economic inequality is through wage stagnation and the decline of labor's share of income. Over the past few decades, while corporate profits have soared, wages for many workers have remained stagnant.[678] This stagnation has been driven in part by corporate strategies aimed at reducing labor costs, such as outsourcing, automation, and the suppression of union activity.

Many businesses have outsourced jobs to nations with lower labor costs as a result of the emphasis on cutting costs to maximize profits; this frequently results in job losses and wage reductions for workers in higher-cost nations.[679] Further adding to wage stagnation and job insecurity is the fact that automation has displaced a large number of workers, especially in manufacturing and other blue-collar industries.

The decline of labor unions has also played a significant role in the erosion of workers' bargaining power. As unions have weakened, workers have found it increasingly difficult to negotiate for higher wages, better benefits, and improved working conditions.[680] This has allowed companies to capture a larger share of the economic value created by their employees, contributing to a growing concentration of wealth among executives and shareholders.

Executive Compensation and the Wealth Gap

Another key factor contributing to economic inequality is the dramatic rise in executive compensation, particularly in the form of stock options and bonuses tied to company performance. Over the past several decades,

---

678. Bivens, J., & Mishel, L. (2015). The Pay Is Too Damn Low: Why Wages Have Stagnated. *Economic Policy Institute*. Retrieved from https://www.epi.org/publication/why-americans-wages-have-stagnated/

679. Autor, D. H. (2014). Skills, Education, and the Rise of Earnings Inequality Among the "Other 99 Percent". *Science*, 344(6186), 843-851.

680. Western, B., & Rosenfeld, J. (2011). Unions, Norms, and the Rise in American Wage Inequality. *American Sociological Review*, 76(4), 513-537.

CEO pay has increased at a much faster rate than that of average workers, leading to a significant widening of the wealth gap within companies.[681]

The shareholder value paradigm has played a central role in driving this trend, as corporate boards have increasingly tied executive compensation to stock performance. This has created strong incentives for executives to focus on short-term financial gains, often at the expense of long-term sustainability and the well-being of employees.[682] As a result, executives have reaped substantial rewards, while the benefits of corporate success have not been shared equally with the broader workforce.

Since the wealthiest people have seen their wealth increase at an unprecedented rate, the concentration of wealth among top executives and shareholders has contributed to wider economic inequality. This concentration of wealth has also had broader societal implications, as it has fueled political polarization, social unrest, and a sense of disenfranchisement among those who feel left behind by the economic system.[683]

Public Health and Corporate Practices

Corporate practices can also have a profound impact on public health, particularly when profit-driven decisions lead to the production and promotion of harmful products or the neglect of safety and ethical standards. The ripple effect of these practices can manifest in widespread health crises, increased healthcare costs, and a decline in public trust in the healthcare system.

The Opioid Crisis and Pharmaceutical Practices

One of the most glaring examples of the impact of corporate practices on public health is the opioid crisis in the United States. The aggressive marketing and promotion of prescription opioids by pharmaceutical companies, particularly Purdue Pharma's OxyContin, played a central

681. Mishel, L., & Wolfe, J. (2019). CEO Compensation Has Grown 940% Since 1978. *Economic Policy Institute*. Retrieved from https://www.epi.org/publication/ceo-compensation-2018/

682. Lazonick, W. (2014). Profits Without Prosperity: Stock Buybacks Manipulate the Market and Leave Most Americans Worse Off. *Harvard Business Review*, 92(9), 46-55.

683. Piketty, T. (2014). *Capital in the Twenty-First Century*. Harvard University Press.

role in fueling this epidemic.[684] Driven by the pursuit of profit, these companies downplayed the risks of addiction and aggressively marketed opioids to healthcare providers, leading to widespread overprescription and a dramatic rise in opioid addiction and overdose deaths.

Public health has suffered greatly as a result of the opioid crisis, which has claimed hundreds of thousands of lives and left millions more addicted. The crisis has also placed a significant strain on the healthcare system, with increased demand for addiction treatment, emergency services, and other healthcare resources. The financial cost of the opioid crisis has been estimated in the billions of dollars, further burdening public health systems and contributing to broader societal challenges.[685]

Pharmaceutical companies' strategies to promote opioids have also undermined public trust in the healthcare system. Many patients and healthcare providers now view pharmaceutical companies with skepticism, questioning the motives behind drug marketing and the safety of new medications.[686] This breach of trust has broader implications for public health, as it can lead to delays in the adoption of new treatments and a reluctance to seek medical care.

Environmental Health and Corporate Responsibility

Through their effects on the environment, corporate policies can make a big impact. Companies that prioritize profit over environmental responsibility can contribute to pollution, climate change, and other environmental health risks.[687] These practices often disproportionately affect low-income communities and communities of color, exacerbating existing health disparities and contributing to broader societal inequality.

---

684. Van Zee, A. (2009). The Promotion and Marketing of OxyContin: Commercial Triumph, Public Health Tragedy. *American Journal of Public Health*, 99(2), 221-227.

685. Kolodny, A., Courtwright, D. T., Hwang, C. S., Kreiner, P., Eadie, J. L., Clark, T. W., & Alexander, G. C. (2015). The Prescription Opioid and Heroin Crisis: A Public Health Approach to an Epidemic of Addiction. *Annual Review of Public Health*, 36, 559-574.

686. Meier, B. (2003). *Pain Killer: An Empire of Deceit and the Origin of America's Opioid Epidemic*. Rodale Books.

687. Bullard, R. D. (2000). *Dumping in Dixie: Race, Class, and Environmental Quality*. Westview Press.

For example, industrial pollution from factories, power plants, and other sources can lead to increased rates of respiratory diseases, cancer, and other health problems in nearby communities.[688] These health impacts are often concentrated in areas with high levels of poverty and limited access to healthcare, further exacerbating the burden on already vulnerable populations.

Climate change, driven in large part by corporate practices such as fossil fuel extraction and deforestation, also poses significant public health risks. The effects of climate change, including more frequent and severe heatwaves, natural disasters, and the spread of infectious diseases, can have devastating consequences for public health.[689] These impacts are often felt most acutely by those who are least able to adapt, including low-income communities, the elderly, and people with pre-existing health conditions.

Corporate practices that contribute to environmental degradation not only harm public health but also undermine efforts to address global challenges such as climate change. The pursuit of short-term profits at the expense of environmental sustainability can have long-lasting and far-reaching consequences, both for human health and for the planet as a whole.[690]

---

688. Brulle, R. J., & Pellow, D. N. (2006). Environmental Justice: Human Health and Environmental Inequalities. *Annual Review of Public Health*, 27(1), 103-124.

689. Watts, N., Adger, W. N., Agnolucci, P., Blackstock, J., Byass, P., Cai, W., ... & Costello, A. (2015). Health and Climate Change: Policy Responses to Protect Public Health. *The Lancet*, 386(10006), 1861-1914.

690. Bullard, R. D. (2000). *Dumping in Dixie: Race, Class, and Environmental Quality*. Westview Press.

Monsanto Disrupting Communities and Reshaping Society

Monsanto, once a leading agribusiness company and now part of Bayer, has long been a polarizing figure in the global agricultural industry. Known for its aggressive marketing of genetically modified organisms (GMOs) and its development of the herbicide glyphosate, marketed as Roundup, Monsanto has faced extensive legal battles and public criticism over health concerns, environmental impacts, and the broader implications of its business practices. Monsanto's marketing of GMOs and the legal battles over health concerns, and it examines the lasting impact of these practices on agriculture and public perception.

Aggressive Marketing of GMOs

Monsanto played a pioneering role in the development and commercialization of genetically modified crops, which have become a significant part of modern agriculture. The company's aggressive marketing strategies and its influence on regulatory frameworks have sparked widespread debate over the safety, ethics, and environmental impact of GMOs.

Monsanto's Role in the Development of GMOs

Genetically modified organisms (GMOs) are plants or animals whose genetic material has been altered using genetic engineering techniques. Monsanto was a pioneer in the development of GMOs, creating genetically modified crops that were resistant to pests, diseases, and herbicides.[691] The company's flagship product, Roundup Ready crops, were engineered to be resistant

691. Charles, D. (2001). *Lords of the Harvest: Biotech, Big Money, and the Future of Food.* Basic Books.

to glyphosate, allowing farmers to use the herbicide without harming their crops. This innovation was marketed as a solution to improve crop yields, reduce farming costs, and support sustainable agriculture.

Monsanto's GMOs quickly gained widespread adoption, particularly in the United States, where crops such as soybeans, corn, and cotton were rapidly converted to genetically modified varieties.[692] By the early 2000s, GMOs had become the dominant form of several major crops in the U.S., and Monsanto was at the forefront of this agricultural revolution.

GMO Marketing and Promotion

Monsanto's success in promoting GMOs can be attributed to its aggressive marketing strategies and its ability to influence regulatory policies. The company marketed GMOs as a solution to global food security challenges, claiming that genetically modified crops could increase yields, reduce the need for chemical inputs, and help feed a growing global population.[693] Monsanto also emphasized the environmental benefits of GMOs, arguing that they could reduce the need for pesticides and herbicides, lower greenhouse gas emissions, and promote conservation tillage practices.

To support its marketing efforts, Monsanto invested heavily in lobbying and public relations campaigns aimed at shaping public perception and influencing policymakers. The company worked closely with regulatory agencies, such as the U.S. Department of Agriculture (USDA) and the Environmental Protection Agency (EPA), to ensure that GMOs were approved for commercial use and that regulatory frameworks were favorable to the adoption of genetically modified crops.[694]

---

692. Crost, B., Shankar, B., & Bennett, R. (2007). Bias from Farmer Self-Selection in Genetically Modified Crop Productivity Estimates: Evidence from Indian Data. *Journal of Agricultural Economics*, 58(1), 24-36.

693. Qaim, M., & Zilberman, D. (2003). Yield Effects of Genetically Modified Crops in Developing Countries. *Science*, 299(5608), 900-902.

694. Robin, M. M. (2010). *The World According to Monsanto: Pollution, Corruption, and the Control of Our Food Supply*. New Press.

Monsanto's marketing strategies also included efforts to discredit critics and suppress dissenting voices. The company has been accused of using its influence to silence scientists and researchers who raised concerns about the safety and environmental impact of GMOs.[695] Monsanto's aggressive legal strategies have also drawn criticism, including the lawsuits it filed against farmers who unintentionally grew genetically modified crops after nearby fields accidentally contaminated them.

Global Spread of GMOs and Public Resistance

Monsanto's aggressive marketing and promotion of GMOs have played a role in shaping the global debate over genetic modification. While the company has successfully promoted GMOs as a solution to agricultural challenges, it has also faced intense criticism for its tactics and the perceived risks associated with genetically modified crops.[696] The global spread of GMOs has sparked a broader conversation about the role of biotechnology in agriculture, the power of multinational corporations in shaping food systems, and the need for greater transparency and public involvement in decision-making processes.

While GMOs have been widely adopted in the United States and some other countries, they have faced significant resistance in many parts of the world. Public concerns about the safety of GMOs, their environmental impact, and the ethics of genetic modification have fueled opposition to their use in agriculture. In Europe, for example, public resistance to GMOs has been strong, leading to strict regulations and bans on the cultivation of genetically modified crops in several countries.[697]

---

695. Center for Food Safety. (2019). *Monsanto: A Legacy of Controversy*. Retrieved from https://www.centerforfoodsafety.org/monsanto

696. Falkner, R. (2007). *The International Politics of Genetically Modified Food: Diplomacy, Trade and Law*. Palgrave Macmillan.

697. Tait, J. (2001). More Faust than Frankenstein: The European Debate About the Precautionary Principle and Risk Regulation for Genetically Modified Crops. *Journal of Risk Research*, 4(2), 175-189.

Legal Battles Over Health Concerns

Monsanto's business practices have led to numerous legal battles, particularly over the safety of its products. The company has faced lawsuits and regulatory challenges related to the health effects of glyphosate, the active ingredient in its Roundup herbicide, and the potential risks associated with GMOs.

Concerns Regarding Roundup and Glyphosate

Glyphosate, the active ingredient in Monsanto's Roundup herbicide, has been the subject of extensive scientific and legal debate over its safety. Roundup has been one of the most widely used herbicides in the world, and its use has been closely linked to the adoption of Monsanto's Roundup Ready crops.[698] However, concerns have been raised about the potential health risks associated with glyphosate exposure, including its possible link to cancer.

The controversy over glyphosate intensified in 2015 when the International Agency for Research on Cancer (IARC), a part of the World Health Organization (WHO), classified glyphosate as "probably carcinogenic to humans."[699] This classification was based on evidence from animal studies and limited evidence from studies on humans, particularly those showing an association between glyphosate exposure and non-Hodgkin lymphoma.

Monsanto strongly disputed the IARC's classification and launched a public relations campaign to defend the safety of glyphosate. The company argued that glyphosate had been extensively studied and that regulatory agencies around the world had consistently found it to be safe when used according to label instructions.[700]

---

698. Mills, P. J., Kania-Korwel, I., Fagan, J., & Thorne, P. S. (2018). The Monsanto Papers: Roundup (Glyphosate) Cancer Case Corroboration of Human Health Risk. *Environmental Sciences Europe*, 30(1), 1-13.

699. International Agency for Research on Cancer (IARC). (2015). IARC Monographs Volume 112: Evaluation of Five Organophosphate Insecticides and Herbicides. *World Health Organization*. Retrieved from https://monographs.iarc.fr/iarc-monographs-volume-112-evaluation-of-five-organophosphate-insecticides-and-herbicides/

700. Bain, C., Ransom, E., & Worosz, M. (2019). Governing the Global Agri-Food System: Challenges, Trends, and Approaches. *Routledge*.

Monsanto also criticized the IARC's decision-making process and accused the agency of ignoring key studies that did not find a link between glyphosate and cancer.

Despite Monsanto's efforts to defend glyphosate, the IARC's classification fueled a wave of lawsuits against the company. Thousands of plaintiffs, many of them agricultural workers and gardeners, filed lawsuits alleging that exposure to Roundup had caused them to develop cancer. In 2018, Monsanto (by then owned by Bayer) lost a landmark case when a California jury awarded $289 million in damages to Dewayne Johnson, a groundskeeper who claimed that his non-Hodgkin lymphoma was caused by Roundup exposure.[701] The jury found that Monsanto had acted with "malice" by failing to warn users of the potential risks associated with glyphosate.

This case was the first of many legal battles that Bayer would face over glyphosate, leading to billions of dollars in settlements and significant reputational damage for the company.[702] The glyphosate controversy has also prompted calls for stricter regulation of pesticides and herbicides, as well as heightened scrutiny of the interactions between regulatory bodies and corporations.

The Debate Over GMO Safety and Labeling

In addition to the legal battles over glyphosate, Monsanto has faced ongoing controversy over the safety of GMOs and the labeling of genetically modified foods. While Monsanto has consistently argued that GMOs are safe and have been thoroughly tested, critics have raised concerns about the potential health risks associated

701. Bellon, T. (2018). Monsanto Loses First Glyphosate Cancer Trial, Ordered to Pay $289 Million. *Reuters*. Retrieved from https://www.reuters.com/article/us-monsanto-cancer-lawsuit/monsanto-ordered-to-pay-289-million-in-glyphosate-cancer-trial-idUSKBN1KV2HB

702. Bellon, T. (2018). Monsanto Loses First Glyphosate Cancer Trial, Ordered to Pay $289 Million. *Reuters*. Retrieved from https://www.reuters.com/article/us-monsanto-cancer-lawsuit/monsanto-ordered-to-pay-289-million-in-glyphosate-cancer-trial-idUSKBN1KV2HB

with genetic modification, including the possibility of allergenicity, antibiotic resistance, and unintended effects on human health.[703]

The debate over GMO safety has been compounded by the lack of consensus within the scientific community and the limitations of current testing methods. While many regulatory agencies, including the U.S. Food and Drug Administration (FDA) and the European Food Safety Authority (EFSA), have declared GMOs to be safe, critics argue that the long-term health effects of genetically modified foods have not been adequately studied.[704]

One of the most contentious issues in the GMO debate has been the labeling of genetically modified foods. In the United States, Monsanto and other agribusiness companies have lobbied against mandatory GMO labeling, arguing that it would be misleading and could lead to unnecessary fear among consumers.[705] However, public support for GMO labeling has been strong, with many consumers demanding the right to know whether the foods they purchase contain genetically modified ingredients.

In response to public pressure, several states and countries have introduced laws requiring the labeling of GMOs. For example, in 2016, the United States passed the National Bioengineered Food Disclosure Standard, which requires food manufacturers to disclose the presence of genetically modified ingredients on product labels.[706] While this law represented a victory for GMO labeling advocates, it also highlighted the ongoing tension between consumer rights and corporate interests in the debate over GMOs.

---

703. Antoniou, M., Robinson, C., & Fagan, J. (2012). *GMO Myths and Truths: An Evidence-Based Examination of the Claims Made for the Safety and Efficacy of Genetically Modified Crops*. Earth Open Source.

704. *Ibid.*

705. Lucht, J. M. (2015). Public Acceptance of Plant Biotechnology and GM Crops. *Viruses*, 7(8), 4254-4281.

706. *Ibid.*

Wider Ethical and Legal Consequences

The legal battles over glyphosate and GMOs have broader implications for the relationship between corporations, regulators, and the public. These cases have raised questions about the transparency and integrity of the regulatory process, the influence of corporate lobbying on public policy, and the ethical responsibilities of companies in protecting public health and the environment.[707]

Monsanto's aggressive defense of its products, coupled with its efforts to influence scientific research and regulatory decisions, has fueled public skepticism about the safety of GMOs and the motivations of the agribusiness industry.[708] As the global population continues to grow and demand for food increases, the decisions made by companies like Monsanto will have far-reaching consequences for the future of agriculture and the sustainability of food systems.The Lasting Impact on Agriculture and Public Perception

Monsanto's development and promotion of GMOs have had a profound impact on global agriculture. The adoption of genetically modified crops has contributed to increased agricultural productivity, particularly in regions where pests, diseases, and environmental challenges pose significant threats to crop yields. GMOs have also facilitated the use of conservation tillage practices, which can reduce soil erosion and improve soil health.[709]

However, the widespread adoption of GMOs has also raised concerns about the long-term sustainability of industrial agriculture. The reliance on glyphosate-resistant crops has led to the emergence of glyphosate-resistant weeds, requiring farmers to use higher doses of herbicides or resort to alternative chemicals. This has contributed to the problem of herbicide resistance and

---

707. Robin, M. M. (2010). *The World According to Monsanto: Pollution, Corruption, and the Control of Our Food Supply*. New Press.

708. Falkner, R. (2007). *The International Politics of Genetically Modified Food: Diplomacy, Trade and Law*. Palgrave Macmillan.

709. Qaim, M., & Zilberman, D. (2003). Yield Effects of Genetically Modified Crops in Developing Countries. *Science*, 299(5608), 900-902.

increased chemical use in agriculture, raising concerns about the environmental impact of GMOs.[710]

Concerns have also been raised regarding the loss of biodiversity and the degradation of farmers' rights due to the concentration of seed ownership in the hands of a small number of powerful companies, such as Monsanto. The patenting of genetically modified seeds has given companies like Monsanto significant control over the seed market, limiting farmers' ability to save and reuse seeds and increasing their dependence on proprietary seed technologies.[711]

The impact of Monsanto's practices on agriculture has sparked a broader conversation about the future of food systems and the need for more sustainable and equitable approaches to farming.[712] While GMOs have the potential to address some of the challenges facing global agriculture, their use must be carefully managed to ensure that they do not exacerbate environmental problems or undermine the resilience of food systems.

Its Effect on Public Attitude

Monsanto's reputation has been shaped by both its technological innovations and its controversial business practices. While the company has been praised for its contributions to agricultural productivity, it has also been vilified for its aggressive marketing tactics, legal battles, and perceived disregard for public health and environmental safety.

Public perception of Monsanto has been influenced by a variety of factors, including media coverage, activism, and the company's own efforts to shape public opinion. The controversies surrounding glyphosate, GMOs, and Monsanto's legal battles have contributed to a negative public image, with many people associating the

710. Howard, P. H. (2009). Visualizing Consolidation in the Global Seed Industry: 1996, 2008. *Sustainability*, 1(4), 1266-1287.

711. *Ibid.*

712. Falkner, R. (2007). *The International Politics of Genetically Modified Food: Diplomacy, Trade and Law.* Palgrave Macmillan.

company with corporate greed, environmental harm, and health risks.[713]

The backlash against Monsanto has been fueled by grassroots activism, including campaigns for GMO labeling, protests against glyphosate use, and efforts to hold the company accountable for its actions.[714] This activism has played a key role in raising awareness about the potential risks associated with GMOs and glyphosate and has contributed to the growing demand for transparency and accountability in the food and agriculture industries.

Monsanto's legacy is also reflected in the broader public debate over the role of biotechnology in agriculture. The controversies surrounding GMOs and glyphosate have sparked a global conversation about the ethical and environmental implications of genetic engineering and the need for more sustainable and equitable approaches to food production.[715]

Long-Term Repercussions for the Agriculture Sector

The long-term consequences of Monsanto's practices for the agriculture industry are still unfolding. The company's merger with Bayer in 2018 has brought new challenges and opportunities for the future of agricultural biotechnology.[716] While the merger has strengthened Bayer's position in the global agriculture market, it has also inherited the legal and reputational challenges associated with Monsanto's legacy.

Future developments in the agriculture sector are probably going to be significantly impacted by the ongoing legal disputes sur-

713. Robin, M. M. (2010). *The World According to Monsanto: Pollution, Corruption, and the Control of Our Food Supply*. New Press.

714. Center for Food Safety. (2019). *Monsanto: A Legacy of Controversy*. Retrieved from https://www.centerforfoodsafety.org/monsanto

715. Falkner, R. (2007). *The International Politics of Genetically Modified Food: Diplomacy, Trade and Law*. Palgrave Macmillan.

716. Bellon, T. (2018). Monsanto Loses First Glyphosate Cancer Trial, Ordered to Pay $289 Million. *Reuters*. Retrieved from https://www.reuters.com/article/us-monsanto-cancer-lawsuit/monsanto-ordered-to-pay-289-million-in-glyphosate-cancer-trial-idUSKBN1KV2HB

rounding glyphosate and the growing public opposition to GMOs. As consumers become more aware of the environmental and health risks associated with chemical-intensive farming, there is increasing demand for alternative approaches to agriculture that prioritize sustainability, biodiversity, and food sovereignty.[717]

Important questions concerning how corporations will influence agriculture in the future and the necessity of increased public participation in decision-making processes are also brought up by Monsanto's legacy.[718] As the global population continues to grow and the challenges facing agriculture become more complex, it is essential to ensure that the benefits of new technologies are shared equitably and that the risks are carefully managed to protect public health and the environment.

The ripple effect of Monsanto's practices on society underscores the importance of transparency, accountability, and ethical considerations in the development and promotion of new technologies. As the global agriculture industry continues to evolve, it is essential to ensure that the benefits of biotechnology are realized in a way that is sustainable, equitable, and protective of public health and the environment.

The lessons learned from Monsanto's experience can inform the future of agricultural policy and practice, helping to create a more just and sustainable food system that meets the needs of all people and protects the planet for future generations.

Food and Beverage Industry and Public Health

Another clear illustration of how corporate practices can have a detrimental effect on public health is the food and beverage sector. The marketing and sale of unhealthy food products, such as those high in sugar, salt, and fat, have contributed to the global rise in obesity and related health conditions, including diabetes, heart disease, and certain cancers.

---

717. Lucht, J. M. (2015). Public Acceptance of Plant Biotechnology and GM Crops. *Viruses*, 7(8), 4254-4281.

718. Falkner, R. (2007). *The International Politics of Genetically Modified Food: Diplomacy, Trade and Law*. Palgrave Macmillan.

Corporate practices in the food and beverage industry, particularly the aggressive marketing of unhealthy products to children and vulnerable populations, have been widely criticized for prioritizing profit over public health.[719] Companies often use misleading advertising, portion manipulation, and the promotion of addictive ingredients to drive sales, despite the known health risks associated with their products.

The impact of these practices on public health is profound. The rise in obesity and diet-related diseases has led to increased healthcare costs, reduced quality of life, and a decline in life expectancy in some regions.[720] The burden of these health issues is often borne by low-income communities, where access to healthy food is limited and where the marketing of unhealthy products is most pervasive.

Growing calls for regulation and reform have also resulted from the food and beverage industry's emphasis on profit at the expense of public health. Public health advocates have pushed for measures such as taxes on sugary drinks, restrictions on junk food advertising, and clearer labeling of nutritional information.[721] These efforts aim to reduce the health impact of unhealthy products and to promote healthier eating habits among the population.

---

719. Nestle, M. (2013). *Food Politics: How the Food Industry Influences Nutrition and Health*. University of California Press.

720. Brownell, K. D., & Warner, K. E. (2009). The Perils of Ignoring History: Big Tobacco Played Dirty and Millions Died. How Similar Is Big Food? *The Milbank Quarterly*, 87(1), 259-294.

721. *Ibid.*

Nestlé's Practices Exploit Communities and Profiteer from Suffering

Nestlé, the world's largest food and beverage company, has faced significant controversy over its business practices, particularly concerning water resources and the marketing of infant formula. These controversies have raised critical questions about the company's impact on communities and the broader societal implications of its practices. Nestlé operates all over the world, so its decisions could have a significant impact on everything from environmental sustainability to public health.

Water Resource Controversies

Nestlé has faced widespread criticism for its approach to water resources, particularly in its bottled water operations. The company has been accused of exploiting water resources in various regions, leading to environmental degradation, water scarcity, and social unrest. These controversies have raised serious concerns about the ethical implications of Nestlé's water practices and their broader impact on communities around the world.

Nestlé's Bottled Water Business

Nestlé is one of the largest players in the global bottled water market, owning several major brands, including Poland Spring, Pure Life, and San Pellegrino. The company sources water from various locations around the world, often tapping into natural springs and aquifers to supply its bottling plants.[722] While Nestlé markets its bottled water as pure and natural, the process of

722. Barlow, M. (2007). *Blue Covenant: The Global Water Crisis and the Coming Battle for the Right to Water*. New Press.

extracting, bottling, and distributing this water has sparked significant controversy.

One of the primary criticisms of Nestlé's bottled water business is the company's practice of extracting large quantities of water from public resources at minimal cost. In many cases, Nestlé pays little or no fees for the water it extracts, even in regions where water scarcity is a pressing issue. For example, in California, a state frequently plagued by drought, Nestlé has been criticized for continuing to extract water from public lands even during periods of severe water shortages.[723] This practice has raised concerns about the company's impact on local water supplies and the fairness of its water extraction practices.

Impact on Local Communities and the Environment

The extraction of water by Nestlé has had significant impacts on local communities and the environment. In some regions, Nestlé's water extraction has led to a decline in local water tables, reducing the availability of water for residents, farmers, and ecosystems.[724] This has exacerbated water scarcity in areas already facing water stress, leading to conflicts between Nestlé and local communities.

Aside from the loss of water supplies, the manufacturing of bottled water has a significant negative influence on the environment. The production of plastic bottles, the energy used in bottling and transportation, and the waste generated by discarded bottles all contribute to environmental degradation.[725] Despite efforts to promote recycling, a large percentage of plastic water bottles end up in landfills or as litter, contributing to pollution and environmental harm.

---

723. Clarke, T. (2015). Nestlé's Bottled Water Controversy in California. *The Guardian*. Retrieved from https://www.theguardian.com/sustainable-business/2015/oct/21/nestle-bottled-water-california-drought

724. Gleick, P. H. (2010). Bottled and Sold: The Story Behind Our Obsession with Bottled Water. *Island Press*.

725. Royte, E. (2008). *Bottlemania: Big Business, Local Springs, and the Battle Over America's Drinking Water*. Bloomsbury.

One of the most controversial examples of Nestlé's impact on water resources is the case of Michigan's Great Lakes region. In the small town of Evart, Nestlé has been extracting millions of gallons of water annually from a local aquifer for its Ice Mountain brand. Local residents have raised concerns about the sustainability of this extraction, particularly in light of the ongoing water crisis in nearby Flint, Michigan, where residents have struggled with access to clean drinking water.[726] The contrast between Nestlé's water extraction for profit and the struggles of communities facing water insecurity has fueled public outrage and calls for stricter regulation of water resources.

Ethical Debate Over Water as a Public Good

A larger ethical discussion concerning the nature of water as a public good has been spurred by the scandals surrounding Nestlé's water practices. Critics argue that water is a basic human right and should not be commodified or controlled by private corporations for profit.[727] They contend that Nestlé's extraction and sale of water undermines the principle that water should be accessible to all, particularly in regions where water scarcity is a significant issue.

Nestlé, on the other hand, has defended its practices by arguing that it adheres to strict environmental and legal standards in its water extraction and bottling operations. The company maintains that its operations provide jobs and contribute to local economies, and it has taken steps to improve the sustainability of its water practices, including reducing water use and promoting recycling.[728] However, these efforts have done little to quell the criticism and public backlash against the company's water practices.

---

726. Clarke, T. (2015). Nestlé's Bottled Water Controversy in California. *The Guardian*. Retrieved from https://www.theguardian.com/sustainable-business/2015/oct/21/nestle-bottled-water-california-drought

727. Barlow, M. (2007). *Blue Covenant: The Global Water Crisis and the Coming Battle for the Right to Water*. New Press.

728. Nestlé. (2019). *Nestlé in Society: Creating Shared Value and Meeting Our Commitments 2019*. Retrieved from https://www.nestle.com/sites/default/files/2020-03/creating-shared-value-report-2019-en.pdf

The ethical debate over water as a public good raises important questions about the role of corporations in managing and profiting from natural resources. As the global population grows and water scarcity becomes an increasingly pressing issue, the practices of companies like Nestlé will likely continue to be a focal point of public debate and scrutiny.

Controversies Over Infant Formula Marketing

As well as to its water practices, Nestlé has faced significant controversy over its marketing of infant formula, particularly in developing countries. The company has been accused of promoting its formula in ways that undermine breastfeeding, leading to serious public health consequences.

The controversy over Nestlé's marketing of infant formula dates back to the 1970s when the company was accused of aggressively promoting its products in developing countries, where access to clean water and adequate healthcare was limited. Nestlé's marketing practices included distributing free samples of formula to new mothers in hospitals, advertising its products as superior to breast milk, and using promotional tactics that targeted vulnerable populations.[729]

These practices were criticized for undermining breastfeeding, which is widely recognized as the healthiest option for infants. The World Health Organization (WHO) and the United Nations Children's Fund (UNICEF) recommend exclusive breastfeeding for the first six months of life, followed by continued breastfeeding along with complementary foods for up to two years or beyond.[730] Breastfeeding provides essential nutrients and antibodies that protect infants from infections and diseases, particularly in environments where sanitation and access to healthcare are limited.

---

729. Muller, M. (1974). *The Baby Killer: A War on Want Investigation into the Promotion and Sale of Powdered Baby Milks in the Third World*. War on Want.

730. WHO (World Health Organization). (2020). *Infant and Young Child Feeding*. Retrieved from https://www.who.int/news-room/fact-sheets/detail/infant-and-young-child-feeding

Despite these recommendations, Nestlé's marketing practices led many mothers to switch from breastfeeding to formula feeding, often with devastating consequences. In regions where clean water was scarce, mixing formula with contaminated water increased the risk of infant illness and death.[731] Families were also severely impacted financially by the price of formula, which caused some mothers to dilute it in order to extend its shelf life, further jeopardizing the health of their infants.

Effects on Public Health

Nestlé's marketing of baby formula has had a significant effect on public health. The company's practices have been linked to increased rates of infant malnutrition, illness, and mortality in developing countries. The widespread use of formula in areas with poor sanitation has contributed to higher rates of diarrhea, respiratory infections, and other preventable diseases among infants.[732]

The controversy over Nestlé's infant formula marketing practices led to the launch of the international Nestlé boycott in 1977, organized by the Infant Formula Action Coalition (INFACT).[733] The boycott aimed to pressure Nestlé to change its marketing practices and to raise awareness about the risks of formula feeding in developing countries. The boycott gained significant international support and brought attention to the broader issue of unethical marketing practices in the food and beverage industry.

In response to the boycott and growing public criticism, Nestlé made some changes to its marketing practices. The company agreed to adhere to the WHO International Code of Marketing of Breast-milk Substitutes, adopted in 1981, which sets guidelines

---

731. Muller, M. (1974). *The Baby Killer: A War on Want Investigation into the Promotion and Sale of Powdered Baby Milks in the Third World.* War on Want.

732. Kent, G. (2011). *Regulating Infant Formula: Can the US Do More?* Environmental Health Perspectives, 119(6), A246-A250.

733. Muller, M. (1974). *The Baby Killer: A War on Want Investigation into the Promotion and Sale of Powdered Baby Milks in the Third World.* War on Want.

for the ethical marketing of infant formula.[734] The Code prohibits the promotion of breast-milk substitutes to the general public and restricts the use of free samples and other promotional tactics that could undermine breastfeeding.

However, Nestlé has been accused of continuing to violate the Code in some regions, particularly in developing countries.[735] Reports of aggressive marketing tactics, including distributing free samples in hospitals and using misleading advertising, have persisted, leading to ongoing criticism of the company's practices.

More Wide-ranging Social and Ethical Consequences

Broader moral and societal concerns regarding the role of businesses in public health are brought up by the controversy surrounding Nestlé's infant formula marketing strategies. The promotion of formula feeding in environments where breastfeeding is safer and more beneficial has been widely condemned as an example of corporate irresponsibility.[736] Critics argue that Nestlé's actions prioritize profit over the well-being of vulnerable populations, particularly infants in developing countries.

The ethical debate surrounding Nestlé's infant formula marketing also touches on issues of social justice and equity. The promotion of formula feeding in developing countries has been criticized for exacerbating health disparities and contributing to the cycle of poverty.[737] Families that cannot afford formula may be forced to make difficult choices that compromise the health and well-being of their children, leading to long-term social and economic consequences.

---

734. WHO (World Health Organization). (2020). *Infant and Young Child Feeding*. Retrieved from https://www.who.int/news-room/fact-sheets/detail/infant-and-young-child-feeding

735. Kent, G. (2011). *Regulating Infant Formula: Can the US Do More?* Environmental Health Perspectives, 119(6), A246-A250.

736. Muller, M. (1974). *The Baby Killer: A War on Want Investigation into the Promotion and Sale of Powdered Baby Milks in the Third World*. War on Want.

737. Kent, G. (2011). *Regulating Infant Formula: Can the US Do More?* Environmental Health Perspectives, 119(6), A246-A250.

Nestlé's Practices' Effect on Communities Around the World

Communities all across the world have been impacted in different ways by the controversies surrounding Nestlé's water resources and infant formula marketing. These effects highlight the need for increased accountability and transparency as well as the wider societal ramifications of corporate practices.

Environmental Degradation and Resource Depletion

Nestlé's water extraction practices have contributed to environmental degradation and resource depletion in many regions. The company's extraction of water from natural springs and aquifers has led to a decline in local water tables, reduced access to water for residents and ecosystems, and increased the risk of drought and water scarcity.[738]

Concerns have also been raised regarding the sustainability of Nestlé's practices due to the environmental impact of producing bottled water, which includes the energy required for bottling and transportation as well as the waste produced by discarded bottles. The production and Disposing of plastic water bottles harms the environment and increases pollution, particularly in places with inadequate waste management facilities.[739]

Nestlé's water practices have an impact on the entire world, which emphasizes the need for more equitable and sustainable natural resource management. As water scarcity becomes an increasingly pressing issue, the practices of companies like Nestlé will continue to be a focal point of public debate and environmental activism.

738. Gleick, P. H. (2010). Bottled and Sold: The Story Behind Our Obsession with Bottled Water. *Island Press*.

739. Royte, E. (2008). *Bottlemania: Big Business, Local Springs, and the Battle Over America's Drinking Water*. Bloomsbury.

Public Health and Social Inequality

Nestlé's infant formula marketing has had a significant negative influence on social inequality and public health, especially in developing nations. The promotion of formula feeding in regions where breastfeeding is safer and more beneficial has contributed to increased rates of infant malnutrition, illness, and mortality. The financial burden of formula feeding on low-income families has exacerbated health disparities and contributed to the cycle of poverty.[740]

Nestlé's marketing strategies for infant formula have had a worldwide impact, which emphasizes the value of moral business conduct and the necessity of stricter laws to safeguard vulnerable groups. It also highlights the broader social and economic consequences of corporate actions, particularly in regions where access to healthcare and other essential services is limited.

Betrayed Trust and the Fight for Corporate Responsibility

Trust in Nestlé and the larger food and beverage sector has been eroded as a result of the scandals surrounding the company's operations.[741] The perception that Nestlé prioritizes profit over the well-being of communities and the environment has led to public backlash, including boycotts, protests, and calls for greater corporate accountability.

It is clear from the decline in trust in Nestlé and other companies how important accountability and transparency are in business operations. Companies that fail to adhere to ethical standards and prioritize the well-being of communities and the environment risk damaging their reputation and losing the trust of consumers and other stakeholders.

---

740. Kent, G. (2011). *Regulating Infant Formula: Can the US Do More?* Environmental Health Perspectives, 119(6), A246-A250.

741. Muller, M. (1974). *The Baby Killer: A War on Want Investigation into the Promotion and Sale of Powdered Baby Milks in the Third World.* War on Want.

Stronger regulation and enforcement of ethical standards in the food and beverage industry are also necessary, as evidenced by Nestlé's practices' worldwide impact. As consumers become more aware of the social and environmental impact of corporate practices, there is growing demand for greater transparency, accountability, and responsibility from companies like Nestlé.

Particularly with regard to water resources and the marketing of infant formula, the Nestlé case study emphasizes the wider societal effects of corporate practices. The controversies surrounding Nestlé's practices have had significant global impacts, affecting communities around the world in various ways. Nestlé's practices have raised critical questions about the role of corporations in managing natural resources, protecting public health, and promoting social equity.

As the global population grows and environmental and social challenges become increasingly pressing, the practices of companies like Nestlé will continue to be a focal point of public debate and scrutiny. The ripple effect of corporate practices on society highlights the need for a more balanced approach to corporate governance, one that prioritizes the well-being of communities and the environment alongside financial performance. By adhering to ethical standards and promoting transparency and accountability, companies can help to build a more sustainable and equitable future for all.

The Decline of Institutional Trust

Corporate practices that prioritize profit over ethical considerations can also contribute to the diminished integrity in institutions, including businesses, governments, and the media. This loss of credibility can have far-reaching consequences for society, undermining social cohesion, fueling political polarization, and weakening the effectiveness of public policy.

Trust in Corporations

The repeated failures of corporations to act in the public interest, whether through environmental degradation, public health crises, or exploitation of workers, have led to a decline in trust in the business sector.[742] Many people now view corporations as self-serving entities that prioritize profits over the well-being of their employees, customers, and the broader community.

This decline in trust can have significant consequences for businesses. Consumers may become more skeptical of corporate claims, less loyal to brands, and more likely to support regulatory measures aimed at curbing corporate power. The collapse of confidence can also make it more difficult for companies to attract and retain employees, particularly among younger workers who place a high value on corporate social responsibility.[743]

Trust in Government and Regulatory Institutions

Corporate practices that undermine public health, environmental sustainability, and economic equality can also erode trust in government and regulatory institutions. When governments fail to effectively regulate corporate behavior, or when they are perceived as being influenced by corporate interests, public trust in these institutions can decline.

The perception that governments are more responsive to corporate interests than to the needs of ordinary citizens can fuel political polarization

742. Edelman. (2020). *Edelman Trust Barometer 2020*. Retrieved from https://www.edelman.com/trust/2020-trust-barometer

743. *Ibid.*

and social unrest.[744] This erosion of trust can also weaken the effectiveness of public policy, as people may be less likely to comply with regulations or to support government initiatives aimed at addressing social and environmental challenges.

Democracy and governance may be more broadly impacted by the erosion of public confidence in the government and regulatory agencies. When people lose faith in the ability of their governments to act in the public interest, they may become disillusioned with the political process and less likely to participate in democratic institutions.[745] This ending of reliability can contribute to a decline in social cohesion and a weakening of the social contract.

Media Influence and Public Perception

The media also plays a critical role in shaping public perceptions of corporate practices and their broader societal impact. However, the media's ability to hold corporations accountable has been challenged by the concentration of media ownership, the rise of fake news, and the increasing influence of corporate interests on news coverage.

Faith in media is faltering due to bias, misinformation, and corporate influence. This decline hinders the public's ability to make informed choices about products, companies, and policies. This erosion of trust can also contribute to the spread of misinformation, political polarization, and social fragmentation.[746]

In order to preserve public confidence and make sure that business operations serve the interests of the general public, the media must play a crucial role in holding companies responsible.[747] However, the increasing commercialization of the media and the rise of new information technologies have complicated this role, making it more difficult for the public to discern truth from falsehood and to hold powerful actors accountable.

---

744. Gilens, M., & Page, B. I. (2014). Testing Theories of American Politics: Elites, Interest Groups, and Average Citizens. *Perspectives on Politics*, 12(3), 564-581.

745. Putnam, R. D. (2000). *Bowling Alone: The Collapse and Revival of American Community*. Simon & Schuster.

746. Fukuyama, F. (1995). *Trust: The Social Virtues and the Creation of Prosperity*. Free Press.

747. *Ibid*.

Beyond the immediate actions of individual companies, corporate practices have a significant impact on society. The pursuit of profit, particularly within the framework of the shareholder value paradigm, has contributed to growing economic inequality, public health crises, and the shattered assurance in institutions. These societal challenges are interconnected, with corporate practices often exacerbating existing inequalities, undermining public health, and weakening the social fabric.

To address these challenges, there is a need for a more balanced approach to corporate governance that takes into account the interests of all stakeholders, including employees, customers, communities, and the environment. This approach requires stronger regulation, greater transparency, and a renewed commitment to corporate social responsibility. By prioritizing the well-being of society as a whole, rather than focusing solely on short-term profits, corporations can help to build a more equitable, healthy, and sustainable future.

KEY TAKEAWAYS

Corporate-driven economic inequality
Corporate practices focused on profit maximization have widened the wealth gap by suppressing wages, outsourcing jobs, and prioritizing executive compensation over employee welfare.

Public health risks and corporate negligence
The pursuit of profit has led to crises such as the opioid epidemic and the promotion of unhealthy food products, highlighting how corporate actions can negatively impact global health.

Environmental degradation and corporate responsibility
Companies prioritizing short-term profits often contribute to pollution, climate change, and resource depletion, disproportionately harming vulnerable communities.

Declining institutional trust
Corporate misconduct, government inaction, and media influence have fueled public distrust in businesses, regulatory agencies, and political institutions, weakening social cohesion.

The need for ethical corporate governance
Addressing corporate harm requires stronger regulations, transparency, and socially responsible business models that balance profitability with sustainability and public well-being.

Chapter 12

Restoring Purpose, The Call to Humanize Corporate Culture

The future of work is a topic of great importance and urgency in today's rapidly evolving global economy. As technological advancements, globalization, and shifting societal values reshape the nature of work, there is a growing recognition of the need to humanize the workplace. This involves reimagining the employer-employee relationship, rebuilding trust, and creating environments where both parties work together toward common goals and objectives. At the heart of this vision is the concept of corporate social responsibility (CSR) and sustainable business practices, which prioritize not only profitability but also the well-being of employees, consumers, and the broader community.

Rebuilding Trust Between Employers and Employees

Trust is the foundation of any successful relationship, and this holds true for the employer-employee relationship as well. In recent decades, trust between workers and their employers has been eroded by practices such as wage stagnation, job insecurity, and the prioritization of shareholder value over employee well-being. Rebuilding this trust is essential for creating a future of work where employees feel valued, engaged, and motivated to contribute to the success of their organizations.

How Crucial Trust Is in the Workplace

Building a positive work environment, increasing employee engagement, and boosting organizational performance all depend on trust in the workplace. When employees trust their employers, they are more likely to be committed to their work, collaborate effectively with colleagues, and go the extra mile to achieve organizational goals.[748] Conversely, a lack of trust can lead to disengagement, high turnover rates, and a decline in productivity.

Rebuilding trust requires a commitment from employers to treat employees with respect, fairness, and transparency. This includes providing fair wages, opportunities for career development, and a safe and supportive work environment.[749] Employers must also be transparent about their decision-making processes and involve employees in discussions about the future direction of the company. By fostering a culture of open communication and mutual respect, employers can build trust and create a more positive and productive workplace.

Collaborative Goal Setting and Shared Objectives

One way to rebuild trust and enhance the employer-employee relationship is through collaborative goal setting and the establishment of shared objectives. When employers and employees work together to define the goals and objectives of the organization, it fosters a sense of ownership and accountability among workers.[750] Employees are more likely to be motivated to achieve these goals when they have had a hand in shaping them and when they understand how their work contributes to the overall success of the organization.

Collaborative goal setting also encourages employers to consider the needs and aspirations of their employees. By aligning organizational goals with the personal and professional goals of employees, companies can

---

748. Dirks, K. T., & Ferrin, D. L. (2001). The Role of Trust in Organizational Settings. *Organization Science*, 12(4), 450-467.

749. Mayer, R. C., Davis, J. H., & Schoorman, F. D. (1995). An Integrative Model of Organizational Trust. *The Academy of Management Review*, 20(3), 709-734.

750. Carroll, A. B. (1999). Corporate Social Responsibility: Evolution of a Definitional Construct. *Business & Society*, 38(3), 268-295.

create a more engaged and motivated workforce.[751] This alignment can be achieved through regular feedback sessions, performance reviews, and open discussions about career development and growth opportunities.

In addition to enhancing employee motivation and engagement, collaborative goal setting can also improve organizational performance. When employees are aligned with the goals of the organization and understand their role in achieving these goals, they are more likely to work efficiently and effectively.[752] This, in turn, can lead to higher levels of productivity, innovation, and overall business success.

Corporate Social Responsibility and Sustainable Business Practices

Corporate social responsibility (CSR) and sustainable business practices are essential components of a humanized workplace. These practices involve considering the social, environmental, and economic impact of business operations and making decisions that benefit not only the company but also its employees, customers, and the broader community.

The Role of CSR in Humanizing the Workplace

By addressing social and environmental issues, corporate social responsibility (CSR) aims to create value for the company and society. By incorporating CSR into their business plans, companies can show that they are committed to social justice, ethical behavior, and environmental sustainability, which can help to humanize the workplace by giving workers a sense of direction and significance.

Initiatives for corporate social responsibility (CSR) can take many different forms, such as lowering carbon emissions, encouraging diversity and inclusion, aiding in community development, and guaranteeing ethical labor practices. By engaging in CSR activities, companies can build a positive reputation, attract and retain top talent, and enhance employee

---

751. Carroll, A. B. (1999). Corporate Social Responsibility: Evolution of a Definitional Construct. *Business & Society*, 38(3), 268-295.

752. *Ibid.*

satisfaction.[753] Employees who work for socially responsible companies are often more engaged and motivated, as they feel that their work contributes to a greater good.

CSR can help to create a more inclusive and equitable workplace. By prioritizing diversity and inclusion, companies can ensure that all employees have equal opportunities for success, regardless of their background or identity.[754] This not only fosters a sense of belonging among employees but also leads to better decision-making and innovation, as diverse teams bring a wider range of perspectives and ideas to the table.

Sustainable Business Practices and the Future of Work

Sustainable business practices involve making decisions that ensure the long-term viability of the company while minimizing negative impacts on the environment and society. This includes efforts to reduce waste, conserve resources, and promote ethical sourcing and production methods.[755] By adopting sustainable business practices, companies can contribute to the well-being of future generations while also enhancing their reputation and competitiveness in the market.

Sustainability is increasingly becoming a priority for both consumers and employees.[756] As awareness of environmental issues grows, people are more likely to support companies that demonstrate a commitment to sustainability. This has led to a growing demand for sustainable products and services, as well as for workplaces that prioritize environmental responsibility.

---

753. Page, S. E. (2007). *The Difference: How the Power of Diversity Creates Better Groups, Firms, Schools, and Societies*. Princeton University Press.

754. Elkington, J. (1997). *Cannibals with Forks: The Triple Bottom Line of 21st Century Business*. Capstone.

755. Cohen, B., Smith, B., & Mitchell, R. (2017). Toward a Sustainable Conceptualization of Dependent Variables in Entrepreneurship Research. *Business Strategy and the Environment*, 26(7), 898-910.

756. Cohen, B., Smith, B., & Mitchell, R. (2017). Toward a Sustainable Conceptualization of Dependent Variables in Entrepreneurship Research. *Business Strategy and the Environment*, 26(7), 898-910.

In the context of the future of work, sustainable business practices can help to create a more resilient and adaptable workforce. By investing in sustainable technologies and practices, companies can reduce their environmental footprint, lower costs, and improve efficiency. This, in turn, can lead to greater job security and stability for employees, as well as opportunities for growth and development in emerging sectors such as renewable energy and green technologies.[757]

Building Institutions and Corporate Culture for a Humane Work Environment

Creating a humane work environment requires not only changes at the organizational level but also the development of institutions and corporate cultures that prioritize the well-being of employees and the ethical delivery of goods and services.

Regulation plays a crucial role in ensuring that companies adhere to ethical standards and provide humane work environments. Government regulations related to labor rights, workplace safety, and environmental protection are essential for protecting workers and ensuring that companies operate in a socially responsible manner.[758] These regulations help to create a level playing field, where all companies are held to the same standards and are accountable for their impact on society.

However, regulation alone is not enough to create truly humane work environments. It must be complemented by a strong corporate culture that values ethics, transparency, and employee well-being. Companies should go beyond compliance with regulations and strive to create workplaces that are inclusive, supportive, and empowering for all employees.[759] This requires a commitment from leadership to prioritize the well-being of workers and to foster a culture of respect and collaboration.

---

757. *Ibid.*

758. Freeman, R. E., Harrison, J. S., & Wicks, A. C. (2007). *Managing for Stakeholders: Survival, Reputation, and Success.* Yale University Press.

759. Freeman, R. E., Harrison, J. S., & Wicks, A. C. (2007). *Managing for Stakeholders: Survival, Reputation, and Success.* Yale University Press.

Corporate Culture and the Humanization of Work

Corporate culture plays a central role in shaping the work environment and influencing employee behavior and attitudes. A positive corporate culture that values diversity, inclusion, and employee well-being can help to humanize the workplace by creating a sense of belonging and purpose among workers.[760] This, in turn, can lead to higher levels of engagement, satisfaction, and productivity.

Building a positive corporate culture requires intentional efforts to align the company's values with its practices. This includes setting clear expectations for ethical behavior, promoting open communication, and providing opportunities for employee growth and development. Leaders play a critical role in shaping corporate culture by modeling the behavior they expect from others and by creating an environment where employees feel safe and supported.[761]

One of the key elements of a humanized work environment is the promotion of work-life balance. Companies that prioritize work-life balance recognize that employees have responsibilities and interests outside of work and that a healthy work-life balance is essential for overall well-being.[762] By offering flexible work arrangements, paid time off, and support for employee mental and physical health, companies can create a more humane work environment that fosters long-term employee satisfaction and retention.

Delivering Goods and Services in a Caring Way

The humanization of work extends beyond the internal operations of a company to the way it delivers goods and services to consumers. Companies that prioritize ethical and responsible business practices can build stronger relationships with their customers and contribute to a more caring and just society.

---

760. Schein, E. H. (2010). *Organizational Culture and Leadership*. John Wiley & Sons.

761. *Ibid.*

762. Kossek, E. E., Baltes, B. B., & Matthews, R. A. (2014). How Work, Family Research Can Finally Have an Impact in Practice. *Industrial and Organizational Psychology*, 4(3), 352-369.

Delivering goods and services in a caring way involves considering the impact of business practices on consumers and the broader community. This includes ensuring that products and services are safe, high-quality, and ethically produced.[763] It also involves being transparent about business practices and engaging with consumers in a respectful and honest manner.

By prioritizing ethical business practices, companies can build trust with consumers and create a positive brand reputation. Consumers are increasingly seeking out companies that align with their values and are willing to pay a premium for products and services that are produced in a socially and environmentally responsible manner.[764] This shift in consumer behavior presents an opportunity for companies to differentiate themselves in the market by demonstrating their commitment to ethical and sustainable business practices.

The future of work presents an opportunity to reimagine the employer-employee relationship and create a more humane and just workplace. By rebuilding trust, fostering collaboration, and prioritizing corporate social responsibility and sustainable business practices, companies can create environments where employees feel valued, engaged, and motivated to contribute to the success of the organization.

Building institutions and corporate cultures that prioritize employee well-being, ethical behavior, and the responsible delivery of goods and services is essential for creating a more humane work environment. This requires a commitment from both employers and employees to work together toward common goals and objectives and to ensure that business practices benefit not only the company but also the broader community.

As companies embrace the principles of CSR and sustainability, they can play a leading role in shaping the future of work and creating a more equitable and sustainable world. By humanizing work and prioritizing the well-being of employees and consumers, companies can build a better future for all.

---

763. Kotler, P., & Lee, N. (2005). *Corporate Social Responsibility: Doing the Most Good for Your Company and Your Cause*. John Wiley & Sons.

764. *Ibid.*

KEY TAKEAWAYS

- **Rebuilding trust is key to a productive workplace**,
  Employers must prioritize transparency, fair treatment, and employee engagement to restore trust and create a collaborative, motivated workforce.

- **Corporate social responsibility (CSR) strengthens businesses and communities**
  Companies that embrace ethical labor practices, environmental sustainability, and social equity can build stronger relationships with employees, consumers, and society.

- **Sustainable business practices drive long-term success**
  Investing in sustainability not only benefits the environment but also enhances corporate reputation, improves efficiency, and ensures job security in emerging industries.

- **Corporate culture shapes the employee experience**
  A positive workplace culture that promotes inclusion, work-life balance, and ethical leadership fosters engagement, innovation, and long-term employee satisfaction.

- **Delivering goods and services responsibly builds consumer trust**
  Businesses that prioritize ethical sourcing, product quality, and transparent communication can differentiate themselves in the market and create lasting customer loyalty.

Chapter 13

Building for the Future, Proven Strategies to Create a Stronger Workplace

In today's dynamic business landscape, companies are increasingly understanding the value of cultivating a workplace culture that attracts talent, enhances employee satisfaction, and drives productivity and commitment. A thriving workplace values, supports, and empowers employees, enabling them to perform at their best while aligning with organizational goals. Achieving this requires a multifaceted approach, including developing skilled managers, ensuring fair compensation, offering meaningful benefits, prioritizing employee training, fostering autonomy, building trust, and creating an inclusive, collaborative culture.

Training Managers in Employee Development

Managers play a crucial role in shaping the work environment and influencing employee engagement and performance. To create a better workplace, companies must invest in training managers to be effective leaders who are capable of developing their teams and helping employees reach their full potential.

The Importance of Managerial Training

Managerial training is essential for equipping managers with the skills and knowledge they need to effectively lead and develop their teams. Training should cover a range of competencies, including communication, conflict resolution, performance management, and coaching.[765] By providing managers with the tools to support employee development, companies can create a more engaged and motivated workforce.

Effective managers understand the importance of providing regular feedback, setting clear expectations, and recognizing employees' achievements. They also play a key role in identifying employees' strengths and areas for improvement and providing opportunities for professional growth. When managers are trained to focus on employee development, they can help create a work environment where employees feel valued and supported in their career progression.[766]

Coaching and Mentorship

In addition to formal training programs, companies should encourage managers to take on coaching and mentorship roles. Coaching involves helping employees develop specific skills and achieve their professional goals, while mentorship provides long-term guidance and support for career development.[767] Both coaching and mentorship are valuable tools for employee development and can help create a culture of continuous learning and improvement within the organization.

When managers act as coaches and mentors, they build stronger relationships with their employees, foster trust, and create an environment where employees feel empowered to take on new challenges.[768] This not only benefits individual employees but also contributes to the overall success of the organization by developing a more skilled and capable workforce.

---

765. Hogan, R., & Kaiser, R. B. (2005). What We Know About Leadership. *Review of General Psychology*, 9(2), 169-180.

766. Luthans, F., & Avolio, B. J. (2003). Authentic Leadership: A Positive Developmental Approach. In *K. S. Cameron, J. E. Dutton, & R. E. Quinn (Eds.), Positive

767. *Ibid.*

768. Hogan, R., & Kaiser, R. B. (2005). What We Know About Leadership. *Review of General Psychology*, 9(2), 169-180.

Paying Fair Wages and Salaries

Employees who are paid fairly for their work are more likely to be satisfied, motivated, and committed to their organization. Fair compensation is a fundamental aspect of creating a better workplace. Companies must ensure that they offer competitive wages and salaries that reflect the value of the work being performed.

Employee Satisfaction and Fair Compensation's Effect

Fair compensation is directly linked to employee satisfaction and retention. When employees feel that they are being paid fairly, they are more likely to be engaged in their work and committed to the organization.[769] Conversely, employees who perceive their compensation as unfair are more likely to experience dissatisfaction, lower productivity, and higher turnover rates.

To determine fair wages and salaries, companies should conduct regular market research to ensure that their compensation packages are competitive within their industry and region. This includes considering factors such as cost of living, industry standards, and the skills and experience required for the job.[770] Companies should also be open and honest about their pay policies, giving workers a clear understanding of how their salary is decided.

Equity and Pay Transparency

In addition to offering competitive pay, companies should focus on ensuring pay equity across the organization. This means addressing any disparities in compensation that may exist based on gender, race, or other factors. Pay equity is not only a matter of fairness but also a critical component of creating an inclusive and supportive work environment.[771]

---

769. Levine, D. I. (1993). *Fairness in Markets and Organizations: An Essay on Equity in Compensation*. Oxford University Press.

770. Bloom, M., & Michel, J. G. (2002). The Relationships Among Organizational Context, Pay Dispersion, and Managerial Turnover. *Academy of Management Journal*, 45(1), 33-42.

771. Lips, H. M. (2013). The Gender Pay Gap: Challenging the Rationalizations, Perceived Equity, Discrimination, and the Limits of Human Capital Models. *Sex Roles*, 68(3-4), 169-185.

Pay transparency is another important aspect of fair compensation. By being open about pay scales and compensation practices, companies can build trust with their employees and reduce the potential for misunderstandings or perceptions of unfairness.[772] Transparency also encourages accountability and can help prevent pay discrimination within the organization.

Offering Realistic Benefits

In addition to fair wages, companies must offer realistic benefits that meet the needs of their employees. Benefits play a significant role in attracting and retaining talent, as well as in supporting employees' overall well-being.

Designing a Comprehensive Benefits Package

A comprehensive benefits package should include health insurance, retirement savings plans, paid time off, and other perks that contribute to employees' financial and physical well-being. Companies should consider the specific needs of their workforce and offer benefits that are both competitive and relevant to their employees' lives.[773]

In addition to traditional benefits, companies can offer flexible work arrangements, wellness programs, and professional development opportunities. Flexible work arrangements, such as remote work and flexible hours, allow employees to balance their work and personal lives more effectively. Wellness programs, including mental health support and fitness incentives, help employees maintain their health and well-being.[774] Professional development opportunities, such as training and education reimbursement, support employees' career growth and development.

772. Babcock, L., Recalde, M. P., Vesterlund, L., & Weingart, L. (2017). Gender Differences in Accepting and Receiving Requests for Tasks with Low Promotability. *American Economic Review*, 107(3), 714-747.

773. Barber, A. E., Dunham, R. B., & Formisano, R. A. (1992). The Impact of Flexible Benefits on Employee Satisfaction: A Field Study. *Personnel Psychology*, 45(1), 55-75.

774. Miller, D., & Allen, K. (2016). The Building Blocks of a Supportive Workplace: Strategies for Enhancing Employee Well-Being and Productivity. *Journal of Organizational Development*, 34(2), 123-139.

Aligning Benefits with Employee Preferences

To ensure that benefits are effective, companies should regularly assess employee preferences and satisfaction with the benefits offered. This can be done through surveys, focus groups, and one-on-one discussions.[775] By understanding what employees value most, companies can tailor their benefits packages to better meet their needs and preferences.

Offering benefits that align with employee preferences not only enhances satisfaction but also demonstrates that the company values its employees and is committed to their well-being.[776] This can lead to higher levels of employee engagement and loyalty, as well as a stronger employer brand that attracts top talent.

Training Employees for Success

Continuous learning is essential for employee development and organizational success. In today's fast-paced business environment, employees must constantly update their skills and knowledge to stay competitive and meet the evolving demands of their roles. Companies should invest in training programs that provide employees with the tools they need to succeed, whether through formal education, on-the-job training, or professional development courses.

Training should be tailored to the specific needs of employees and the organization. This includes offering a mix of technical skills training, soft skills development, and leadership training. By providing a comprehensive approach to training, companies can ensure that their employees are well-equipped to handle the challenges of their roles and contribute to the organization's success.[777]

---

775. Barber, A. E., Dunham, R. B., & Formisano, R. A. (1992). The Impact of Flexible Benefits on Employee Satisfaction: A Field Study. *Personnel Psychology*, 45(1), 55-75.

776. Miller, D., & Allen, K. (2016). The Building Blocks of a Supportive Workplace: Strategies for Enhancing Employee Well-Being and Productivity. *Journal of Organizational Development*, 34(2), 123-139.

777. Salas, E., Tannenbaum, S. I., Kraiger, K., & Smith-Jentsch, K. A. (2012). The Science of Training and Development in Organizations: What Matters in Practice. Psychological Science in the Public Interest, 13(2), 74, 101. https://doi.org/10.1177/1529100612436661

Encouraging a Growth Mindset

In addition to formal training programs, companies should foster a growth mindset among employees. A growth mindset is the belief that abilities and intelligence can be developed through effort and learning.[778] Employees with a growth mindset are more likely to embrace challenges, persist in the face of setbacks, and view feedback as an opportunity for improvement.

To encourage a growth mindset, companies should create a culture that values learning and development. This includes providing opportunities for employees to take on new challenges, offering constructive feedback, and celebrating both successes and learning experiences. By promoting a growth mindset, companies can create a more resilient and adaptable workforce that is better equipped to navigate change and achieve long-term success.[779]

Teaching Autonomy and Teamwork

Autonomy in the workplace refers to the degree of control and independence that employees have over their work. When employees have the autonomy to make decisions and solve problems on their own, they are more likely to feel empowered, motivated, and engaged in their work. Autonomy also fosters creativity and innovation, as employees are free to explore new ideas and approaches.[780]

To foster autonomy, companies should provide employees with clear goals and expectations while allowing them the freedom to determine how to achieve those goals.[781] This includes giving employees the authority to make decisions, providing them with the resources and support they need, and encouraging them to take ownership of their work. By promoting autonomy, companies can create a more dynamic and productive work environment.

---

778. Dweck, C. S. (2006). *Mindset: The New Psychology of Success.* Random House.

779. Ryan, R. M., & Deci, E. L. (2000). Self-Determination Theory and the Facilitation of Intrinsic Motivation, Social Development, and Well-Being. American Psychologist, 55(1), 68, 78. https://doi.org/10.1037/0003-066X.55.1.68

780. Gagné, M., & Deci, E. L. (2005). Self-Determination Theory and Work Motivation. *Journal of Organizational Behavior*, 26(4), 331-362.

781. *Ibid.*

Promoting Teamwork and Collaboration

While autonomy is important, it must be balanced with teamwork and collaboration. Effective teamwork involves working together toward a common goal, sharing knowledge and resources, and supporting one another's efforts.[782] Teamwork is essential for achieving complex tasks, solving problems, and driving innovation.

A culture of open communication, where employees feel comfortable sharing their thoughts and ideas with others, and team-building activities, cross-functional projects, and collaborative workspaces are some ways that companies can foster teamwork by giving employees the chance to work together on projects, exchange ideas, and develop relationships with their coworkers. By fostering both autonomy and teamwork, companies can create a balanced work environment where employees feel empowered to take initiative while also benefiting from the support and collaboration of their colleagues.

Focusing on Trust

Transparency is key to building trust in the workplace. When companies are open and honest about their goals, decisions, and challenges, employees are more likely to trust their leaders and feel confident in the organization's direction.[783] Transparency also fosters a sense of belonging and inclusion, as employees feel that they are part of the decision-making process and are kept informed about important developments.

To build trust through transparency, companies should communicate regularly with employees about the organization's performance, goals, and challenges. This includes sharing information about financial results, strategic plans, and key decisions that impact the workforce. Additionally,

---

782. Hackman, J. R. (2002). *Leading Teams: Setting the Stage for Great Performances*. Harvard Business School Press.

783. Mayer, R. C., Davis, J. H., & Schoorman, F. D. (1995). An Integrative Model of Organizational Trust. The Academy of Management Review, 20(3), 709, 734. https://doi.org/10.5465/amr.1995.9508080335

companies should be open to feedback and encourage employees to share their thoughts and concerns.[784]

Trusting Employees to Make Decisions

Trust is a two-way street. In addition to building trust between employees and leadership, companies must also demonstrate trust in their employees by empowering them to make decisions and take ownership of their work.[785] When employees feel trusted, they are more likely to take initiative, make informed decisions, and contribute to the organization's success.

To foster trust, companies should delegate authority to employees and provide them with the resources and support they need to succeed.[786] This includes offering opportunities for employees to take on leadership roles, make decisions, and contribute to important projects. By trusting employees to make decisions, companies can create a more dynamic and innovative work environment.

Creating a Social Culture of Inclusiveness, Support, Understanding, Learning, and Collaboration

Inclusiveness and diversity are critical components of a positive workplace culture. Companies that prioritize inclusiveness create an environment where all employees, regardless of their background or identity, feel valued and respected. This not only enhances employee satisfaction but also leads to better decision-making and innovation, as diverse teams bring a wide range of perspectives and ideas to the table.

To promote inclusiveness, companies should implement policies and practices that support diversity and equity. This includes offering diversity

---

784. Robinson, S. L. (1996). Trust and Breach of the Psychological Contract. *Administrative Science Quarterly, 41*(4), 574-599.

785. Dirks, K. T., & Ferrin, D. L. (2001). The Role of Trust in Organizational Settings. *Organization Science*, 12(4), 450-467.

786. Mayer, R. C., Davis, J. H., & Schoorman, F. D. (1995). An Integrative Model of Organizational Trust. The Academy of Management Review, 20(3), 709, 734. https://doi.org/10.5465/amr.1995.9508080335

training, establishing employee resource groups, and creating opportunities for underrepresented groups to advance within the organization. By fostering a culture of inclusiveness, companies can create a more supportive and collaborative work environment.

Encouraging Support and Understanding

A supportive work environment is one where employees feel that they can rely on their colleagues and leaders for help and guidance. Supportive workplaces are characterized by open communication, mutual respect, and a commitment to helping one another succeed. Understanding is also crucial, as it involves recognizing and valuing the unique experiences and perspectives of others.[787]

To encourage support and understanding, companies should create opportunities for employees to build relationships with their colleagues, such as through team-building activities, social events, and mentorship programs. Companies should also cultivate a culture of empathy and compassion so that workers feel their needs and well-being are given priority.

Fostering a Culture of Learning and Collaboration

A culture of learning and collaboration is essential for creating a dynamic and innovative workplace. Companies that prioritize learning provide employees with opportunities for growth and development, while collaboration encourages employees to work together to achieve common goals. Together, these elements create an environment where employees feel empowered to take on new challenges and contribute to the organization's success.

To foster a culture of learning and collaboration, companies should offer continuous learning opportunities, such as training programs, workshops, and professional development courses. Additionally, companies should create opportunities for employees to collaborate on projects, share ideas,

---

787. Eisenberger, R., Huntington, R., Hutchison, S., & Sowa, D. (2001). Perceived Organizational Support. *Journal of Applied Psychology*, 71(3), 500-507.

and learn from one another.[788] By promoting learning and collaboration, companies can create a more engaged and productive workforce.

Developing a Mindset of Collectivism

A collectivist mindset can lead to a more cohesive and collaborative work environment. When employees prioritize the success of the team and the organization, they are more likely to work together to achieve common goals, share knowledge and resources, and support one another's efforts.[789] This, in turn, can lead to higher levels of productivity, innovation, and job satisfaction.

In addition to fostering collaboration, a collectivist mindset can also enhance employee engagement and commitment. When employees feel that they are part of a larger team working toward a common goal, they are more likely to be motivated and invested in the success of the organization. This can lead to lower turnover rates, higher levels of job satisfaction, and a stronger sense of loyalty to the company.

Promoting a Collectivist Culture

To promote a collectivist culture, companies should emphasize the importance of teamwork and collaboration in their values and practices. This includes setting team-based goals, recognizing and rewarding collective achievements, and encouraging employees to prioritize the success of the group over individual accomplishments.[790] Companies should also give their staff members the chance to connect with their coworkers and foster a spirit of support and friendship.

By fostering a collectivist mindset, companies can create a more cohesive and supportive work environment where employees feel that they are part of a larger team working toward a common goal. This, in

788. Schein, E. H. (2010). *Organizational Culture and Leadership* (4th ed.). Jossey-Bass.

789. Hofstede, G. (1980). *Culture's Consequences: International Differences in Work-Related Values*. Sage.

790. *Ibid.*

turn, can lead to higher levels of engagement, productivity, and overall organizational success.[791]

Creating a better workplace requires a multifaceted approach that addresses the needs and aspirations of employees while aligning with the goals of the organization. By training managers in employee development, paying fair wages, offering realistic benefits, providing comprehensive employee training, fostering autonomy and teamwork, building trust, and creating a social culture of inclusiveness, support, and collaboration, companies can create a work environment that promotes employee satisfaction, engagement, and long-term success.

By developing a mindset of collectivism, companies can foster a sense of shared responsibility and collaboration that enhances both individual and collective performance. As companies implement these strategies, they can create a better workplace that not only benefits employees but also contributes to the overall success and sustainability of the organization.

791. Triandis, H. C. (1995). Individualism and Collectivism. Westview Press.

KEY TAKEAWAYS

- **Effective leadership development is key to a thriving workplace**
Training managers to coach, mentor, and support employee growth fosters a culture of engagement, trust, and professional development.

- **Fair compensation and benefits drive employee satisfaction**
Competitive wages, pay equity, and comprehensive benefits contribute to retention, motivation, and a sense of value within the organization.

- **A culture of learning strengthens workforce adaptability**
Continuous training, skill development, and fostering a growth mindset help employees stay competitive and prepared for evolving industry demands.

- **Balancing autonomy and teamwork enhances productivity**
Empowering employees with decision-making authority while promoting collaboration ensures a dynamic, innovative, and engaged workforce.

- **Inclusivity and shared purpose create a strong corporate culture**
Encouraging diversity, trust, and a collectivist mindset fosters a supportive environment where employees feel valued and invested in organizational success.

Conclusion

Renewing Accountability, Restoring Trust, and Reclaiming Excellence

This book has journeyed through the labyrinth of corporate culture, exposing its flaws, highlighting its ripple effects, and offering actionable solutions to reimagine its future. From uncovering the disastrous consequences of prioritizing profit over people to showcasing innovative models that prioritize sustainability, equity, and humanity, the narrative has revolved around one central theme: the urgent need to humanize corporate practices and realign them with societal well-being.

Reflecting on Corporate Accountability

The case studies of Boeing, Purdue Pharma, Facebook, and Monsanto are just some of many that have revealed how corporate missteps can devastate public trust, harm communities, and deepen systemic inequalities. These chapters underscored the dangers of unchecked shareholder capitalism, where the relentless pursuit of profit often blinds organizations to their ethical obligations. The resulting erosion of trust in corporations, government institutions, and even the media serves as a stark reminder of the interwoven fabric of societal trust and corporate responsibility.

Beyond individual scandals, the broader societal impacts of corporate practices highlighted the far-reaching consequences of decisions made in boardrooms. Whether through exacerbating economic inequality, compromising public health, or fueling environmental degradation, corporate behavior often leaves lasting scars on society. The interconnected nature of these issues demands holistic solutions that address not only the symptoms but also the underlying causes.

This book also explored alternatives to the current corporate model, such as B Corporations, conscious capitalism, and collectivist cultures. These frameworks demonstrate that profitability and ethical behavior are not mutually exclusive. Companies can thrive while also promoting social equity, environmental sustainability, and employee well-being. By fostering inclusiveness, building trust, and prioritizing long-term value over short-term gains, corporations can evolve into entities that serve all stakeholders.

The Path Forward

The final chapters proposed actionable strategies to create better workplaces and more responsible corporations. Training managers to support employee development, ensuring fair compensation, promoting transparency, and fostering cultures of inclusion and collaboration are not mere aspirations, they are achievable goals. When implemented effectively, these strategies can transform organizations into spaces where employees, consumers, and communities thrive together.

The lessons learned from corporate failures and successes are clear: humanity must become central to the corporate ethos. Companies wield immense power, and with that power comes the responsibility to contribute positively to society. This is not just a moral imperative but also a strategic necessity in an age where consumers, employees, and investors increasingly demand accountability and sustainability.

As readers close this book, the hope is to inspire a collective reimagining of what corporations can and should be. By advocating for humane practices, supporting ethical businesses, and holding organizations accountable, we all play a role in shaping a future where business becomes a force for good, a future where profit and purpose coexist harmoniously.

Let this book serve as a reminder that change begins with awareness and flourishes through action. Together, we can build a world where corporations not only thrive financially but also stand as pillars of trust, integrity, and humanity.

Index

A

B

C

D

E

F

G

H

I

J

L

M

N

O

P

Q

R

S

T

U

V

W

www.ingramcontent.com/pod-product-compliance
Lightning Source LLC
LaVergne TN
LVHW010636110826
845149LV00014B/2853